D1155976

The Chinese Family
in the
Communist Revolution

Ting-jui 140
March 13, 1962
Harvard

C. K. YANG

Professor of Sociology
University of Pittsburgh

The Chinese Family
in the
Communist Revolution

with a Foreword by Talcott Parsons

A publication of
THE TECHNOLOGY PRESS, Massachusetts Institute of Technology
1959

Distributed by
Harvard University Press, Cambridge, Massachusetts

© Copyright 1959 by the Massachusetts Institute of Technology

Library of Congress Catalog Card Number 59–14897

Printed in the United States of America

Foreword

It is a pleasure to have the opportunity to say a word about this study of the Chinese family under the Communist regime. In my opinion Dr. Yang has with unusual success accomplished a dual purpose: he has made an important contribution to the general sociology of the family, and has also contributed to our understanding of the background of momentous events in the Far East which have such an important bearing on our own political responsibilities and destiny. Though probably a larger proportion of readers will be more interested in the latter contribution than in the former, I would like to emphasize their intimate connection: unless he had done an excellent piece of sociological analysis, Dr. Yang could not have produced a document of such practical significance.

For a generation in the sociological literature China has provided the stock example of a "familistic" society, one in which the family, and the kinship system ramifying from it, had an unusually strategic place in the total society, and, it has often been held, the family itself was unusually stable. The first of these generalizations has undoubtedly been true of the "classical" Chinese social system. But insufficient attention has been paid to defining the conditions under which the second held true. Dr. Yang shows us very convincingly that the old system generated very considerable tensions, both in the relation between the generations and that between the sexes.* As long as the old family system was reinforced by the old ideological, political, and class systems and certain features of a predominantly agricultural economy, the consequences of this strain could be successfully counteracted and the system as a whole remain substantially unchanged.

* Dr. Yang's most important predecessor in this line of analysis of the Chinese family is probably Marion J. Levy. See his *The Family Revolution in Modern China*, Cambridge, 1949.

The stability of these conditions has, however, broken down in the long series of social changes which have occurred since the revolution of 1911. The impact of the West, through missions, trade, education, medicine, and political intervention has upset the old equilibrium. In these circumstances there has been a strong pressure of the "disadvantaged" groups, the younger people and women, to be relieved of the handicaps to which they were subjected in the old family system, the subordination of the young to the authority and interests of the older generation, and of women to men. For understandable reasons the spearhead of these movements has been found in the cities, and in the intellectually and culturally more "emancipated" sections of the population; but they have by now spread far and wide.

Dr. Yang's essential thesis in this respect is that the Communists did not originate this fundamental process of change in the family, but that its roots go very deep into the constitution of the older society and the much more general process of change to which it has been subjected. Much of it was well under way before the Communist movement became very prominent. What the latter has done is to exploit and help along a process of change which is rooted in forces much bigger than itself. But it was given its opportunity by the tendency of the Kuomintang in its later phases to form an alliance with the older conservative elements which, in this as in several other respects, tended not only to try to check the process of change but even actually to turn the clock back.

In its more specifically sociological aspect, then, Dr. Yang's study takes the step beyond the more "static" view of the Chinese family as a structural type to a dynamic analysis of the conditions of its equilibrium, both internally and in relation to the other structures of the society. In its more political aspect the study brings forcibly and effectively to the reader's attention the fact that what has been happening in China is not the consequence of mere machinations of a conspiratorial cabal, but constitutes a fundamental process of change in the structure of a society, something that surely more Americans need to realize than the public discussion would seem to indicate is yet the case. Unfortunately the literature on which a sound appraisal of this process can be based has been seriously limited both in amount and in quality, and this book is hence a particularly welcome addition.

It cannot but strike the American reader that, on the background of the old system, the *direction* of change sponsored by the Communists, but only very partially brought about by them, has been precisely to make Chinese family conditions far more like our own than they were in the old system. What American now contests the right of young people to marry the persons of their own choice, or of married women to hold property in their own right? Yet these are typical of the things which the Communists have been promoting. Perhaps this makes a little more intelligible why intelligent people in China can favor the Communist movement.

What of the prospects for the future? The type of family organization with which we are familiar has never been typical of peasant societies, particularly those with a very high density of population. I strongly suspect that the success of the Communist movement in making its family reforms "stick" depends, more than on any other factor, on the success of its industrialization program in its *social* rather than economic consequences. This will not be primarily a question of the internal organization of families, but of their relation to the rest of the society in which they exist. But furthermore, it is highly questionable whether an industrial society, once fully developed and stabilized, can remain a "communist" society. So far the Communist movement has been a conspicuously successful agent of social change in the direction of industrialization of previously agrarian societies. How well it can survive success remains to be seen. It is not impossible that the type of family organization which has so far been developing under Communist auspices in China (as substantially also in the Soviet Union) will in the long run prove to be one of the most important foci of a shift from a Communist to something more like a "democratic" organization of society.

                                                                                                    Talcott Parsons

Harvard University

Acknowledgments

In the preparation of this volume I am deeply indebted to the following: Dr. John K. Fairbank for helping to initiate my research and for the encouragement given by him and his wife, Mrs. Wilma Fairbank, in reading and criticizing the manuscript; Dr. Talcott Parsons for his stimulating ideas, valued suggestions, and generosity in writing the Foreword; Dr. and Mrs. Robert Redfield for reading the manuscript and contributing much to its improvement. The generous financial support from the Center for International Studies of Massachusetts Institute of Technology, the Trustees of Lingnan University, the Rockefeller Foundation, and the Social Science Research Council made possible the fruition of this work and is deeply appreciated. Special acknowledgment is due the University of Pittsburgh for partial relief from teaching duties during revision of the manuscript. I wish especially to thank Mr. Richard W. Hatch of the Center for International Studies, Massachusetts Institute of Technology, for carefully editing the entire text and Mr. Howard Linton of Columbia University Library for his kindness and generosity in providing library resources. Last but not the least, my wife, Louise Chin Yang, unselfishly contributed long hours improving the manuscript and sharing the ordeal of its preparation.

C. K. Yang

University of Pittsburgh
March 1958

Contents

The Chinese Family
in the
Communist Revolution

change and not by the coordinated and conscious planning of an organized political power.

It is obvious that the domestic aim of the Chinese Communist regime is not limited to gaining political rule over the country. The declared purpose of the regime is the remaking of the total structure of China's political, economic, and social life. During the first ten years (1949–1959) of the regime its policies and action have encompassed wide grounds of institutional revision of Chinese society, including the imposition of a new national orthodoxy by relentless "thought reform;" the recasting of the economic institution through land reform, collectivization of agriculture, nationalization of industry and commerce, large-scale industrialization, liquidation of landlords and remolding of the urban business class; the introduction of a political institution based on the power of a large, formally organized elite; the enforcement of an educational system different from the old in its universality and its literary and technical content; the organized development of new forms of recreation carefully geared to the cultivation of the new ideological orientation; the concerted attack on the religious institution; and, as the focus of our special interest, the reform of the traditional family. Thus in the brief period of ten years there have been simultaneous attempts to alter the basic character of the entire institutional framework of Chinese society.

The importance which is attached by the Communist leadership to the remaking of the Chinese family institution is shown in the numerous directives issued by the major Communist agencies such as the Chinese Communist Party, the New Democratic Youth League, the Democratic Women's League, the Political Department of the People's Revolutionary Military Committee, and many other vital organizations ordering the effective implementation of the new Marriage Law.[1] There is little question about the earnest intention of the Communists to introduce basic changes in the Chinese family institution by concerted application of political, economic, and social pressure.

But the Communist regime is still new, and its effort to alter the family institution on a national scale did not formally begin until the promulgation of the new Marriage Law in May 1950. Within the limited time, it is hardly possible to see a nationwide change in such an ancient, deeply rooted institution as the traditional family. Nevertheless, events pointing to a broadening change of the family have been occurring in all parts of China under Communist rule. It is the purpose of the present study to analyze developments in Communist China which may disclose consistent trends in the change of the family institution,

CHAPTER I

The Communist Revolution and the Change of Chinese Social Institutions

WHEN THE famed Communist general Ch'en I led his victorious troops into conquered Shanghai in the early spring of 1949, he told the apprehensive citizens of that city that China was going to see the "first real change" in two thousand years. Epitomizing the principles and programs of the Communist regime in China, his statement marked the distinction between the present Communist revolution and the political changes of the past.

In the past two thousand years of recurring dynastic cycles, of alternations of order and chaos, there had been a general continuity and consistent development of the institutional framework of Chinese society. There had been changes and innovations from time to time in Chinese history, to be sure, but they were generally limited in institutional scope and spaced at rather long intervals which allowed them to be gradually assimilated by the traditional institutional system. When any sudden change took on too drastic and extensive a character, it usually soon succumbed to the forces of tradition. Hence the frequent assertion that, for some two millennia, no major social revolution had successfully introduced extensive alterations in the basic pattern of Chinese society.

In the modern scene, the immediate vital effect of the Republican revolution of 1911 was limited mainly to the disintegration of the traditional system of central political control; there was no sweeping introduction of any new pattern of society. The subsequent four decades of the Republican period brought a gradual disintegration of China's traditional institutions and a rather chaotic beginning of a new social pattern, but these came largely by the spontaneous process of social for, although such trends are now visible only in certain segments of the population, with the consolidation of Communist political power and the continued implementation of its policies, they are spreading to increasing portions of the population.

The Chinese Family in Traditional Society

Communist consideration of the remaking of the family as one of the basic measures in the transformation of traditional Chinese society shows that the Communist leadership has a full realization of the vital role of the family and the broader kinship system in the traditional social structure. Economically, the family has been the most important unit of organization in production, for not only has agriculture been almost exclusively a family undertaking but also in industry and commerce the family has been the most numerous organizational unit in investment and operation. There is hardly one major aspect of traditional social life that is not touched by the ties and influence of the family. It is somewhat difficult for an upper- or middle-class urban Chinese in his twenties today to visualize how dominant a part the family once played in public and private life during the earlier part of his father's generation.

In the early years of the twentieth century many of society's economic, educational, religious, recreational, and even political functions were intimately tied to the family institution. From cradle to grave the individual was under the uninterrupted influence of the family regarding his physical and moral upbringing, the formation of his sentiments and attitudes, his educational training, his public career, his social associations, his emotional and material security. In the Chinese community, particularly in the rural areas, there have been only a few social organizations or associations outside the family to serve the individual's social needs. Consequently, throughout his life the individual constantly struggled with problems concerned with the relations of parents and children, husband and wife, elder and younger brothers, the "in-laws," uncles, cousins, nephews, grandparents and grandchildren, and other members in the complex kinship circle.

Beyond the kinship circle the individual might have to deal with government officials, with his teacher or craft master, his colleagues, his employer or employees, and his neighbors and friends. But many of these social relations came through direct or indirect kinship contacts, and they were often patterned after the family system in structure and in values. Hence government officials were often referred to as "parent-officials" (fu mu kuan) and the people as "children people" (*tzu min*). The relationship between master and apprentice, or between teacher and student, operated on a simulated father-and-son basis. A solemn ceremony of a sacred character was used to introduce a new student to his teacher and an apprentice to his master, in order to establish the pseudo-kinship bond. And the devotion and reverence expected of a student or apprentice by the teacher or master was of the same type expected from a son by his father. Stores, handicraft shops, and farms employed mainly relatives, and the kinship bond was pervasive in the system of basic economic relations. Friends and neighbors addressed each other in fraternal or other kinship terms. Conversations between friends were punctuated with appellations like "elder brother" and "younger brother" and "uncle," even though the parties were not related as such.

Various forms of fraternal and sororal organizations stood out prominently among the few organized associations which existed beyond the kinship ties. The membership of most traditional social associations, from fraternities, sororities, and literary societies of the gentry to the business and craft guilds of the urban centers, was structured according to age and generation factors. The secret societies regarded their founders as "ancestors" and treated them with ancestor-worship rites. Their organization was patterned closely after the kinship structure, and authority was exercised through a hierarchy of generational status and age levels. The initiation of a new member was frequently done by drinking a few drops of each other's blood so as to establish the "blood tie" and to impart a measure of realism to the simulated kinship bond. Secret societies have played an important part in the life of certain segments of the traditional society, particularly among traveling entertainers, patent-medicine venders, and urban transportation workers, who had to operate outside the home territory where the kinship system was based, and among the poor peasants whose kinship ties were insufficient to meet their social and economic needs.

Under a social situation so thoroughly permeated with actual or simulated kinship ties it is to be expected that many of the kinship values should have general validity for society as a whole, and that the family should perform the function of being the training ground for general citizenship for society and for the state. An example is the so-called Five Cardinal Relations (*wu lun*, meaning the five basic norms of social order), which constituted the foundations of traditional social values. Mencius states that in "the relations of humanity — between father and son there should be solidarity and affection; between sovereign and minister, righteousness; between husband and wife, attention to their separate functions; between old and young, a proper order; and between friends, fidelity." [2] It is to be noted that heading the Five Cardinal Relations of humanity is the relation between father and son, and that of the five relations three belong to the kinship realm. The two non-kinship relations, those between ruler and officials and between friends, also rely partly for their actual operation on the moral strength of loyalty and status concepts required of the three kinship relations. In this sense, the mores of non-kinship relations may be regarded as an extension of the mores of kinship relations.

These Five Cardinal Relations, centering upon kinship ties, formed the core of social and moral training for the individual almost from the beginning of his consciousness of social existence until he became so conditioned to it that his standard of satisfaction and deprivation was based upon it, and the complex and extensive web of kinship ties created a feeling of a closed universe from which there seemed to be no escape, except perhaps death. The large number of suicides resulting from the strain of family relations among women (see chapters IV and VI) is a reflection of this situation. Here, for the unfortunate few, social pressure from the family institution appeared weightier than life itself, and the pain of death was considered lighter than the torture of living in a society which provided little outlet and security for a deviant from the traditional ideal of the family institution.

Such was the place of the traditional Chinese family and the broader kinship system in the general picture of social life about half a century ago. At present this situation still exists widely in rural communities and to a lesser extent among certain sections of the urban population. This is particularly so in mountainous sections of the country where confinement of the population in valleys discourages migration and accentuates the earthbound character and the kinship orientation of the peasant communities.

Organization of the Traditional Family

As an institution that has come to perform a multiplicity of functions and to play a vital role in the general organization of social life, the average Chinese traditional family seems surprisingly simple and small. If a family is taken to mean a biologically related group belonging to a single household sharing property and income together, the average Chinese family ranges in membership from four persons to six persons. From more recent statistical information we have the censuses of nine counties in Szechwan Province in 1942–43 giving an average range of 4.4 to 5.3 persons per family and a government report on

twenty-three provinces presenting an average range from 4.1 persons
in Jehol Province to 5.9 persons in Anhwei Province per family. The
frontier province of Kirin in Manchuria had an unusual average of
6.9 persons per family,[3] which is reminiscent of the large frontier family in early American history.

To assume a multiplicity of functions and a vital social role in the
fairly complex organization of traditional Chinese society, such a small
membership appears inadequate — hence the expansion of the effective
family relations beyond the confines of the household and the importance of the greater kinship circle to the life of the common man.
Such a circle centers upon the nucleus of the parents-children relation
and extends along the paternal lineage for generally three generations.
The possible separation of married sons into independent households
among the poor class weakens the parental control somewhat, but the
parents-children relation is still intimate, and filial obligations remain
strong. Under the leadership of and dominance by the parents, the
married sons and their children, though in separate households, continue to operate as an effective organization performing many common
functions.

In traditional social life there is the term *liu ch'in*, or "six kinship
relations," which suggests a delimitation for the larger kinship circle
as a functioning unit. Interpretations vary as to what constitutes the
"six kinship relations," but a commonly accepted version is that they
are the relations (1) between husband and wife, (2) between parents
and children, (3) between brothers, (4) between the children of brothers,
(5) between brothers' grandchildren, and (6) between brothers' great
grandchildren.[4] In actual social life, however, the first four categories
of relations are comparatively more intimate, and the last two types
belong more to the organization of the clan than to the intimate kinship circle of the extended family. Nevertheless, kinship obligations
of some degree are effectively present in all six categories of relations.
The number of persons in an organizational unit of this type exceeds
considerably that of the average household. In addition, the kinship
relations of the fourth and fifth generations, as well as those of the
immediate household of the maternal side (mainly those of the mother's
and wife's), also involve a certain amount of mutual obligations, thus
further expanding the effective unit of kinship organization for the
common people whose households are usually small. It is the greater
collective strength of the kinship circle, not the household alone, that
accounts for the prominence of the family in the traditional pattern
of social organization, although the household always remains the
fundamental nucleus of the kinship structure.

A significant and well-known aspect of the Chinese traditional family is the integration of the extended kinship circle, normally within three generations along the paternal lineage, into a single household whenever economic conditions permitted. The Chinese family in this sense was like a balloon, ever ready to expand whenever there was wealth to inflate it. As soon as there was enough land or other forms of production to employ the married sons, they would remain in the father's household, with property and income managed in common under the leadership and authority of the parents, and the process of expansion of the small household into a "big family" began. Should wealth increase, the membership of the family would expand further by adding concubines and their children. The longer life span of the well-to-do also augmented the size of the expanding family. Sufficient economic means being a necessary ingredient, the "big family" was more common among large landowners and well-to-do merchants than among the average peasants and workers.

With the advantage of education, coupled with the more favorable operation of the law of chance in a large family (as compared with a small family), it was fairly inevitable that within three generations one or more of the sons would, in the days of monarchical government before 1911, pass one of the official examinations, become the holder of an imperial academic degree, and possibly enter officialdom. With this accomplishment, the family entered the ranks of the gentry. Even in the Republican period the advantage of education, particularly modern higher education, for the young sons brought the family into the group of local political leadership, which functioned somewhat like the old gentry. Hence the frequent association between the big family and the gentry group.

In comparison with the smaller family and the limited kinship circle of the common man, the big family presented a close, effective integration of a large number of members which stood as a source of social and economic strength. It is significant that this form of family organization was intimately associated with the classes having social, economic, and political dominance. Another significance of the big family was its function of serving as an exemplary model of traditional family organization for the common people, thus encouraging them to maintain a strong tie with members of the near-kinship circle in an effort to simulate the advantages of the big family which traditionally brought prestige and success. In this sense, the big family played an important role in the functioning of the traditional kinship system.

The major principle of structure, from the big family of the well-to-do to the smaller family of workers and peasants, is the already noted Confucian canon of kinship relations: "between father and son there should be solidarity and affection; . . . between husband and wife, attention to their separate functions; between old and young, a proper order." One may make the following annotation to this canon from its implicit meaning as well as from the ways it worked out in traditional family life. The relation between parents and children in general and between father and son in particular should be the closest, closer than any other type of kinship relation, including the relation between husband and wife, for this is the nucleus of all family relations and the seat of authority in the power structure of the family; the expansibility of the traditional family is made possible by the use of this relation as the controlling factor in family life. Second in importance is the relation between husband and wife, and here "attention to separate functions" implies a division of labor as well as a stratification of status of all family members in both sexes on the basis of age and generational levels.

This structural principle of dominance by the parents and stratification of status and distribution of functions by sex and age is applicable to the organization of kinship units of all sizes, from the small family of the common people to the big family of the well-to-do, even to the clan with hundreds or thousands of members. Whatever the size of the unit, any individual member can readily find his or her specific place in this organizational scheme. This proved to be a workable principle for the majority of the families, in spite of occasional deviation such as the presence of a dominant wife or the situation in which a man's youngest son was younger than his oldest grandchild should he take on concubines at a late age after his sons have been married for some time. The general applicability of this organizational scheme is particularly adaptable to the expansible character of the traditional family and to the distribution of functions in the kinship system.

The "Family Revolution"

This form of family organization, centering upon parental control of married sons and structuring the membership rigidly according to sex and age, produced in the past a stable family and contributed substantially to the long stability of the traditional culture. In the traditional society dominated by the kinship factor it seems to have served social needs well with its multiplicity of functions.

But the impact of Western ideas and industrial influences since the closing quarter of the last century increasingly altered the picture. In the traditional family a strong authoritarian character is inherent in the rigid parental control and the stratification according to sex and age. Pressure and tension bore down heavily upon the women and the young. The introduction of the Western idea of individual liberty and rights inspired the women and the young to review and to reject their traditional roles of submission in the family.

In the past the traditional family could function rather smoothly in spite of the many innate dissatisfactions of the women or the young with its authoritarian character, chiefly because of the dominance of the kinship factor in the old social pattern. In such a pattern the family and the larger kinship group formed a relatively warm atmosphere in which the individual found not merely economic security but also the satisfaction of most of his social needs. Beyond this warm atmosphere lay what the traditional individual considered the cold and harsh world wherein his treatment and fate became unpredictable. Consequently, the women and the young accepted their traditional status as dictated by the way social life was traditionally organized.

But this pattern of social organization became increasingly incompatible with the new needs that arose with China's gradual integration into the modern industrial and nationalistic world. The past three-quarters of a century of floundering efforts at transferring the family and kinship relations to modern economic and political undertakings produced endless contradictions between the particularistic and the universalistic patterns of social life.[5] From such contradictions developed the accelerating trend of change in the traditional family and its old role in the organization of social life, a change that proceeded by popular demand from the educated young for a "family revolution" from the second decade of the present century. There was little success in overcoming the incongruity between the kinship tie as an organizational requirement in the traditional order and the need for objective qualifications for individuals as components of modern economic and political structures. Moreover, the particularistic nature in the kinship-oriented pattern of social organization divided the population into numerous small, self-confined, and loosely interrelated kinship units, while the mass organization of modern industrial society and the national state demanded intimate integration between the social and economic organs based on universal standards for the individuals.

This incompatibility seems to have been in the awareness of China's modern leading reformers whose ideological movements aimed at guiding China into a modern industrial state. K'ang Yu-wei, who led China's first organized modern reform in 1898, pointed out that the "abolition" of the traditional family was a condition for proper performance of modern public duties.[6] But his reform movement proved abortive. Save for his unwitting pioneering influence in weakening the Confucian orthodoxy by inspiring a change of attitude, he and his reform movement had little direct effect on the traditional kinship system. Sun Yat-sen, the leading revolutionist to rise on the heels of K'ang's failure, sensed the same incompatibility when he urged the expansion of "familism and clannism" into nationalism. Although he advanced no specific steps for such transformation, the Republican revolution of 1911 which he fathered did have serious effects on the subsequent change of the traditional family institution.

Some students underestimate this revolution as merely a change of political formality from monarchy to a nominal republic, devoid of any serious social significance. Actually, it started the trend toward destroying the theoretical applicability of Confucian kinship ethics to the operation of the state, thus undermining the traditional dominance of the family in social and political life. Furthermore, the collapse of the monarchy brought the abolition of the old imperial laws which compelled conformity to the traditional family institution based on Confucian orthodoxy. Subsequent laws on kinship relations promulgated by various governments under the Republic increasingly veered away from the traditional pattern. This had at least the negative significance of undermining the strength of the traditional family institution by reducing that part of its compulsory character which was founded upon formal political control. Also gone with the monarchy was the encouragement given by the government to such acts of devotion to the ideals of the traditional family as erecting memorial arches for unusually chaste widows or temples for outstanding filial sons. The effective symbolistic value of such old objects erected before the Republic steadily wore thin with the passing years. Finally, the revolution of 1911 attracted into its ranks many women whose demand for a new feminine role in a different family institution was no less strong than their demand for a new political order. These women, though few in number, planted the seed for the many subsequent popular movements that were to seriously affect the continued operation of the traditional family institution.

These influences continued to brew in the political chaos of the young Republic while the problem of social and cultural reform claimed increasing public attention. A great ideological upheaval, the New Culture Movement or Renaissance, which started in 1917, broke out in full force in the May 4th Movement of 1919. In this movement of multiple significance the term "family revolution" was introduced

into the consciousness of the public. It was used by leaders and pro-
tagonists of the movement as a slogan, and by the conservative old
generation as a reprimand to rebellious youngsters who struggled to
deviate from the traditional family institution. It became current par-
lance in the rising cry of the times for a change in the way of life as
the political revolution gradually unfolded into its social and cultural
phases.

There was no organized platform for this popular movement called
the "family revolution," but its main objectives were clearly suggested
in its slogans, catch-words, and the increasing volume of its literature.
It demanded a new role for women in the family as well as in society
in general terms of sex equality; it advocated freedom of social association between opposite sexes; it demanded marriage by free choice
and love, not by parental arrangement; it called for greater freedom
for the young; it vaguely urged a new family institution similar to the
Western pattern.

Ill-defined and poorly coordinated as some of these objectives were,
they did form a sufficiently coherent group of new ideas that served
to focus the public's attention upon the problem of remaking the
traditional family and of gathering sympathetic forces for group action.
The roots of Western inspiration were unmistakable in this movement.
From the May 4th Movement to the late 1920's, Ibsen's plays on
women's status and the family gained wide circulation in Chinese, became successful stage productions in large cities, and brought forth
spirited discussions. But the main preoccupation of the movement
then was still with the traditional family institution. Books, pamphlets,
and articles on the family problem appeared in growing numbers, firing broadsides at the ancient institution as being destructive of human
rights, decadent in moral character, and as discouraging the spirit of
independence and progress. The institution that had withstood some
two millennia of dynastic changes and foreign invasions and all their
political and economic devastations now came to be viewed as symbolizing all of China's sins and weaknesses. The new demands and the
proffered solutions, however untried and incoherent in some respects,
were pictured as the road to happiness and strength. Nationalistic
sentiments which began to surge forth with increasing force in the
decade following World War I in China as well as elsewhere helped
to impress these arguments on the minds of the public.

Aside from the rising nationalistic sentiments, many other forces
stimulated by the May 4th Movement added strength to the family
revolution. One was a concentrated attack on the absolutism of the

Confucian orthodoxy and the social institutions modeled after it. Keynotes of the attack were: "skepticism toward all ancient teachings," "down with *Confucius and Company*" (the latter term meaning the traditional schoolroom and its Confucian classical teachings) and the "man-devouring doctrine of ritualism." This branch of the New Culture Movement called for a complete re-evaluation of traditional learning and institutions and for a new cultural orientation in the light of modern science and democracy.

As the "new current of thought" won widening acceptance in a decade of raging polemics following World War I, Confucian orthodoxy together with its kinship values and the family institution molded after it were no longer a matter of "sacred" character enjoying deep reverence and unquestioned conformity from the people and supported by compulsory political power. They became subjects for secular discussions and popular attacks from the educated young — so much so, in fact, that it was fashionable for modern Chinese intellectuals to criticize Confucianism. The result was a serious loss of prestige and strength by the Confucian orthodoxy. As the family institution was deeply enmeshed in the matrix of Confucian ideology and its institutions, it could not help but be weakened by this development.

The call for skepticism toward the old cultural heritage and a new orientation for the future found the most attentive listeners among modern educated young men and women, who felt the most strain from the rigid sex and age stratifications in the traditional family and society. The rise of the youth movement and the women's movement, as phases of the May 4th Movement, lent important support to the family revolution and in fact became inseparable parts of it. In a sense, the family revolution developed as a rebellion of the educated young of both sexes against the traditional social order.

Such a rebellion, breaking out within the family circle, was naturally viewed with alarm and even terror by the older generation, who found the process increasingly difficult to stop. Under the driving and infectious demand for freedom and equality, and in the growing destruction of unquestioned conformity to traditional institutions in general, many traditional families, mainly among the urban upper and upper-middle classes, were forced to undergo certain fundamental changes by the mid-1920's; and the family problem was pushed into the fore of the nation's attention along with other vital political, social, and economic issues of the day.

By this time another great upheaval was rapidly sweeping across China, bringing the stress of a political storm to bear increasingly upon the old social institutions. This was the so-called Second Revolution, which began with the early years of the second decade of the present century and culminated in Chiang Kai-shek's Northern Expedition of 1926 and in the establishment of the Nationalist government in Nanking a year later. The decade from 1927 to the full-scale Japanese invasion of China in 1937 saw the development of the Chinese Communist Party as a military and political power in the "red areas" that studded many parts of the country.

In this turbulent decade social and political forces served to accelerate the pace of the family revolution — although the term was by this time losing its impact of novelty and was less frequently heard. A vital feature of the period was the youthfulness and the Western educational background of the men who came into power, whether in the Nationalist or in the Communist camp. When Chiang Kai-shek led his expeditionary forces northward from Canton in 1926, he was but a young man of forty, and Mao Tse-tung, present head of the Chinese Communist Party, was only thirty-three. Young and modern educated men came to fill an increasing proportion of government offices at all levels.

Although the Republican revolution of 1911 had abolished the imperial laws which supported the traditional family institutions, old officials who manned the government in the early Republican years still exercised their political power largely in the Confucian mode in which they had been raised and trained, and the Republican laws, when enforced at all, were more frequently than not given a Confucian interpretation. But by the late 1920's the gap was fast widening between the Confucian mentality and the attitudes of the young political leadership, and consequently not only the *de jure* but also the *de facto* political control of the traditional family institution dwindled rapidly, particularly in the cities. So overwhelming was the ideological swing away from the Confucian orthodoxy and the social institutions molded by it that repeated restorationist efforts in the 1930's, such as local government orders to reinstate Confucian classics into the school curriculum and the Confucian tenet of the New Life Movement of the Nationalist regime, were unable to turn the tide. Although the scene of ideological struggle was enacted mainly in the cities, the new influence spread to an ever-increasing proportion of the population, especially among those who could afford a modern education.

Against this ideological background, the family revolution persisted on its course set by the previous period. Literature on the subject continued to pour forth from the growing number of mechanical presses.

Increasing social contacts between the young of opposite sexes, growing numbers of marriages resulting from romantic love, and "small families" on the Western model were among the visible results wrought by this process of change. These were living examples of a cause that had come to be embraced by an entire generation of the modern educated young. The youth movement and the women's movement continued to expand and to exert influence upon the development of the family situation. Anti-Communist measures frequently caused setbacks to these movements by hitting many of their organizations as Communist fronts, but this did not affect the spreading struggle among the young against the traditional family and their persistent clamor for its reform.

The Law of Kinship Relations promulgated by the Nationalist government in 1930 incorporated many of the ideological objectives of the family revolution, although many of the basic principles of the traditional family institution were retained.[7] Aside from the question of logical coherence and the lack of effective general enforcement, this compromise law stood as a crystallization of the persistent trend of change in the traditional family, a change which had been brewing for a quarter of a century.

It was true that this trend mainly affected the modern intelligentsia, the majority of whom stemmed from the upper and upper-middle classes in the cities. The importance of this group could not be measured entirely by its small numerical size because of its strategic function in giving direction to the social change and its dominant position in such mechanisms of social control as the government. But the influence of the family revolution in this period was definitely spreading, though slowly, to the urban middle class and a small portion of the city workers. The younger generation of the well-to-do landowners in the countryside also became increasingly affected by the new ideological trends as they went to the cities for a modern education, but, as they soon became identified with the urban intelligentsia and no longer remained members of rural communities, the countryside was not much affected by modern ideological movements.

It is obvious that the gradual change of the traditional family was not the result of ideological agitation alone without the operation of other supporting social and economic factors. The confinement of the family revolution and its related ideological movements mainly to the cities was due precisely to the presence of collaborating social and economic forces in the urban areas and the weakness or absence of such forces in the rural communities.

There was, for example, the concentration of modern educational facilities and the modern press in the cities, which operated as disseminating agents for new ideas about the family and other social institutions which were being challenged by the "new currents of thought." The rapid development of women's education and coeducation since the New Culture Movement was a particularly important influence. Similarly significant was the growth of urban occupational opportunities for women, which provided the economic ground for women's claims for a higher status in the family and in society. The city, with its greater social and economic mobility, offered more fertile ground than the rural community for the dissemination of modern democratic ideas incompatible with the authoritarian characteristics of the traditional family. The growing specialization of social and economic functions, including the commercialization of recreation, undermined the traditional self-sufficiency of the family by reducing many of its functions and thus lessening the individual's dependence upon it. Above all, the accelerating development of modern industry and the emergence of an urban economy geared to its needs after World War I worked to destroy the particularism of the old kinship-oriented social pattern, and compelled some kind of change in the mode of family life.

Growing population mobility, with frequent prolonged physical separation of some members from the family, affected the continued operation of the traditional family organization, which required constant, close contact among the members. Increased population mobility stemmed from a number of social situations, notably the steady deterioration of the handicraft and agricultural economy, the expansion of urbanization, and the high frequency of famines and wars. In the eight years of war against the Japanese invasion (1937–1945), there was no new ideological wave on the reform of the family, but the pouring of millions of modern-minded coastal refugees into the hitherto isolated Southwest undoubtedly aided the disintegration of many traditional families and the formation of new ones on the model promoted by the family revolution. When the curtain of enemy occupation was lifted by the Japanese surrender of 1945, the cities revealed a scene of family life marked by physical separation of members and deviation from the traditional standards, departing further from the Confucian pattern than in any preceding period.

The Communist Revolution and the Chinese Family

In 1949, four years after the Japanese surrender, when the Chinese Communists took over the reins of national political power, China entered upon a period in which drastic political revolution was but one phase of a comprehensive movement aimed at recasting the entire traditional social order by coordinated plans and compulsory measures. The reform of the Chinese family, along with the remaking of other major social institutions, became a part of an over-all drastic social change.

This crisis for the family institution contained no new substance. As already shown, this institution had been changing under constant stress and strain for the preceding three decades; and the Communist crisis, so far as the family was concerned, represented but a more drastic development of the same process, which was now being urged on under a different leadership and in a different manner.

Neither was the effort at altering the family institution anything new with the Communists. Long before the establishment of the Communist regime in 1949, members of the Communist movement had been playing a vital part, along with other reformers and intellectuals, in developing the family revolution and its supporting ideological movements. Ch'en Tu-hsiu, one of the founders of the Chinese Communist Party, ranked with Hu Shih in the New Culture Movement and in the relentless assault against the ideological and institutional citadel of Confucian orthodoxy. Particularly vital was Ch'en's place in initiating and developing the youth movement and the women's movement. Communists in general had been strategic in the agitating and organizing efforts of these movements. The Chinese Communist Party was co-author with the Kuomintang of the Second Revolution, which had serious effects on the development of the family revolution. (Present Communist interpretation of modern Chinese history claims Communist Party leadership in the May 4th Movement and the Second Revolution.) The actual development of the family situation in the "red areas" that came into existence after 1928 has remained largely unrecorded, but scattered information has indicated uncompromising Communist endeavor in changing both the traditional family institution and the kinship-oriented pattern of social organization in those areas.

Many sources of popular information in China for the past thirty years have pictured the Communists as iconoclasts toward the family as a social institution. Ch'en Tu-hsiu was charged by his political enemies with advocating the practice of "communal property and communal wives;" and the charge of practicing "communal wives" was directed against the "red areas" in the early 1930's.[8] There was a disquieting rumor of "forced assignment of wives" by the Communists in 1948 and 1949, a rumor so persistent and widespread that it caused a marriage boom in localities in the paths of the advancing Communist columns in their southward conquest because parents were hurriedly marrying off their daughters in an effort to save them from becoming "assigned wives."

It is probably true that relatively light restrictions were placed upon marriage and divorce in the "red areas" before 1949. This can be seen in such available documents of the period as the Marriage Regulations of the Chinese Soviet Republic and the Temporary Marriage Regulations, both promulgated in 1931 by the Chinese Soviet Republic, and the Marriage Regulations of the Border Area of Shansi, Chahar, and Hopei provinces. But there seems to be no substantiation to the charge of either the practice of "communal wives" or the discarding of the family as a social institution.

Facts as observed in Communist China after 1949 indicate no evidence for any of these allegations. The promulgation of the new Marriage Law on May 1, 1950, and the nationwide efforts at its enforcement by the Communist government through the network of organizations under its command seem clear indications of a Communist policy toward the family which insisted upon drastic reform of the traditional family but fully retained the family as a basic social institution. Even under the people's commune, the family remains the basic social unit, though vastly reduced in its functions. An unmistakable sign of Communist policy was seen in the complex responsibilities involved in divorce by the new Marriage Law, responsibilities that weigh particularly heavy on the husband. (See the English translation of the Marriage Law in the Appendix at the end of this work; see also Chapter IV.) Hence the drastic reform of the traditional family demanded by the Communists should not be taken as an iconoclastic view of the family as a social institution.

The reason for the Communist policy of reshaping the traditional family seems plain. The Communist regime is bent on building an industrial society on the socialistic pattern, and it is fully aware of the incompatibility between such a society and the kinship-oriented structure. Also important for the political purpose of the regime is the incompatibility between the individual's traditional loyalty to the family and the new requirements of his loyalty to the state and to the Communist Party.

Up to the Communist accession to power, the family revolution had proceeded largely as a part of a process of spontaneous social change in modern China. The inauguration of the Communist regime, particularly after the promulgation of the new Marriage Law, brought a

different development. Change of the traditional family is no longer
left to a spontaneous process but is subjected to the compulsory power
of law and the pressure of a powerful, well-organized mass movement;
and it is coordinated with other aspects of the Communist social,
economic, and political revolution.

Traditional Chinese society was composed of numerous semi-autonomous local units, each of which was structured around the kinship
system as its core, and each was only loosely related to the others. As
a national social system, these units were integrated not so much by
extensive functional interdependence and centralized control as by a
fairly uniform institutional framework which enabled Chinese people
everywhere to act together as a group on the basis of a common system
of basic values. At the center of this decentralized system was the kinship structure with its sizable membership, its generational continuity,
its rigid organization, and its multiplicity of socio-economic functions.
In the structural strength and functional effectiveness of this kinship
system lay much of the stability of the traditional social order and the
long continuity of Chinese culture.

Now, under the strain of modern socio-economic influences in general, and of the family revolution in particular, the structural and
functional integrity of the kinship system is sagging notably, and a
new mold of family relationship has been developing to take its place.
With its structural system weakened and its functional importance
reduced, the kinship organization no longer serves as the strategic core
of the social order. Nor is the emerging social order able to function
with a dominant kinship system, for the rapidly developing social pattern is no longer composed of a loose conglomeration of compartmen-
talized local societies in which a strong kinship system is a stabilizing
asset, but is based on a national system of functional interdependence
of the local units and centralized control, a system in which a strong
and dominant kinship organization would have a disruptive influence.
In this sense, the change of the Chinese family and its extended kinship system forms a part of the broad transformation of Chinese society
in the modern age.

As this study is focused on the disorganization of the traditional
family and the development of a new family system, it must stress
the inadequacies of the structural system of the old institution which
caused its progressive disintegration under the pressure of modern
socio-economic influences. Thus, the subsequent pages will disclose

mainly the harsh and tyrannical features of the traditional family and its internal tensions and conflicts. This does not mean that noble qualities are lacking in the traditional Chinese family. The Chinese family has been an object of sentimental praise and even idealization by many Western writers who were generously and kindly disposed toward Chinese culture. And, objectively, the Chinese family has functioned stably and effectively in meeting the multifarious needs of its members and the broad requirements of the traditional social order for a thousand years. The Chinese family must have possessed many attributes of humanitarianism, moral strength, and social wisdom, in order to have been maintained by the people over such a long period of time. Anyone intimately familiar with old Chinese culture can readily reproduce many pictures of family life characterized by affection, mutual sacrifice, orderliness, moral dedication, and a long list of other features that make people feel nostalgic as they face the modern revolutionary scene of violence, chaos, and uncertainty.

But moral evaluation of the Chinese family institution is not the purpose of this study, and presentation of the merits of the old institution has little place in an effort to see why the traditional family is crumbling under the pressure of modern social values and socio-economic influences, or to explain the development of a different family system to better fit into the modern social order. If the reader finds in the subsequent chapters mostly tensions, conflicts, and injustices in the Chinese family, it is because these are the factors most closely associated with the modern change of that ancient institution.

CHAPTER II

Freedom of Marriage

MARRIAGE BEING the first step in the creation of a family, any change in the basic concept of marriage and in the procedure by which it is consummated affects the whole character of the family institution. Inevitably, therefore, the attack on the marriage system shook the foundations of the traditional Chinese family; and, theoretically as well as empirically, the marriage problem is of primary interest in the present analysis.

Marriage in traditional China had been under stifling ritualistic restrictions for a thousand years. In the half century of development of the family revolution the issue of freedom of marriage saw its most dramatic growth and formed the point for the most heated conflict between the younger generation and the traditional family. Inspiring the young was the Western idea of individual freedom and romantic love. Urging the old to reject this demand was the conscious fear of disrupting the long-established order of the family. The clash between generations resulted in untold numbers of tragedies — unreconciled family conflicts, runaway children, broken family ties, and moving stories of suicide. Sentiments and episodes in this clash provided leading themes for modern Chinese fiction and poetry. And the conflict continues in the present period under the Communist regime, spreading from the midst of the modern urban intelligentsia to the multitudes of workers and peasants.

Arranged Marriage and the Traditional Family Institution

To members of the older generation, particularly to the parents, the demand of the modern educated young for freedom of marriage violated the traditional family institution and threatened grave consequences. Fully aware that the form of marriage had a profound effect upon the arrangement of status of the family members, they were not in a mood to relax their traditional control over that critical event. It is therefore necessary to analyze the treatment of marriage by the traditional family in order to see the significance of the demand for freedom in the context of the traditional family institution.

For the traditional Chinese family marriage was not so much an affair of the matured children as an affair of the parents and of the family, with its chief purpose not so much the romantic happiness of the marrying children but fulfilling the sacred duty of producing male heirs for the perpetuation of the ancestors' lineage, the acquiring of a daughter-in-law for the service and comfort of the parents, and the begetting of sons for the security of the parents' old age. Marriage was not a crisis in which a family unit might be reduced and split by the departure of the married son; rather, it was an event not only to expand the family but also to provide additional protection and security to the family unit. To fulfill this purpose, marriage could not be allowed to transfer the center of affection, loyalty, and authority from the parents to the new couple. Hence the traditional discouragement of open affection between husband and wife, particularly when they were newly wed. In every way marriage and its ensuing relationships remained subordinated to the welfare and happiness of the parents and the continuity of the family organization. Such a consideration applied not only to the marriage of a son; the marriage of a daughter was subjected to the same consideration by the husband's family.

To put such traditional principles of marriage into practice was not an easy task. As the children, particularly the sons, were growing up, a centrifugal tendency was already developing away from the family and from parental ties. When marriage took place, the nucleus of an independent unit of family life already had its beginnings. To mitigate the centrifugal tendency, to subject the fresh nucleus to parental control, to force the ways of a grown-up woman, the daughter-in-law, into the mold of intimate family life as dictated by the parents, was very difficult. To achieve this, all the institutional devices of the Chinese family were brought to bear.

In this sense, marriage must of necessity be arranged by the parents. It must come by "orders of the parents and words of the go-between," and not by free choice of the partners. When the marriage had been dictated and arranged by the parents, the son was made to feel that the affair was seriously related to the parents, even though he might not be entirely convinced that his own role in it was totally unimportant. Especially critical was the parents' authority over the choice of a daughter-in-law. This not merely affirmed the dominance of the parents' role and the subordination of the son in the affair of marriage; it also strengthened the control of the parents over the daughter-in-law by making her recognize that she came into the family by their order and choice, not by her personal love for the son. The "words of the go-between" had similar significance. The go-between was an indispensable substitute for open social life between the young of opposite sexes and for romantic love as the medium of marriage.*

Marriage born of romantic love has all the opposite effects of an arranged marriage. The husband-wife relationship is the core, overshadowing the role of the parents, and the intimacy and affection in such a marriage would seriously threaten the dominance of parental affection, loyalty, and authority, if not replace it altogether. If the daughter-in-law should come into the family of her own volition and through affection for her husband, it would be difficult for her to subordinate her role to the will of the parents-in-law.

Thus one device to maintain parental control over the married son and his wife was to deny to the young the ecstatic experience of romantic love and to seek to divert it by other institutional means, such as concubinage and tacit approval of prostitution, while trying to keep the latter from becoming too disruptive an influence to the family organization. For centuries the Chinese school child was made to memorize Mencius' moral exhortation: "If the young people, without waiting for the orders of their parents and the arrangements of the go-between, shall bore holes to steal a sight of each other, or get over the wall to be with each other, then their parents and all other people will despise them." [1] Mencius' explanation for this advice was deeply imbedded in traditionally minded people. "The desire of the child is towards his father and mother. When he becomes conscious of the attraction of beauty, his desire is towards young and beautiful women. When he comes to have a wife and children his desire is towards them. . . . But the man of great filial piety, to the end of his life, has his desire towards his parents." [2] For centuries the traditional thought on marriage took this single track, stifling all romantic dreams.

In addition, there was an economic aspect to parental control over the son's marriage. Normally the parents shouldered the financial responsibility of the marriage and the starting of the new life of the

* The go-between was a diabolical character who specialized in fancy sales talk. It was an important occupation for women in the traditional society, and the practice continued among the majority of the population in recent years, although its place under the Communist regime is in doubt.

couple. To be able to afford their children's marriage was the anxious hope of all parents, and the failure to do so was to have failed in the duty of parenthood and was considered a great misfortune in life. The parents' paying for the expenses of the marriage and letting the son use the family property to start his married life reaffirmed both to the son and to the daughter-in-law who was boss and who was subordinate.

The high cost of the traditional marriage is a well-known story. It was common to see parents sell or mortgage their property to pay for the marriage of their sons, and some of them sank so deeply into debt for this that they could hardly get out of it for the rest of their lives. In the villages in the vicinity of Canton in 1949 it took an average of thirty five piculs of rice for a peasant's son to get married, the equivalent of the net income of a little over a year for a poor peasant. Whatever other significance such sumptuous marriage ceremonies might have, the effect on the minds of the young couple could not be ignored, for it visibly demonstrated to them the dominant role of the parents and the family in their marriage. The more costly the marriage, and, for that matter, the more deeply the parents went into debt, the greater indebtedness the young couple felt toward the parents. When the parents strained their final savings and their last bit of credit in order to give the son a wedding feast, which would be attended by scores of relatives and friends in the cities and hundreds of people in the entire clan in the villages in some parts of the South as required by custom, the couple could not escape the pressure of the claim that their marriage was an affair of the family caused by the parents instead of an affair of the couple themselves motivated by love or personal attraction.

Besides the feast and other ceremonial expenses, a leading item in the cost of the traditional marriage was the amount to be paid the girl's family in kind or in cash or both. Such payment bore a variety of labels, such as the gift of betrothal, or ritual wealth, or body price, depending upon the social class and locality. Whatever the name, such payment was either symbolically or realistically a price for the person of the daughter-in-law, and it compelled the daughter-in-law to reckon with the authority and superiority of the parents-in-law who had paid the price for her.

The elaborate wedding ceremonies served the same general purpose, whatever additional functions they might have. Of foremost importance to the old tradition in a wedding ceremony was the performance of homage and sacrifice to the husband's ancestors. The rite of homage to the parents-in-law carried the same significance. These elaborate ritualistic performances by the new couple inspired in them the feeling that their marriage was only a part of the complex family institution, dramatized for them the importance of the ancestors and the family, dwarfed their own roles as individuals, and demonstrated to them the idea that marriage was a link in the cycle of critical events of the family. The gathering of a large crowd of kinsmen for the ceremony and the feasts also helped to magnify the importance of the family and the kinship group. It is interesting to note here that the bride's family and relatives were not invited to participate in the ceremony and celebration — clearly a means of preventing interference by the bride's family in the exercise of authority over the new daughter-in-law. There was no part of the traditional marriage procedure in which the two families gathered together for any kind of common celebration.

Families that could not afford an elaborate wedding as required by custom commonly resorted to the practice of taking a "child bride." A very young girl, sometimes even an infant, was purchased by a poor family which would raise her along with the young son. When they both reached marriageable age, they were married with a simple ceremony. While the ritualistic function was not outstanding in such a situation, the economic bondage of the couple to the parents was strong, for the parents had not merely raised the son but also the girl. The subordination of the child bride was even greater than that of brides normally married into the family, for she owed directly to the parents-in-law the efforts and expense of bringing her up. Consequently, the parents-in-law's treatment of a child bride was frequently more tyrannical than normally. It is obvious that in such circumstances the son or the wife could not consider their marriage as an affair that they themselves had sponsored or entertain the moral possibility of leaving the parents' household and setting up an independent family unit by themselves.

Taking a child bride as a form of marriage was still common in many rural sections throughout China proper in the early years of Communist rule.[3] While more will be said about this subject later, the following case serves to indicate the current character of this practice. In the immediate vicinity of the county seat of Yi-shi county, Shansi Province, Kao Chuan-wah, was taken as a child bride at the age of twelve. On the day of her betrothal, when the bridal chair was already at her door, she was still playing with other childern on the street, blissfully ignorant of what was taking place. At last, crying and kicking, she was dragged into the bridal chair by her parents and carried away "to suffer inhuman treatment under the cruel hands of the parents-in-law." [4]

Similarly, weird but rare forms of marriage, such as "marrying the spirit" and taking a "daughter-in-law-in-anticipation," which were occasionally practiced in some parts of China, particularly in the South, were products of the same situation. When a woman was betrothed to a man and the man died before the marriage, "marrying the spirit" in full wedding ceremony was sometimes arranged with the consent of the parents of both families, and the bride went through all the ceremonies next to a wooden tablet with the dead man's name and dates of birth and death written on it. Taking a "daughter-in-law-in-anticipation" was a practice in which a couple, having no son as yet, took in a bride in anticipation of the birth of a son. When the right of divorce was emphatically asserted by the Communist Marriage Law in 1950, a twenty-eight-year-old woman in Hupeh Province brought her eight-year-old husband in her arms to the court for a divorce. She had been a "daughter-in-law-in-anticipation." [5] While the economic factor played a part in these practices, they were primarily a product of an institution which considered marriage an affair of the family and dictated by the parents for the purpose of perpetuating and operating the traditional family organization. They illustrate the extreme to which marriage could be carried, even without a male spouse in actual existence, all for the purpose of completing this link in the cycle of events in the family in order that the organization of the family could at least symbolically approach the traditional ideal form.

Another factor contributing to the consolidation of the family organization and assertion of parental authority was the traditional practice of marrying the son as young as possible if the parents' economic means allowed. It was considered glorious to have grandchildren at an early age; and there is the folk tale of a well-known man who, at the age of thirty-six, was displaying his grandchild with pride. There is no systematic quantitative data to show how far this ideal was realized in the traditional society. As a general urban practice some three decades ago, it was common for sons to be married between sixteen and eighteen; for a daughter, marriage at nineteen was considered rather late. This practice is still current in rural districts today, as substantiated by sample population studies in rural areas. For instance, in the rural district of Cheng Kung in Yunnan Province, during the period 1940–1944, the age of first marriage for males was concentrated in the range of sixteen to twenty-one with the median at nineteen; for females the range was between fifteen and twenty, with the median at seventeen.[6]

A young boy of sixteen to eighteen was obviously unable to afford the expenditure of a traditional marriage and the support of a new family, especially in the traditional society in which employment opportunity outside of the family was limited and the struggle for existence was hard. Hence, the younger a son was married, the more dominant was the role of the parents in the marriage and in his married life. The daughter-in-law was subjected to the same influence owing to the dependency of the husband. In addition, marriage at an early age made it easier for her to conform to subordination to the mother-in-law than if she were married at a later, less pliable age.

To strengthen the effectiveness of these institutional devices and practices and to guard against their possible failure in meeting individual situations, the supernatural influence of religion was invoked to play a part in the traditional institution of marriage. After the go-between had brought two prospective partners together, the parents of both families would take the next step of consulting the oracles to see if the dates of birth of the boy and the girl were in harmony or in conflict with each other. Should they harmonize, the marriage had the approval of the spiritual world, and it was fate that had brought the two matrimonial partners together. The god in the moon had tied their legs together with a red ribbon, as the folk tale goes. The lengthy and elaborate wedding ceremony was permeated with religious acts of paying homage and sacrifice to the ancestors and the gods, all to impress the young couple with the irresistibility of fate and the sanction of institutional ideals and practices by the spiritual powers. After this, if the individuals still found the married state unsatisfactory, they would be advised to submit to fate, which would punish them for their individual failures.

Traditional marriage made possible the expansion of the conjugal family into the patriarchal "big family" to include married brothers and their wives who were organizationally integrated under the dominant role of the parents. At the death of the parents, if the big family was not to break up but to continue, as frequently was the case, the eldest son acted as the head of the family after the parents had set up the organization and laid down the pattern. Obviously, should marriage be considered primarily an affair of the young couple, initiated by themselves in the Western style of romantic love, it would be difficult to organize the married brothers and their wives into a tightly knit and delicately balanced unit. Without the dominant and coordinating role of the parents as expressed in the traditional marriage and in other ways, it would be difficult to settle the numerous family disputes between brothers and between their wives who occupied relatively equal status.

The system of arranged marriage and all of its institutional devices helped to assure the parents of the continued discharge of filial duties by their children after marriage. The preservation of the parents' dominant role after the children's marriage also strengthened the age and generational structuring of the family membership, for control over an individual by age and generational factors tended to weaken as he grew older, and marriage was a distinct mark and reminder of the advancement of age. Similarly strengthened by the institution of arranged marriage was intra-class selection of mates. When a marriage was arranged by the parents, the choice of a mate was less influenced by emotion and more by conventional considerations such as expressed by the proverbial admonition of "matching a bamboo door with a bamboo door, and a wooden door with a wooden door." * Organizationally, intra-class marriage tended to facilitate the assimilation of the daughter-in-law by the new family due to the greater similarity of ways of life between the two families. In short, the ramifying influences of the system of arranged marriage made it an inseparable part of the traditional family organization.

Weakening of Arranged Marriage under the Republic

Institutional devices succeeded in severing the connection between romantic love and formal marriage but not in completely suppressing the emotional appeal of romantic love, which cropped up in concubinage and such forms of extramarital relations as prostitution, and burst out in lamenting poetry and fiction. The strong desire for romance by the young constantly posed a serious potential threat to arranged marriage and frequently acted as a disruptive influence to the traditional family by behavior such as squandering money on other women at the expense of family necessities or taking in a nonconforming prostitute as a concubine. For the woman, since arranged marriage required her to enter abruptly into intimate relations with a man with whom she had had no previous contact, the secret desire for marriage through love had a strong appeal. Thus, a structural strain in the traditional family provided the wedge for the entry of a new and highly disruptive influence.

* The word "door" in the Chinese context carries the meaning of the prestige and status of a family.

When the cry for freedom of marriage through love was raised with the swelling tide of revolution soon after the turn of the century, the effect on the educated young was infectious, and acceptance of the new idea was ready and eager. While the revolution of 1911 was mainly a political event, it nevertheless signified the general call for a new order of life, leading many young men and women to hope for marriage through love and to make attempts which often resulted in tragedy. In 1912 a woman teacher in a Shanghai primary school openly made friends with a male colleague, fell in love with him, and the two secretly decided to be married. When the affair became known to others there was gossip accusing the two of promiscuity. The woman was especially attacked as one of immoral character. Under the crushing attack of public opinion and stern warnings from parents of both parties, the man weakened and told the woman he could not marry her. She now found society turned against her, and after leaving the man a heart-rending letter, she committed suicide. In some cases both the man and the woman were driven to suicide by group pressure in the form of social ostracism and public gossip.[7]

Although the stone wall of traditional mores stood firm in the first two decades of the present century, the movement for freedom of marriage continued to spread, mainly among the modern intelligentsia. The forceful impact of each subsequent revolutionary wave, such as the May 4th Movement of 1919 and the Second Revolution in the mid-1920's, gave the movement added impetus, and it became increasingly difficult for parents and social institutions to enforce the concept that marriage was primarily not a couple's own business but the business of the family and the parents. Other social and economic changes, wars, and political disturbances, resulting in identification of the individual with new group interests and in physical separation of family members, converged to loosen parental control over the young and increased the difficulty of retaining the arranged marriage system.

When the Nationalist government was established in Nanking in 1927, large numbers of modern young intellectuals came to occupy responsible positions in it, bringing with them the concepts of the family institution developed in the family revolution during the previous three decades. The consequence was the promulgation of a new kinship law which permitted marriage by free choice of partners conditioned upon parental approval. While this Nationalist law did not prohibit marriage by compulsory parental arrangement, it nonetheless provided for the first time legal recognition of marriage which realized the importance of the young couple's own interest. A major limitation of this legal act was the lack of active enforcement among the common people, who largely remained ignorant of its existence.

The years toward the mid-century found most parents of the urban intelligentsia facing the formerly bitterly contested issue with a spirit of resignation. The movement spread rather slowly to other segments of the population not benefited by modern education, the workers and the peasants, and the conflict between the generations over the form of marriage continued on a steadily increasing scale. When the Communists took over the country in 1949, the great change lay not in the introduction of a totally new concept of marriage but in steadily extending the new marriage movement to the workers and peasants whose family life so far had remained little touched by the new ideal.

Freedom of Marriage under the Communist Regime

The struggle for freedom of marriage based on love has always been stressed by the Communist movement, and this freedom had been written into laws and regulations on marriage in the "red areas" for two decades previous to Communist accession to national power in 1949.[8] The new Marriage Law, promulgated in May 1950, was one of the first major laws ensuing from the new regime. This law abolishes the "arbitrary and compulsory" form of marriage and establishes the "New Democratic" form of marriage.[9] Interference of parents in their children's marriage is ruled illegal.[10] The practice of paying a price for the bride, whether in the form of money or goods or articles, whether under the name of "body price" or "ritual gift of wealth," is prohibited.[11] To get married, the couple have only to register in person with the local government, and the marriage becomes legal if it is found to be in conformity with the provisions of the marriage law. Should the marriage be found contrary to the legal provisions, it is given no legal recognition.[12] Such legal provisions consist of the "complete willingness of the two parties"[13] and the prohibition of the following: the use of compulsion or the interference by third parties including parents,[14] the committing of polygamy by taking concubines or other polygamous behavior, child brides, interference with the remarriage of widows, the exaction of money or gifts,[15] violation of minimum age requirements for marriage,[16] and marriage between close kin, by the sexually impotent, or by those afflicted with loathsome diseases.[17] There is no requirement such as the ceremonial celebrations provided in the traditional marriage and in the marriage law of the Nationalist government.

The basic points of the Marriage Law had been developed in the family revolution in the pre-Communist period, and many of them, such as the prohibition of concubinage and other forms of polygamy, are found in the Nationalist marriage law. Instead of breaking any new ground, the Communist marriage law represents the continued advancement of the family revolution in two major respects, the extension of the new marriage concept to a larger proportion of the population and the use of political power to achieve institutionalization of the new marriage system. It is obvious that the form of marriage defined by the new law is unacceptable to the traditional mind. In the urban upper and upper-middle classes, from which the intelligentsia mostly stem, the long process of family revolution has broken down much of the resistance of the older generation, but resistance to the new form of marriage remains strong among the working class and the peasantry, where the voice for freedom of marriage has not been widely raised. It is in the latter segment of the population that the greatest change is being brought about by Communist propaganda, indoctrination, and enforcement of the new Marriage Law (see Chapter XII on propaganda). Political power, with many forms of social and economic pressure at its command, is thrown directly into the conflict on the side of the new marriage system against the old one. The development of the new family institution, hitherto mainly part of a spontaneous process of social change, is now being aided by the leverage of political power and law.

One means of using political and legal power to gain popular acceptance of the new form of marriage, especially among the multitudes of workers and peasants, is the new legal requirement of the registration of all new marriages. Couples intending to get married come before the Communist official in charge of marriage registration for the locality. He asks the couple whether the intended marriage is taking place with the consent of both parties, whether duress from any third party has been exerted, whether polygamy or concubinage is involved. If the answers agree with the legal provisions, and if the results of an investigation check with the answers, a marriage certificate is issued and the couple is legally married. In the cities, medical examination is required in addition to the above procedure.[18]

Although marriage registration is stipulated in the Marriage Law as promulgated in 1950, the Communist government issued a supplementary Rules for Marriage Registration in 1955 [19] to insure universal enforcement. This legal document introduces two new features. The first is the addition of marriage registration as one of the functions of the large number of lower-level government agencies such as the neighborhood offices in the cities and the People's Committees of village districts and towns in the rural areas, thus vastly increasing the accessibility of the registration facilities to the common people. Secondly, the registering officials are required to explain to the registrants the stipulations of the marriage law so as to acquaint them with their own legal rights and obligations before proceeding with interrogations and examination of the case for approval or disapproval of the registration. The measure has the merit of informing the common people of the contents of the new law as a vital step in its effective enforcement, which is in contrast to the conditions under the Nationalist government, when the majority of the population were ignorant of the existence of a new marriage law.

There is no systematic quantitative data on the extent of the success of these means in establishing the new form of marriage. Fragmentary figures in reports from various parts of the country show that a beginning of the new system is being made in rural communities which had not been generally influenced by the family revolution in the pre-Communist period. In 178 villages of Huailai county of Chahar Province, in the period of ten months following the promulgation of the Marriage Law on May 1, 1950, there were altogether some 400 marriages, of which some 300 were based on the free will of the contracted parties "plus the agreement of the parents on both sides." [20] In other words, about 75 per cent of all the marriages in the stated period followed the new form, although the expression of agreement of the parents on such marriages shows that some influence of the old tradition still exists among these new marriages. Again, in two rural subdistricts of Hailien county of Shantung Province, in an unspecified period of 1951, there were 290 traditional "selling-and-buying" marriages as against 227 marriages based on the free choice of partners and love.[21] There are fragmentary figures which do not provide any comparison with the number of traditional marriages in the same locality in the same period. Thus, it is stated that in the rural county of Yaoyang in Hopei Province 120 couples were married according to the provisions of the new law.[22] In the rural town of Pochen of Shantung Province, within the period of a year following the promulgation of the Marriage Law, 488 young men and women married of their own free will and for love, and many of them won parental consent only after a "bitter struggle." [23] All these localities are a part of North China. Statistics on other regions are available only in a few instances. A report covering seven counties in Chiahsing Special District of

Chekiang Province, four counties of the Hsuanch'eng Special District in the southern part of Anhwei Province, and Jukao county in the northern part of Kiangsu, a total of twelve counties, shows that "34 per cent of all women who were married [time unspecified] did so of their free will." [24] Such is the reported picture of the East China Region. In the Central-South Region "according to incomplete statistics, during the period from January to April, 1951, 23,600 new couples registered their marriage with the government." [25]

There are questions of accuracy and comparability regarding the above figures, particularly the percentages in the twelve rural counties of the East China Region. Nevertheless, they indicate that the idea of the new form of marriage is being widely disseminated among the conservative rural population. The new marriages in the hitherto isolated countryside, although few in number, are becoming fermenting agents, causing local youth to react against the repressive traditional family and to challenge its authority.

In terms of individual situations, these statistical figures represent an increasing number of cases of struggle by young peasants and workers for the freedom of marriage. Typical among the peasants is the case of Li Ta-kuei, a peasant girl in Hsiawan village of Luchiang county, Anhwei Province. She was betrothed to a maternal cousin against her wish. The engagement was so unpleasant to her that she once attempted suicide as a means of forcing its cancellation. When the propaganda corps of the Marriage Law came to the village to explain the new legal stipulations on marriage, she became emboldened. After some struggle with the family, she went to the subdistrict government and obtained a legal cancellation of the betrothal. Finally she married a young peasant with whom she had fallen in love.[26]

Among the urban workers the enforcement of the new Marriage Law yields similar cases of struggle between the young and the older generation. Typical is the experience of Yen Ts'ai-nü, a nineteen-year-old girl who worked in a Shanghai cotton mill. Her father and grandmother, in accordance with the old custom, betrothed her to a worker in a grocery store. Her first knowledge of the betrothal came when relatives arrived for the ceremonial feast. She was very angry and demanded that the betrothal be nullified. Her father and grandmother beat her for protesting. When she could not stand the mistreatment any longer, she went to the family of her deceased mother for support and appealed to the Association of Family Women (an affiliated organization of the Democratic Women's League) requesting assistance in the cancellation of the betrothal. The father and grandmother heard of this and rushed to the maternal relatives to raise trouble. The ensuing quarrel stirred up the whole neighborhood, and the case was taken to the people's court. The court ruled that the betrothal should be canceled.[27]

There are, however, less tortuous circumstances by which new marriage has come to the workers. Tai Yu-lan (woman) and Chao Ch'uan-yung were both workers in Cotton Mill Number 1 in Tientsin. They had been in love with each other for some time, but owing to the traditional stigma placed upon free choice of partners and love, had not dared talk about getting married. After they learned of the new Marriage Law in May 1950, they became engaged, and in March of 1951 they were married by the legal formality of registering with the local government.[28]

The preceding cases illustrate the re-enactment of social conflicts centering upon the marriage problem, a familiar scene among the modern urban intellectuals in the pre-Communist period, now being extended to the peasants and workers. But such cases may not represent a universal picture of the marriages reported as being in conformity with the new law. Thus, in the 178 villages in Chahar Province all the 300 new marriages were reported to be based on the free will of the partners as well as the consent of their parents, but it is hard to judge the relative weight between free will and parental consent. The latter in some instances might mean actual parental arrangement and verbal profession of free will by the boy and girl before the local official, an act of formality under previous instruction from the parents. On the other hand, there were many instances even in the pre-Communist period when a couple were married on the basis of love but, after going through the new simple form of marriage, again went through the full ceremony of the traditional marriage in order to appease the family and to gain institutional recognition from the local community.

At least, it is an established fact that the idea of the new form of marriage is being spread by propaganda and other means among the workers and peasants, and that those who wish to fight for the new privilege have the help of the law in places where local officials are sufficiently indoctrinated in the Marriage Law and are willing to enforce it. In such places members of the older generation no longer possess the coercive power that they held in the pre-Communist period in maintaining the traditional institution of marriage. The increasing accessibility of legal assistance to the people, as suggested from the fragmentary figures, points to the accelerating trend of the new form of marriage and to the rapid undermining of the authority and solidarity of the traditional family institution.

Resistance by Tradition against the New Marriage Ideas

A recurrent problem in an age of revolution is the relative effectiveness of law as a means of uprooting old institutions which have passed their days of usefulness. A new law imposed by a progressive minority upon a conservative public naturally meets popular opposition motivated by the still strong values and structure of the traditional institutions; and the conservative force of the opposing majority slows down the operation of a new law despite the vigor and absolutism of a fresh revolutionary political power. This problem is particularly pertinent to a country like China where the maintenance of the traditional social order has relied much more heavily on the operation of social institutions than on the functioning of formal government and law.

Thus there has been opposition to the new Marriage Law among local Communist officials, even though enforcement of the new law is a part of their functions. Indications point to the possibility that a large number of them neither understand nor accept the new legal principles of marriage. In October of 1951, almost a year and a half after the promulgation of the new Marriage Law, the Department of Interior of the Communist central government stated in a directive urging local political leaders to study the law carefully: "A very common phenomenon is . . . the adopting of antagonistic attitudes toward the Marriage Law by some subdistrict and village cadres . . . . Some even use imprisonment and torturing to handle marriage cases [in an effort to enforce the traditional institution]." [29] Similar directives and statements have been issued by other official and semi-official organizations.

It is significant that resistance against the new Marriage Law by the cadres is a reflection of the popular attitude among the local population. The requirement of marriage registration is strange to the common people whose social life, especially marriage, has been regulated hitherto mainly by tradition rather than by law. Traditionally, government and law enter into the picture only on the occasion of a grave violation of institutional practices. Even in the modernized city of Shanghai, where the people are more legal-minded than in the countryside, when a factory girl who was to be married was advised by a woman member of the labor union, "Don't forget to register with the government," two other women workers standing on the side asked, "Even marriage has to be registered?" Some other workers chimed in: "From ancient times to the present day, whoever has heard of having to register a marriage with the government, and what is the new fashion for?" [30] This attitude is especially common among many local officials in rural areas. The Preparatory Committee of the Democratic Women's League of the Central-South Region stated in October 1951: "Some cadres consider that the marriage problem is a private matter which the government and the court should not interfere with." [31]

If the requirement of marriage registration astonished the people, freedom of marriage and the new principle of marriage by love raised roars of objection. People charged that marriage by free choice of partners was to make marriage "a loose affair." Others said that "this will make a mess of the relationship between men and women." Still others were certain that "freedom of marriage will lead the world into general promiscuity." [32] The relaxation of the sex mores and the consequent fear of a general moral degeneration have been familiar charges from the opposition in family-reform movements in other lands in modern times, and its recurrence in China is but a part of a typical picture long known to students of sociology of the family.

Like registration, the practice of free choice in marriage met opposition not only from the common people but also from an appreciable proportion of party leaders and local government officials. In Shiht'ang village of the third subdistrict, Yungch'un county of Kwangsi Province, during the period from May 30 to June 6, 1951, the village head ordered the militia to arrest and cruelly torture ten women, forced them to parade in the streets, and made them the object of "struggle" in mass "struggle meetings." The charge was that these women manifested bad behavior. The case was later discovered by the people's court, and the village head was sentenced to four months' imprisonment,[33] for the women's "bad behavior" was their attempt to make love to men or to marry for love. Similarly, in P'uk'ou village of Chinhua county, Chekiang Province, when a peasant girl fell in love with the secretary of the village Youth Corps, soldiers and some of the members of the Youth Corps raised a "struggle" against the couple, accusing them of promiscuity because they had been seen once together in the same room. A "public trial" was held, and the two were told to confess to having been promiscuous.[34] In a suburban village of Hankow, when a young peasant couple fell in love, they were immediately made the object of "struggle" by the village women's association, in which the local militia and the village leaders participated. Deeply shamed, the woman unsuccessfully attempted suicide by hanging. Later, when the "corps of examination of the enforcement of the Marriage Law" arrived in the village, help was given the couple, enabling them to be legally married according to the new law.[35] In a village near the town of Shaohsing in Chekiang Province a village schoolteacher, Ch'ang Jui-p'eng, a member of the Youth Corps, fell in love with a "progressive" girl who was also a member of the Corps. When they became engaged and asked for consent from parents on both sides, they met objection from both families and from the villagers. Even the Youth Corps called a membership meeting to launch a "struggle" against them, saying that "our Corps is morally pure, but the relationship of these two is not pure." A decision was made to dismiss the two from Corps membership. Group pressure closed in on them. The man attempted suicide but failed. The girl became mentally ill. Later, the case was brought to the attention of the people's court, which straightened out their trouble, and they were married.[36]

These cases cited from official Communist reports, which show the new political leaders acting together with the local population in a common attempt to protect the traditional institution of marriage against the new principle of marriage based on free choice of partners and romantic love, indicate clearly the limitation of the power of law alone as a means of changing an age-old social institution. The high Communist leadership appears to be aware of this. Hsieh Chueh-tsai, Minister of the Department of Interior, has stated:

> The Marriage Law, once promulgated . . . cannot be expected to see unobstructed enforcement. China is a very ancient society, with many remnants of bad customs of feudalism . . . still existing strongly in not a few places. Therefore, the enforcement of the Marriage Law should not be regarded as a matter for the government alone, but should be a common object of study and propaganda for the cadres and the people before it can be thoroughly realized as a correct legal standard in the problem of marriage.[37]

Pursuing this theme, the Communist authorities emphasize "study" (indoctrination) of the new Marriage Law, especially for local leaders, and the acceleration of propaganda campaigns by both government agencies and public organizations such as the youth and women's organizations.

It is claimed that an intensive indoctrination campaign in 1953 yielded some 3,500,000 lower-echelon leaders trained in the understanding and interpretation of the new Marriage Law. They were distributed over 1,118 counties and 111 cities throughout the country to directly administer the new law among the people.[38] In view of the widespread ignorance of the new law among local Communist officials, many of whom were recruited from the hardly literate peasantry when the Communists came into power, such training of the local leaders was a logical first step in any attempt to effectively enforce the new marriage principles. In some localities, indoctrination and propaganda campaigns have produced to a certain degree a change of attitude among the leaders and people (see Chapter XII).

The New Marriage Law and the Traditional Family Organization

Granting a measure of success in the dissemination of the new marriage concept through indoctrination and propaganda, the introduction and stabilization of the new family institution still depends not only on the enforcement of the new law but also on a number of socioeconomic factors that affect the functions and structure of the family.

Marriage now becomes an affair of the marrying couples themselves, intended for their own common life,[39] and no longer an affair intended for the perpetuation of the ancestral lineage. The prohibition of polygamy, even to assure the birth of a son, and the new right of a wife to have custody of her children in a divorce show that begetting male descendants is no longer a guiding principle of marriage, a change by which the sacred character of the traditional family is seriously undermined. The strong traditional bond between parents and the married son is obviously weakened under the new arrangement since free choice of a partner greatly reduces the parents' role in their children's marital affairs, a change with grave consequences for the traditional family which relied upon parental authority over the children's marriage as a leading integrating factor. The economic aspect of the parents' role is likewise affected. Parents continue to contribute to the marriage expenses of the children, particularly sons, but these expenses tend to decline; and there is a consequent decline in the importance of parental economic control over the children's marriage and the children's moral obligation to the parents.

One part of the traditional marriage expenditure, the often ruinously heavy purchase price of the bride, is now forbidden by law and is no longer in practice where marriage is conducted in the modern form. As will be seen later, the husband's attempt to recover the purchase price of the bride, if she should subsequently insist upon a divorce, is rejected by the people's court on the ground that paying a price for a bride is neither legal nor in harmony with the moral standard of the "new democracy." [40] Should this verdict be universally held, as the result of the accelerating indoctrination of the judicial workers to the new standard, even traditionally minded ones will hesitate to pay a heavy price for a bride, particularly in view of the idea of freedom of divorce now being introduced by the new ideology and guaranteed by the new law. No doubt, gifts may still be exchanged by the two families involved, but such gifts do not approach the amount of the traditional bridal price.

In the new marriages the girl's family now receives prepared food and some chickens or ducks, or even some grain, but these are given freely and not as the result of any bargaining. Frequently the girl's family receives nothing at all (see Chapter VI on the status of women). This particularly affects the traditional relation between the mother-in-law and daughter-in-law, for now the stigma of the latter's bondage and subordination, as symbolized by the traditional bridal price, is removed.

Another taxing burden in the traditional marriage expenditure, the ceremonial expenses which included the heavy item for feasts, is now also sharply reduced. The simplification of marriage ceremonies has been a pre-Communist trend since the early 1920's, culminating in the "group ceremony of marriage" in the 1930's developed under the Nationalist regime for the purpose of saving marriage expenses. Such group ceremonies involved scores or even a hundred couples at a time, and a local government official such as the head of the municipal bureau of social welfare or the mayor of a city officiated. More popular in the pre-Communist period than the "group ceremony" was the "civilized marriage ceremony" patterned closely after the Western style, with the presence of the parents of both families, a "witness," and a circle of relatives and friends. In either case, the ceremony was less elaborate and expensive than the traditional type. Under Communist rule, sumptuous weddings are not only condemned by the new ideology, which emphasizes utilitarian practicality, but are also discouraged by the general fear that any conspicuous display of wealth such as elaborate ceremonies and feasts is dangerous. Thus the pre-Communist trend toward ceremonial simplification has been accelerated by political pressure; and in practice most modern marriages under the Communists have been consummated by registering with the government followed by a simple "tea party" of light refreshments instead of the former lavish feasts, and attended only by a small group of close relatives and friends. Young couples now insist upon this type of wedding as a part of the fashion of the times, however much it may be against the parents' sense of values.

The simplified wedding ceremony has two implications for the traditional family. First, it reduces the expense of marriage and thus decreases the importance of the parents' role in the marriage of their children. Second, the attendance at such weddings by only a few close relatives instead of by the large extended family circle or clan mitigates the importance and the social pressure of the general kinship system on the matrimonial affairs of the young. Hence, the simplification of the wedding ceremony has the effect of dramatizing the role of the marrying couple and dwarfs the importance of both the parents and the kinship system since it focuses public attention on the marrying individuals and not on the kinship group.

The new ceremony differs from the old in still other aspects. While the bride and groom often put on special wedding clothes, such garments do not compare with the heavy elaborateness of the traditional costumes. In addition, others attending the occasion are no longer decked in gorgeous ceremonial clothing as in the traditional form. These changes make the wedding appear more secular than the deeply impressive affair of the family as emphasized by the elaborately costumed circle of relatives who attend the ceremony. Above all, the various religious acts such as offering sacrifices and bowing to the ancestors are now expunged from the ceremonies in a large number of the new marriages upon the insistence of the young couples. This secularization of the new marriages reduces the sacred character of both the family and the marriage and consequently weakens the dominance of the parents and the family over the married son and the daughter-in-law, a dominance which was strengthened by sacred sentiment in the traditional ceremonies. Most couples who are married under the new system no longer perform such religious acts as consulting oracles on the compatibility of the fates of the two persons intending to get married and ignore the tale about the god in the moon who predetermines matrimonial partnership, even though such superstitions may still persist among the uneducated common people.

Change in the marriage age is another important feature of the new marriage situation. Among the upper and middle classes for some three decades there has been a tendency toward later marriage. Previously for the man, the breadwinner of the family, marriage was common before the age of twenty; now the general practice is marriage after the age of twenty. It is very common now for a girl to be married between the ages of eighteen and the early twenties, whereas previously marriage after eighteen was considered late and it was difficult to find a suitable man for a girl over twenty. Among workers and peasants the man's marriage age has generally been two or three years later than for the upper and middle classes, and dislocation of the traditional economy in the past half century has had the effect of postponing it even later. The Communist Marriage Law now sets the minimum legal age of marriage as twenty for men and eighteen for women, instead of eighteen for men and sixteen for women as provided in the Nationalist law.

The effect of later marriage on the relation of the married son and daughter-in-law to the parents and the family can be plainly seen. The man is usually economically more independent after the age of twenty. He can better afford not only the expenses of marriage, now much lighter than before, but the support of a new family as well — or, if he works on the parents' farm or in their shop, he can at least make a greater contribution toward the support of the new family. His greater economic value significantly reduces the importance of the role of the parents and the family in marriage and consequently undermines the authority of the latter over his married life. An older daughter-in-law is also a less malleable person to be molded into her traditional position in a complex family situation. Her husband's greater economic value at marriage strengthens her attitude of independence toward the parents-in-law and other members of the family. Above all, an independent income brought in by the daughter-in-law in a rapidly collectivizing economy elevates her family status (see Chapter VIII). All these have serious effects on the role structure of the traditional family.

If marriage as arranged by parents is a significant factor in maintaining intra-class marriage, free choice of partners contributes somewhat to the weakening of class demarcation in matrimonial affairs. Present facts show no sign of inter-class marriage becoming a general phenomenon even among the ideologically progressive young men and women. Class factors still have a strong influence on the choice of mates. But when the class distance between a couple is not too great, the traditional barrier against their marriage seems to break down in the case of modern marriages.

The inter-class marriage of Lin Yi-k'ai, daughter of a small landowner in Shunteh county, Kwangtung Province, to Lo Jen-ch'eng, her father's farmhand, is an illustration. The two fell in love after Lo had been working on Lin's farm for three years. In 1951 the girl summoned enough courage to ask her parents for permission to marry Lo. The father was horrified; he thought the boy, only a farmhand, too poor and that the marriage would be one of "inviting the husband into the wife's house," a humiliation to the family of Lin. Clansmen in the village also raised objections to the marriage as a violation of the clan's tradition. The girl eloped with Lo to his village, intending to be married there. The peasants' association and women's association of the girl's village learned about the case, and representative members of the two organizations visited the girl's father to carry out a "struggle by reasoning," demanding that the couple be permitted to return to the village and be married. The old man became remorseful, for he was too old to farm and could not afford to lose these two young laborers from the family, and he acceded to the demand. The subdistrict government was quick to capitalize on the propaganda value of the event by turning the wedding into a public affair for the whole village, attended by four hundred people.[41]

Marriages of an upper-class son and a poorer middle-class girl or vice versa have been common among the intelligentsia in recent decades, but among the peasantry similar cases were rare until the Communists took power and promulgated the Marriage Law. The entrance of a daughter-in-law into the family from another class status adds obstacles to the assimilation of the new member and makes it harder to maintain the complex and delicate family organization of the traditional form. In a broader perspective, the situation accelerates the reshuffling of the population into a new class alignment under Communist rule.

When a couple initiate and control their own marriage, there is, of course, no longer ground for the continuation of abnormal forms of traditional marriage such as the taking of a child bride, "marrying the spirit," or taking a "daughter-in-law-in-anticipation." The new Marriage Law [42] and the interpretation given it by Communist judicial authorities [43] vehemently attack the practice of taking child brides because of its widespread existence and the acute suffering of the little girls.

It can be readily seen that the many changes of the marriage institution from traditional principles and practices to the new form affect the role of the parents in relation to the married son and the daughter-in-law so seriously that it has become difficult for the family organization to continue to operate as formerly. The shift of the center of marriage control from the parents to the young couple, the change in marriage procedures, together with other new social and economic factors, necessitate a new balance of roles involving the relation of the parents to their married sons and daughters-in-law and the relation between the wife and husband. The setting up by the married son of an independent household, thus ending the expansibility of a small family into a big one, a basic feature of the traditional family system, occurs increasingly as families come under the new influence.

While the new form of marriage based on free choice of partners has an obviously disintegrating effect on the structure of the traditional family, it is not yet clear what new form of family will emerge. In the urban centers, where the socio-economic functions of the family are being drastically reduced by the emerging socialistic economy, there is a strong tendency toward the development of a conjugal family of the Western type. But even here, whether the aging parents will become members of a married son's family is still a serious problem prior to the development of an effective collective program to meet the social and economic needs of the aged. In the rural communities, where kinship relations have always been a supreme social factor, the development of a conjugal, two-generation family to replace the old institution meets even more problems than in the urban areas. During 1949–1958, neither the land reform nor the subsequent collectivization movement produced any effective socio-economic pattern capable of systematically replacing the economic structure of the traditional family. But the people's commune, if successfully stabilized, may become a significant factor in inducing the development of a two-generation conjugal family in the rural communities because the commune system of remuneration seriously restricts the individual worker's ability to support his family, and because the commune assumes direct responsibility for supporting all individuals within its confines, including the young and the aged. However, the commune system remains a radical social experiment in 1959, with results uncertain, thus making it difficult to predict the new form of the family which may eventually emerge under its influence.

CHAPTER III

Associated Problems of Marriage

THE PREVIOUS chapter analyzed arranged marriage as a structural factor in the traditional family and the rise of marriage by free choice of partners as an influence destructive to the old kinship system but also conducive to the development of a new one. Associated with the traditional form of marriage are several secondary problems concerning the stability of the family, namely, the remarriage of widows, the practice of polygamy, and the related issue of prostitution. The traditional restrictions against the remarriage of widows was an important device in enforcing the solidarity of the family group; the institutional recognition of polygamy was partly a means to insure the continuity of the family organization; and polygamy together with the tacit approval of prostitution had the function of mitigating men's tension under arranged marriage and retaining their loyalty toward the old family institution. Thus, recent institutional alterations regarding the remarriage of widows, polygamy, and prostitution have obvious effects on the ability of the family to continue functioning in the traditional form and on the trend toward a different kinship system.

Remarriage of Widows under the Traditional System

We have noted that the traditional form of marriage was characterized by its rigid subordination of the marrying individuals to the consideration of the husband's family headed by his parents. The question arises as to how such a marriage, reinforced by the religious idea of fate, dealt with a serious situation such as the death of a spouse, which affects both the continuation of the family organization and the status and welfare of the surviving spouse as an individual.

If the wife died, there was little institutional problem involved. Tradition allowed the widowed husband to take another wife or a concubine, whichever he desired. The membership vacancy in the family was thus filled, the weakened organization was restrengthened, and the process of family assimilation of the new member began all over again. In localities for which statistical information on this point is available widowed men were from 7 per cent to 10 per cent of all married men.[1] Their failure to remarry was usually due to poverty or old age and not institutional restriction. An outstanding institutional problem involved in the remarriage of widowed men was the frequent mistreatment of the deceased wife's children by the new wife or concubine, which was a disruptive factor to the family organization. Under the traditional system the paternal grandparents attempted to prevent such mistreatment, but, if the grandparents died while the children of the deceased wife were still very young, the only protective force for the unfortunate children except their father would be close relatives sensitive to such situations in an intimately integrated kinship system. In fact, a devoted father who had serious concern for his children's welfare often refrained from remarriage.

But it was entirely different for the widowed woman. Institutional restriction against the remarriage of widows is strongly reflected in fragmentary statistical sources which show a high ratio of widows among married women. Sample census figures of nine counties in Szechwan Province of Southwest China in 1947 show a ratio of one widow to every 3.15 married women.[2] Sample studies of nine localities in northern, eastern, and southwestern regions show a range of one widow for every 3.02 to 4.15 married women fifteen years of age and over.[3] Compared with one widow for every 5.55 married women of fifteen years of age and over in the United States,[4] these ratios of widows in China are much higher. Only in India, where there is one widow to every 3.14 married women, can the situation in China find a counterpart.[5]

The general traditional situation was that a widow seldom remarried as long as the husband's family could support her. A certain number of widows in poor families did remarry on account of economic pressure, in which case the husband's family usually exacted a price as a condition of her remarriage. The higher frequency of the remarriage of widows among the poor indicates a weaker family organization in the lower than in the middle and upper classes; but even among poor families it was common to find that after the death of the husband the widow became the only adult in the family with income-earning capacity, the parents-in-law, if living, being too old to work. In such cases the widow frequently remained in the family in order to support the parents-in-law as well as her own children.

The institutional interpretation of the restriction against the re-marriage of widows is fairly obvious. The mores of chastity required a woman to be married to only one man to the end of her life. The strength and universality of this custom are expressed in the ubiquitous stone memorial arches that stud the landscape of China in memory of chaste widows. Since the traditional marriage cemented a wife not only to her husband but also to the husband's parents and family, morally the death of the husband did not dissolve the bond of marriage or change the widow's status and obligations as a daughter-in-law. The function of these mores was plainly to preserve the integrity and solidarity of the family by preventing the widow from leaving it, re-gardless of her personal interest or sacrifice.

Besides the moral assumption of a lifetime bond, a widow who wanted to remarry faced many other institutional obstacles. The hus-band's family had invested heavily in the marriage through the price for her person. Hence the family's claim to the right of preventing her remarriage and the right to exact a price in case permission for re-marriage was granted.

The children posed a difficult problem. Even if the husband's family granted the widow remarriage, she was not permitted to take the chil-dren, particularly her sons, who belonged to the family, not to her. The children were liable to be mistreated after her departure, and their rightful share of the family property was frequently encroached upon by predatory relatives, especially if the children were too young to defend their own rights. In some cases, such as the death of the paternal grandparents, or if the widow should be living in a city or at some distance from the deceased husband's family where his parents could not exercise effective control over her, the widow might be able to take her children into a new marriage. But even in such cases the general discrimination and mistreatment of them by her new husband and his family still posed a thorny problem. Even the local community discriminated against children brought along by a remarried widow, and the new husband's clan would not take them into clan member-ship, a serious matter in rural communities, especially in the southern part of the country where the influence of the clan is strong.

There were still other considerations which helped to discourage the remarriage of widows. If she left a family to remarry, she was not permitted to take any family property except her own belongings of jewelry and clothing, and at times not even these, owing to the tradi-tional concept of communal ownership of property. Her chance of finding a husband with a comfortable livelihood was generally poor.

Because of social discrimination against marrying a widow ("taking a second-hand article") motivated partly by the value of chastity, a man earning a comfortable livelihood would prefer to marry a virgin. Merry widows were few in traditional China, and those few seldom enjoyed any merry ending.

The operation of institutional restrictions against the remarriage of widows can be seen in local situations in various parts of the country, especially in connection with clan regulations. The Preparatory Committee of the Honan Provincial Women's Association under the Communist regime reported in 1949 that in the northern part of Honan, the current rule of the clans was that a widow could not remarry. Should she remarry against the objection of the family, the whole clan had the right to interfere, even the right to kill her. If she should persist, the family of the widow's own parents and the family of the deceased husband had the right to sell her to another man as wife. The following incident in 1949 in Honan Province is testimony to the effectiveness of this rule:

> A woman whose family name was Ch'en was married to a man named Hsu. The husband died eight years after the marriage, and both the woman's and the husband's families did not permit her to remarry. In 1949 the widow took the matter into her own hands and married the head of a neighboring village. Two months after this, the woman's uncle, a local bully, and her own brother, ordered her to hang herself. She begged for mercy from her own brother, saying, "Brother, I have worked for you for years, won't you have mercy on me as my brother?" and she turned to her uncle saying, "Uncle, won't you do some talking for me?" Both turned a deaf ear to her pleas. She then requested to see her children and to put on her good clothes before dying, but this was also denied. She adamantly refused to hang herself; so her own brother strangled her to death, then hung her body up below the roof.[6]

At times a local bully might sell a widow without the knowledge of the widow or her families. The buyer and his helpers would arrive and take her away by force. Such cases have been reported fairly recently in many rural areas.[7]

The Wang clan in Shiyiao village in Linch'uen county of Kiangsi Province had a rule that widows might not remarry and that a widow committing fornication would be tortured to death by the clansmen. In 1950 a widow in that village wanted to marry the cousin of her deceased husband. Being afraid of the clan's punishment, they had secret sexual relations, and she became pregnant. This fact terrified her into fleeing the village and hiding in her mother's home in another village, but when the baby was born her brother wished to evict her from the house, accusing her of shaming the family. Her mother intervened and succeeded in having her live in the farm tool shed. The brother attempted to kill the baby. A Communist Party worker heard the commotion, prevented the killing, took the case to the subdistrict government, and had the widow and the man legally married.[8] In T'anghsia village in Chuchih county of Chekiang Province there was a clan rule prohibiting the remarriage of widows. A widow fell in love with a widower in the same village and they had sexual relations. When the situation was discovered by the clansmen the man was beaten up and chased out of the village, the woman was subjected to public humiliation, and her house and all her other property were taken over by the clansmen.[9]

Remarriage of Widows in the Pre-Communist Period

It is obvious that preventing the remarriage of widows was an institutional device to strengthen the family organization at the expense of the widow's interest. In this sense, a widow's lack of freedom to remarry constituted a point of potentially disruptive tension in the general stability of the traditional family institution. In the traditional social setting this tension was kept under control by institutional pressure bearing directly upon a widow's remarriage and by general social and economic pressure against the widow who contemplated remarriage. But such tension was bound to erupt in an age when the individual's interest becomes a criterion of social values, and when an individual's role receives dominant consideration in the matter of marriage. Abolition of the traditional restriction in the remarriage of widows thus became a logical part of the Chinese family revolution. Sacrifice of widows' interests by the once-commanding value of chastity, the threat against their security, and the actual mistreatment they were subjected to — all contributed to the turbulence of the family-reform movement and to the violence which has characterized the movement in certain areas under the Communist regime.

In the pre-Communist period the remarriage of widows was not an active issue. While there was general agitation against the traditional value of chastity and condemnation of the institutional restrictions on widows' remarriage, the problem received no independent emphasis either in the family revolution or in the marriage law under the Nationalist government. The remarriage of widows as an issue thus gained only implicit recognition in the family-reform movement.

The reason for the relative lack of independent agitation on the issue lies in the fact that the main force of the family revolution had been unmarried young urban intellectuals whose focus of attention was on freedom for the first marriage. Widows were not numerically important in the movement. True, in the course of the past three or four decades' development of the movement many educated young women who were married in the modern fashion became widows. For them the problem was simple. They fully assumed the freedom to re-marry should they choose to, for they entered the husband's family as "free" women on an entirely different basis from the traditional mar-riage, and the family could not effectively prevent them from leaving. When the individual's interest as expressed in the free choice of partners became the basis of marriage, death of a spouse which dis-solved that marriage also theoretically ended the obligatory bond be-tween the widow and the deceased husband's family. This represents the attitude of the modern-minded widow.

Economically, since such women were almost invariably from the upper or upper-middle class, the problem of financial difficulty weighed less. The traditional concept of family property remained strong as a last bulwark for a weakened institution, and the modern widow who chose remarriage still could not take along a part of her deceased hus-band's family property into her new marriage. But her own parents' family would support her should she wish to leave the husband's family and wait for the development of a new marriage. Among young male intellectuals the discrimination against marrying a widow be-came much weaker than before, owing to the gradual devaluation of the old concept of chastity. So it became possible for a modern widow to find a suitable mate who could afford a comfortable livelihood. Such cases were not rare among modern urban intellectuals. The problem of children still remained a serious one, though the modern widow occasionally succeeded in taking her children into the new marriage.

Thus in the pre-Communist period the problem of widows' remar-riage arising among urban intellectual women was individually treated on the basis of new concepts introduced by the family revolution. But as a family issue it enjoyed no independent prominence in the move-ment, and its modern solution was not clearly defined in the Nation-alist kinship law. As to workers and peasants, remarriages proceeded along traditional arangements, and the modern issue of marital free-dom was scarcely raised. The integrity of the traditional family institu-tion among the lower class was not affected by this change as was the case with middle and upper-class families having modern educated women as daughters-in-law.

Change in Widows' Remarriage under Communist Rule

When the Communists rose to power in 1949, the issue of widows' remarriage assumed a different status under the general acceleration of the family revolution. The scope of marriage reform was broadened from first marriage to other aspects of the marriage institution, including remarriage of widows. The issue thus became an independent subject in the family revolution and gained formal clarification in the Communist Marriage Law. In the general prohibition of interference on the freedom of marriage by any third party the law specifically forbids interference in the freedom of a widow's remarriage (Marriage Law, Articles 2 and 3). The stipulation on the prohibition of "exaction of money or gifts in connection with marriage" (Article 2) explicitly includes the forbidding of the sale of widows or the exaction of a price for their remarriage.[10]

Furthermore, when the main motivating force of the family revolution shifted from intellectual agitation in the pre-Communist period to enforcement of the new Marriage Law under Communist rule, an inevitable effect was the spread of the movement from urban intellectuals to other segments of the population owing to universal application of the law. Widows among workers and peasants, who previously were little affected by the movement, now awakened to the new privilege of remarriage. In North China "some widows long repressed by feudalistic public opinion have now chosen their partners and have been married on the basis of free choice." [11] It is reported that in the six months following the promulgation of the Marriage Law, 469 widows were married of their own free choice in thirty-four rural subdistricts in the Chengchow Special District of the province of Honan.[12] Fragmentary figures and reports such as these appear widely in published statements and discussions on the marriage question in various parts of the country. The anti-Communist press in Hong Kong printed frequent reports of large numbers of widows in the villages of Kwangtung Province being forced by Communist political workers to remarry. While the report of the use of force in such cases appears to be obvious anti-Communist opinion, Communist statistics indicate the rapid weakening of the rigid traditional restriction on the remarriage of widows under the encouragement of the propaganda drives of the new Marriage Law and the enforcement of it in cities as well as in villages.

Widows' freedom to remarry has also been facilitated by new views regarding the problems of children and property. On the question of a widow's children Communist law completely rejects the traditional view of treating children primarily as a means of carrying on the family lineage. Under the new law raising children is considered a responsibility of parenthood, and the custody of the children in case of the remarriage of a widow is based on the interests of the children and the widow, not the interests of the deceased husband's family.[13] Thus runs a legal interpretation by the Communist court:

> Can a widow take her own children into the new marriage? This question should be clarified. This question is particularly relevant in case the grandparents possess the economic means of raising the children and are gravely concerned over the possible extinction of the family lineage should the children be taken away to a new marriage. . . . The solution of the question depends on the wish of the widow. If the widow agrees, the children can be left with the grandparents to raise. But if the widow does not agree, the grandparents have no right to stop her from taking her own children. In the common traditional pattern, if there is a child still in the nursing period, a widow may take her child along to another marriage. But when the child grows up, the grandparents usually insist upon taking the child back, thinking that the child must return to and acknowledge the ancestors, and that the child of the Chang family cannot possibly be allowed to adopt the surname of the Li family. People also generally call the children brought along by a widow to a new marriage "taking along a calf," and regard this as an extremely disreputable thing. Actually, all this is feudalistic thought, incompatible with the idea of protecting the children's interests. For between the mother and the children, there exists a blood-and-flesh relation and a natural emotional tie; the mother is more devoted to and more concerned over the raising and the education of her children than anybody else. For the children, the mother sacrifices everything. Therefore, when a widow remarries, it is at once natural and to the interest of the children that she should take them along to the new marriage, and nobody should have the right to interfere.[14]

On the problem of a widow's property at the time of her remarriage, the Communist legal view is given as follows:

> When a widow remarries, she may take along the part of the property that is her proper share, for men and women have equal rights in the new society. In land distribution [of the land reform], a widow in the villages is given her share of land, so it is her right to take along her own property. If she cannot manage her own land or house and other property when she goes away to a new marriage, and cannot find someone to manage it for her, she can convert it into cash or commodities and take it along. . . . In short, a widow has the independent and free right toward the disposal of her own property, and no one has the right to interfere. Any interference is illegal. For example, in Milaweitzu village . . . the widow Meng

Li-shih was taking along some things to her new marriage. The head of the village, Yu Chin-sheng, came out to prevent her from taking these things. The widow said to him, "All these are my personal belongings, and moreover, old man Meng and the family agreed that I take these along." But he said, "Hurry up and leave these things, if you talk any more, I'll tear the clothes off your body." Unreasonable interference such as this is an offense against the law according to the stipulation of the Marriage Law.[15]

Instances of widows remarrying in accordance with this new principle have been reported from widely different parts of the country. The following report, while obviously tinged with propaganda, presents such an event:

Hsieh Hou-hai is a widow who used to live in the village of Yang-an in the rural county of Li-shih of Shansi Province. Her husband died, leaving a son, now eleven years old. Poverty-stricken, hungry most of the time, and short of even tattered clothes, her life as a widow was an extremely difficult one. The husband's mother and two married brothers discriminated against her in every way. She thought of remarrying, but did not dare to for fear of reprisals by feudalistic influences. When land reform took place, her husband's family received land, and her own share was clearly written in her own name. Under the encouragement of propaganda mass meetings on the Marriage Law, she decided to remarry. A friend recommended a peasant to her, Lo Chun-mao, in the neighboring village of Hung-lo-kou. She arranged to meet him in person, and found him likable and satisfactory. They were soon married. At the time of her marriage, she took both her son and her share of the land into the new family. The deceased husband's family objected, but the objection was overruled by the subdistrict government. Later, she said in gratitude at meetings of the village women's association: "Women suffered all the misfortunes in the old society, and widows were not treated as human beings. . . . Now I can remarry, and furthermore, I can take my son and my property with me. Under the new principles, we women have really risen up." [16]

After the land reform, the collectivization of land and other means of production under the agricultural producers' cooperatives and later the people's communes further reduced property as a restriction against widows' remarriage. A similar trend is found among urban workers as illustrated by the following case in Shanghai. Describing the rebellion against traditional widowhood by family authority and the religious idea of fate, it is written in the style of propaganda literature, but the event itself is probably factual.

Ah Hsiang is a woman worker in the Yungta Cotton Mill. She had been

a widow for nearly seven years. During the previous year [1949] she became acquainted with Chia Lung-ch'ang, a mechanic for her unit, and
the two fell in love. Chia wanted to marry her, and she was willing, but
both the mother-in-law and her own mother were very feudalistic. The
mother-in-law said to her frequently, "Your widowhood is your fate.
Quiet down and burn more incense for the good of your next life." And
her own mother said to her, "Don't have so many ideas. You are a member
of the Wang family when alive, and a ghost of the Wang family when
dead." Hence, she did not accept Chia's proposal. Yuan, her big sister, was
a woman committee member of the labor union. She knew about Ah
Hsiang's troubles, and went to talk to the mother-in-law and the mother.
But the trips were in vain, and Yuan was scolded by the two old women
who just could not understand. Yuan let the heat cool down a bit, then
told Ah Hsiang to move into the factory dormitory. She also told Chia to
prepare a house and buy some furniture and utensils. When things were
ready, Yuan took the two to court, and served as witness to their legal
marriage.[17]

Although there is no quantitative data on how much the traditional
restriction of the remarriage of widows has given ground, such cases
indicate a spreading of the new trend among both urban workers and
conservative peasants in rural communities.

Polygamy and Prostitution

In the traditional system polygamy had the formal function of insuring the perpetuation of the family lineage as well as the informal function of providing for men the romantic experience that was suppressed
in arranged marriage. The informal function of providing romantic
experience was also related to the traditional existence of open prostitution.

Traditionally, polygamy was practiced by the upper-middle- and
upper-class minority, but the family among the poorer majority was
usually monogamous. This class difference was caused solely by the
economic ability of the well-to-do to support more than one wife and
the resulting larger number of children, for, institutionally, there was
no class restriction on polygamy in recent centuries. Polygamy therefore
was the luxury of the rich minority.

One form of polygamy was the taking on of a "parallel wife" (p'ing
ch'i) by a married man with the full wedding ceremony, which admitted
the second wife to equal status with the first wife. A similar form was
taking a "secondary wife" (p'ien fang) whose status was beneath the
first wife but above that of the concubines. These forms were not com-

monly practiced even in the traditional social order, for they generally aroused violent objections from the first wife and her own family, at times leading to litigation against the husband's family. But the traditional family institution recognized these two forms of polygamy when they were practiced on socially approved grounds such as the first wife being found to have lost her virginity before marriage, her commission of an unusually offensive act against the husband or the parents-in-law, or, above all, her failure to bear a son for the perpetuation of the ancestral lineage.[18]

It is to be noted again that an underlying principle for the approval of such practice was the institutional consideration of the family as the dominant factor in marriage, not the married couple themselves, much less so the wife. Another underlying principle was the dominance of the male in the traditional family.

A much more common form of polygamy was concubinage, a concubine being an informal wife taken into the house with no formal wedding ceremony and thus with no ritualistic recognition or institutional guarantee for her security or the permanency of her position in the family. The same institutional principles underlying approval of the preceding forms of polygamy applied to the social recognition of concubinage. To obtain sons for the family's lineage was a common traditional reason for men to engage in this practice. The idea of "letting one trunk support two branches" is a clear illustration of this. Should an uncle have no son, he might pay the expenses for a married nephew to take a concubine (sometimes a "secondary wife"), and the son born of this concubine would be considered the uncle's adopted son. This son would perform the rites of ancestor worship for the spirit of the uncle when he died, and he would thus be acting as the perpetuator of the uncle's branch of the family.

The fact that a man's wealth and prestige were frequently measured by the number of concubines he possessed might also be considered a motivating factor in concubinage. An additional motivation was the economic value of a big family, for concubines could bring more children, especially sons, as economic assets. But the deeply rooted human factor was the desire for more variegated sex experience and romance, and the complete dominance of the male role in the traditional family facilitated the practice of concubinage for this purpose.

Thus, although the traditional institution of marriage minimized the importance of the individual, it did not completely ignore the personal desires of men, who held the dominant role. Should the formal marriage fail to satisfy a man's desires, he had institutional approval for seeking satisfaction in less formal ways. In the formal marriage he conformed to the requirements of the family organization, leaving the choice of his wife to parental authority and accepting such practical social considerations as the class status of the wife's family; but in taking a concubine such considerations for the family and for the parents were institutionally exempt, and a man could base his choice almost completely on personal desire.

Should a son object to the choice of a mate made by the parents for family reasons, such as to cement a connection with a wealthy family, the parents might tell the boy that he could take a concubine later. Again, a son might have illicit relations with a female servant with the tacit knowledge of the parents, and if he sincerely liked her, she could be made a concubine after the boy's formal marriage. A female servant could not meet the traditional family requirements for a wife, but for a concubine, since almost any choice would do so long as it pleased the man, he might take a servant girl, a singsong girl, or even a prostitute. In fact, taking prositutes as concubines was by no means uncommon. Should the choice prove too much against the wish of the parents or too disruptive to the family organization, the son could set up a separate household for her; and there was no limit to the number of choices except his financial ability to support the concubines and their children.

Because of the lack of family and parental supervision over the taking of concubines, and because of the general inferiority of the concubines in class origin (they were usually bought from poor families), concubines were neither dignified by formal marriage ceremonies nor accorded full membership status in the family. They held inferior positions, performed unpleasant household tasks, and did not enjoy any recognized share of the family income as did the wife — although they could win favorite consideration from the husband and received private gifts from him. Their children, including sons, did not have ceremonial status and family opportunities equal to those of sons born of the wife; they could not claim an equal share of inheritance with the latter, except when the wife had no son. The role differentiation between the wife and the concubines and between the wife's sons and the concubines' sons was a means of maintaining the sanctity of family authority over formal marriage, a device to carefully stratify the members of a family in order to facilitate the exercise of hierarchical authority in the administration of a fairly complex domestic situation, and to prevent the taking over of the control of the household by female members generally originating from an inferior social class, particularly in view of their greater romantic influence over a husband who was frequently the head of the family.

Such was the institutional device to remedy the suppression of romantic love by arranged marriage, a device to prevent the man's romantic disappointment from becoming a disruptive factor to the institution of arranged marriage from which the stability of the traditional family drew much of its strength. The same principle furnished grounds for institutional approval of cohabitation with a woman on the side, and for frequenting prostitutes — except when carried to the point of financially ruining the family.

Although always classified as a vice, prostitution was tacitly approved of by traditional society. Traditional merchants as well as government officials transacted much of their business, and traditional scholars wrote some of their best lines of poetry, in whorehouses.* Prostitutes were considered sources of romance since love had been ruled out in formal marriage. If prostitution was ill-regarded by traditional mores, the basic reason was the frequent economic ruin of the wayward son and not any intrinsic moral abhorrence. A recent well-known Chinese writer who used to entertain his father in houses of prostitution in Peking was praised by friends as a filial son who catered to his father's desires. In a society where women's interests were consistently sacrificed for the welfare of the family and men's pleasure, there was little question of the moral degradation of a human being in "trading skin and flesh as a livelihood." The use of houses of prostitution as a center of social entertainment continued until the Communist government seriously tried to stamp out open prostitution.

Like many other aspects of the traditional family, old concepts of polygamy and prostitution were shaken by the impact of modern values emphasizing the intrinsic dignity and rights of the individual. From its beginning the family revolution and the women's movement which became its strong motivating force made polygamy a major target of attack, holding it to be a gross infringement of the dignity and rights of womanhood and a factor in the Chinese family institution that must speedily be removed as incompatible with the spirit of the modern age. The consecration of the monogamous marriage by Christian mis-

---

* The romantic school of the branch of Chinese poetry known as *Tz'u* drew much of its motif from love affairs with prostitutes. For example, the famous line by Ch'in Kuan of the eleventh century, "The willow-lined river bank, the dawn-breeze, and the night-worn moon," is in fact depicting the pre-dawn scene in which the poet himself was emerging from one of the houses of prostitution that used to line the banks of the Ts'in Huai River in Nanking.

sionaries encouraged this movement. By the 1930's monogamy had established itself as the dominant moral standard among the urban intelligentsia; Nationalist law adopted it as the legal form of marriage; and polygamy in its traditional forms was no longer practiced by the "new youth," the modern educated young of the well-to-do urban families who came under the influence of the family revolution. But the reform was limited to urban modern intellectuals, and its propelling force was informal group pressure generated by the modern social movements, the legal recognition of monogamy by the Nationalists remaining largely on paper. Polygamy continued to flourish among the financially well-to-do; and merchants in the cities, landlords in the villages, warlords, and unregenerated officials in the government continued to take concubines or practice polygamy in its various forms to the end of the Nationalist days on the Chinese mainland.

When the Communist government promulgated the new Marriage Law in 1950 the long-demanded abolition of concubinage and polygamy was once more written into the statute (Marriage Law, Article 2), and monogamy became the only legal form of marriage (Article 1). The Communist Marriage Law went further than the Nationalist reform by giving the children of concubines (previously taken) full and equal status with those born of the first wife, thus disregarding the organizational principle of the traditional family.

In the new concept of marriage as an affair of the marrying couple for their own interest and not primarily an affair of the family for the perpetuation of the ancestral lineage and for the welfare of the husband's parents, polygamy obviously cannot be justified as a means of assuring sons to carry on ancestral sacrifice or to provide security for the couple's old age. And since marriage is the outcome of free choice and love instead of parental authority, a man's need for romantic experience is supposedly satisfied, thus theoretically invalidating polygamy as a compromise measure to arranged marriage. Furthermore, even in the traditional family the wife was usually in opposition to the taking of concubines, and now the wife's objection becomes important, for she comes as a free person, owes much less socially and economically to her husband and his family, and is no longer bound by many of the traditional requirements of the family institution such as having to bear a son.

The new attitude toward polygamy, fully developed in the pre-Communist family reform movement among the urban intelligentsia, is now crystallized into legal interpretations under the Communist regime. In ruling against the practice of "letting one trunk support two branches" and of polygamy in general, the Communist Judicial Department of the Northeast Regional Government rendered the following typical opinion:

> In the old society, the feudalistic ruling class treated women as a tool for enjoyment, and openly practiced polygamy. Many things were utilized as excuses for taking concubines, including the wife's inability to bear a son. . . . Today, in our new society, both sexes enjoy equality, and women are no longer men's tools for enjoyment. . . . Should men take on additional wives on the excuse of begetting sons, they not merely violate the principle of sex equality, but also breach the rule of monogamy. The law can never permit this.
>
> All people like children and wish to have them, but ways of having them should be found in a reasonable direction, and the problem should not be solved in violation of the principles of sex equality and monogamy. First, it should be understood that a woman's inability to bear children may be due to physiological defects of either the man or the woman, and some care in medical examination before marriage will help solve this part of the difficulty. If the defect is discovered after marriage, and there is no way of inducing fertility, then the contracted parties must content themselves with the situation, for the bearing of children is not the only purpose of marriage.
>
> Some people cannot break away from the old thought that without offspring, the ancestors will be without religious sacrifice, and they consider it a tragedy of the first magnitude to see the "sacrifice of incense" discontinued. Actually, what good will it do the dead ancestors to continue the sacrifice of incense, and what harm will it do them to have it discontinued? This is nonsensical superstition, and it is incorrect.
>
> Some others think that without sons in their old age, they will be helpless and without support. Actually, this worry is rather unnecessary. If we labor actively and put effort into the development of production, when the reconstruction of the state is completed, the state will aid the aged who cannot labor and have no means of support, such as shown in the case of the Soviet Union. But, if you must worry about this point, you may adopt children. This will help the children who are without parents, meanwhile it will satisfy your desire for children.[19]

Statistical information is not available on the extent to which this legal principle has been put into practice in stamping out polygamy, but case histories and circumstantial evidence indicate trends regarding the practice of polygamy both in new marriages since the Communist Marriage Law went into effect in 1950 and in old marriages consummated before that date.

With repeated propaganda campaigns from 1951 to 1953 on the new

Marriage Law and continued discussion of this subject since then in various group meetings, particularly in women's organizations, it would seem that the common people in urban and rural communities have learned directly or indirectly that polygamy is no longer approved by law and that monogamy is the only legal form of marriage. With the obviously serious effort to enforce the new Marriage Law and with large numbers of local officials having received special training for this task, it is likely that the new legal requirement of marriage registration and investigation has succeeded in checking polygamy in most of the new marriages. Even if the process of registration and investigation should fail to reveal or prevent a polygamous marriage, later events may bring legal interference. A new concubine or "secondary wife" cannot be hidden from the neighbors for long. Even if the majority of the neighbors remain traditional-minded and regard the event with approval, the young people who are indoctrinated in the new Marriage Law would soon report the case to the local authorities. Furthermore, domestic jealousy and conflict between the wife and the concubine would probably soon lead either or both of them to appeal to the law, now that most women have heard of the new prohibition on polygamy. In addition, supporting more than one wife requires larger financial means than most people have under Communist rule. It is therefore reasonable to assume that among new marriages there is little polygamy practiced as a fully institutionalized affair where a man openly takes more than one wife with public acknowledgment and approval.

There must remain many cases of non-institutionalized polygamy among marriages of the "new youth" who grew up in the family revolution. In the Republican period many educated young men who were married under parental authority and were disappointed in the culturally backward wife later married a girl of their own choice and went off to live in another locality. The new wife might or might not be aware of the husband's previous marriage, which remained socially and legally effective; the husband considered the previous marriage unjust and void insofar as he was concerned, and refused to acknowledge the polygamous nature of the situation. With all its domestic and legal complications, this type of polygamy is of a transitional nature in the sense that it involves modern educated men being caught between the traditional parental authority and a new age of marriage by romantic love. Since under Communist rule legal approval and registration cannot be obtained for a new marriage by a man who already has a wife at home, if that fact is known to the registration official, the only way for a man to enter into a new marriage is to keep his still effective first marriage a secret. Such cases of "surreptitious polygamy" cannot last long without institutional approval or legal recognition.

Communist literature has dealt at length with this particular form of polygamy. One instance involved a twenty-nine-year-old Communist Party member, K'ung Hsien-sun, who married a peasant girl, Chao Ming-fen, also a party member, in 1947 while he was working for the Communist revolution in the rural areas of Shantung Province. With an urban intellectual background, K'ung soon tired of his peasant wife, and in 1947 he left her for advanced training in Manchuria, where two years later he secretly married another woman whom he tried to take to Tientsin when he was assigned there in 1954. When the first wife learned of his transfer to Tientsin and did not receive any call for her to come, she became suspicious and hurried to Tientsin to stay with him. She continued to live with him for over a year, at which time she intercepted a letter from the second wife and uncovered the truth. By this time she had a five-month-old baby girl. She took her case to the party cell and eventually to court. As a consequence, the Communist Party dismissed K'ung from membership, the court sentenced him to one year's imprisonment for polygamy, and he was ordered to contribute to the support of the baby girl after the completion of his prison term.[20]

The large number of existing traditional polygamous marriages constitutes a problem for the Communists. Communist law does not force the dissolution of a polygamous marriage already in existence if no suit is brought to court; if suit is brought, it is settled according to the new Marriage Law. The following instance occurred in the rural district in the northern province of Shantung in 1951:

> Ch'en Shou-tuan, 61 years old, lived in Ch'enshuang-lou village in Feng county of Shantung. In 1943 he bought a concubine, Chu Nien, 18 years of age, for the price of about 160 pounds of wheat. The concubine gave birth to a daughter but had no son. Both Ch'en and his wife mistreated the concubine. Unable to stand the cruelty, the concubine ran away to a neighboring village and lived with a village Communist cadre there. This was soon discovered, and Ch'en brought the case to the county people's court. The court ruled that the case was one of fornication by the concubine, reprimanded her, and ruled that the baby girl should be given back to Ch'en for custody. This decision was along the line of the traditional principle in the institutional approval of concubinage. The case was later appealed to the superior people's court in T'eng county, which reversed the decision and ruled that the daughter should be in the custody of the mother, that the buying of a concubine has no legal effect, and that full legal recognition should be given to the marriage between the concubine and the village cadre.[21]

Thus, although Communist policy seems to be not to disturb existing polygamous marriages until they are challenged, cases such as this serve to undermine existing polygamous bonds. The mistreatment and grievances of concubines are generally known, as is the buying of young concubines by much older men, and many concubines would run away if the law would guarantee them safety and they could find a livelihood. Now, in a sense, they are encouraged to do so.

Following the pre-Communist tenet of the family revolution, Communist ideology attacks prostitution as the product of sex inequality, the treatment of women as merchandise, and the outcome of traditional suppression of inter-sex social life and romantic love. When such factors are removed and replaced by the socialistic economic and social order, it is held, prostitution will disappear. Disregarding the question of validity of this claim for the moment, one may note the fact that the new moral standard no longer lends even tacit approval to prostitution. The drastic suppression of the some two hundred brothels in Peking in 1950, and the re-education of the prostitutes for respectable occupations and a new form of life, first dramatized the new moral standard. Similar measures of government suppression of open prostitution have been carried out in Shanghai and other cities. Strict Communist police supervision of hotels serves to check covert prostitution. It is true that in published reports of the Three-Anti movement in the first part of 1952 many officials in the Communist government were charged with visiting prostitutes; [22] and the anti-Communist press in Hong Kong has continued to report stories of prostitution as a result of economic hardship in Canton and other cities. Nevertheless, the government drive has the significance of actively using political power to set up a new marriage institution which no longer condones prostitution.

Aside from prostitution, there has been a certain amount of extramarital relations among the Communists, especially during the years of struggle for power which sent them marching and wandering all over the country. But Communist Party principles have regarded such behavior as a deviation, not as a moral norm. Chu Teh, the old chief of the Communist Army, once lectured the young party workers in Yenan, "I have heard of people dying of hunger, but not of people dying of the sexual urge." The Marriage Law gives illegitimate children a legal kinship status with the father, who is required to support them (Article 25), thus discouraging licentious behavior. The stabilization of normal married life among the party members after their accession to national power also tends to reduce such deviational conduct.

CHAPTER IV

Freedom of Divorce

TRADITIONALLY THERE was rigid institutional restriction on divorce so as to enforce family solidarity. Although the chief significance of the changes in the marriage system lies in the development of a new family institution among the young generation, leaving the existing traditional marriages undisturbed, the new freedom of divorce may affect all marriages, new as well as old. As an overwhelming majority of existing families in China are still based upon traditional marriage, any widespread application of the new freedom of divorce may shake the foundations of large numbers of families and affect the stability of the social order in general.

In the Republican period the voice for freedom of divorce had already been raised, but obtaining a divorce, though permitted under Nationalist law, was held in abeyance by the influence of traditional institutions. Under Communist rule the situation has changed appreciably. Communist policy professes not to disintegrate by decree the existing traditional marriages,[1] but the Communist Marriage Law unequivocably provides for freedom of divorce as a means of dissolving any marriage, new or old.[2] Ch'en Shao-yü, a leading Communist who took an active part in drafting the Marriage Law, stated explicitly:

> In the New Democratic society the legal protection for freedom of divorce, just as the legal protection for freedom of marriage, serves as a necessary means to oppose and to abolish the old feudalistic marriage institution. It will give physical and mental emancipation to men and women who have been forced to suffer under the old marriage institution to insist upon divorce.[3]

The operation of Communist law as guided by this pronouncement not only affects the integrity of a large number of Chinese families but also has significance for the stability of the social order under Communist rule.

Divorce in Traditional Marriage

To analyze the effect of the new freedom of divorce on the family in modern China, particularly under Communist influence, it is necessary to consider the institutional control over divorce under the traditional system. Traditional matrimony was an event by which the husband's family acquired a daughter-in-law (*ch'ü hsi fu*), and for the woman it was an event by which she found a home. The Chinese character for marrying off a daughter, *chia*, is composed of two radicals, one meaning woman and the other meaning home. In common traditional usage the term marriage was seldom employed; the event was usually mentioned as *ch'ü hsi fu* or *ch'u chia* (finding a home elsewhere).

So far as the woman was concerned the bond to a new home was meant for life, not to be broken even upon the death of the husband. Hence there was no institutional ground upon which a woman could obtain a divorce. Should she become dissatisfied with the marriage, even on justifiable grounds such as extremely cruel treatment, she was advised to tolerate the situation and preserve family unity by exercising forbearance and self-sacrifice and by resignation to fate. The folk adage, "When you marry a chicken, stick with the chicken; when you marry a dog, stick with the dog," was a constant reminder to her in her moments of depression or despair. Should she forget, others in the family would remind her by similar adages such as, "Obey Heaven and follow Fate." And the idea of fate as a reinforcing factor for the institutional bond was instilled in her through every step of the elaborate and religiously colored ceremony of her marriage. Should she still attempt to leave her husband against institutional sanction, she would face the charge against her from the family and the community as an "immoral character," as a wife who "does not observe the womanly ways." This would ruin her chance of remarriage and her respectable status in the community. If she did not stop at such discouragement, authority and even physical punishment might be brought upon her by the family, the clan, or even the government.

A wife traditionally came into a family with a price paid for her person and a heavy family investment in her wedding. She was reminded of this should she threaten to leave. Even in the modern city of Shanghai in 1950 there was the case of a traditional wife who had been married into a family as a child bride at the age of nine. Both the mother-in-law and the husband had given her repeated beatings and scoldings in her ten years of married life. After the Communist Marriage Law was promulgated, she heard of the possibility of divorce but was discouraged by the traditional requirement of paying back the price of her person. A labor union officer in the factory where she worked told her that such a refund was no longer necessary under the new law. Bolstered by this information, she went to court and won her divorce free of charge.[4] Such traditional demands on a wife who wished to get a divorce were universal except among the well-to-do minority where money was a secondary matter and the restraint was mainly one of a moral and social character.

In addition, the difficulties of children and property were as strong obstacles against divorce by a woman as against a widow's remarriage. If divorced she was not permitted to take her chldren out of the family, particularly sons, and, since she had no share in the family property, she could not take anything with her. A divorce would mean the difficulty of a livelihood if her own parents were not wealthy or willing to support her, and opportunity for women's employment in traditional society, especially in the rural community, was very limited. As in the case of widows, the possibility of a divorced woman getting married again into a comfortable family was slim because of social discrimination. And if the husband's family continued to object to the divorce, although the wife might have actually departed from that family, they might forcibly prevent her remarriage by abducting her or by making trouble with her parents and her new husband's family.

In extremely unbearable situations a traditional wife might leave her husband's family and go back to her parents' family, particularly if she had no children; but this was regarded as deviant conduct and as a separation, not as a divorce in the institutional sense. The husband and his family would continue to try to get her to come back. Economic difficulties and concern for her children, or the husband's threat to take another wife might well persuade her to return; and it was not infrequent to see such separations occur repeatedly in a single marriage.

At times, under excessively unbearable situations, suicide was the way out; and the large number of women who took their own lives on account of domestic difficulties is vivid testimony to the lack of any traditional institutional formula for readjustment of a wife's matrimonial relationship in case of absolute failure to achieve harmony between the wife and her husband or other family members, especially the mother-in-law. The following Communist report furnishes some idea of the rigidity of the old marital bond.

In sixteen counties in southern Shansi, from July to September of 1949, there were twenty-five women who died of inhuman treatment by their husbands or their fathers- or mothers-in-law. In Hotsin and Wanchuan counties of the same province, in the second half of 1949, twenty-nine women committed or attempted suicide by hanging themselves or jumping into the well for the same reason. In the months of July to September in Wenshui county and in November in Taiku county there were twenty-four legal cases involving the loss of human lives; among these fourteen were women who met death for the same reason. In Pingyao county the wife of Chao Ping-sheng demanded a divorce and Chao killed her. In Lingchuen county Li Shao-hai, a young married woman, committed suicide on account of mistreatment by her husband and mother-in-law.[5]

Such rigidity of the marital bond, of course, did not apply to men in a male-dominated institution. Tradition allowed a husband to return a wife to her own family on a large number of grounds. But even such a return did not constitute divorce in the modern sense of the word, for a wife who was returned to her own family still retained many claims against the husband and his family. Actually, the return of a wife occurred only rarely. In a poor family the husband and his parents could ill afford to lose a wife, not merely because her service as a housewife would be lost but also because it would be difficult to find the financial means to take another wife. Should a wife prove unsatisfactory, the husband and the parents-in-law could try to force her into submission. Should this fail, the husband and the family would have to be content with a dominant wife, and wife-dominated families were not uncommon even in traditional China, as attested by the numerous hen-pecked-husband jokes. In a well-to-do family a wife could be put aside and ignored and a concubine or "parallel wife" could be taken to fill her position.

It is natural, then, that one seldom heard of divorce in traditional families. In a sample population study of nine localities distributed in various parts of China in the pre-Communist period, five localities reported no divorce for women and four reported no divorce for men. In the three localities reporting divorce among women, the rates of divorced women were 0.02 per cent, 0.115 per cent, and 0.885 per cent of all married women. In the four localities reporting divorces for men the rates of divorced men among all married men were 0.034 per cent, 0.273 per cent, and 0.510 per cent.[6] In a sample census of nine rural counties in Szechwan Province in Southwest China, the rate of divorced women in 1947 was 0.126 per cent of all married women and that of divorced men 0.57 per cent of all married men.[7] These figures may err, but in a general way they reflect the negligible proportion of divorces as a general phenomenon among traditional families in the pre-Communist period.

These figures attest to the proverbial stability of the Chinese family, but, if modern divorce rates in the West are an indication of typical high tension in family relationships, the very low divorce rates in Chinese traditional communities do not signify a low degree of family tension. In fact, since divorce was not given institutional approval by the Chinese family, any tension remained unrelieved and bore especially heavily on the wife; and the Chinese family stability implied by the figures above was achieved at the price of personal sacrifice made largely by the women.

Freedom of Divorce in the Communist Law

A strong demand for the right of divorce formed an important part of the family revolution. After half a century of agitation and struggle, the right of divorce for both men and women had gained acceptance at least among the new intelligentsia in the Republican period. To the newly educated generation the demand was altogether reasonable since the basic premise of marriage itself had already shifted and marriage was no longer considered a bond tying a woman to a family for life but the result of love between two individuals. If the two individuals could not get along together, the new generation saw no reason for the continuation of their suffering. Gone from the young minds was the once dominant consideration of marriage as a means for the perpetuation of the family, and ancestral lineage was no longer a matter of grave concern.

By 1930 the Nationalist government had translated the demands of the young into law permitting divorce. Although the new law retained many favorable considerations for the perpetuation of the ancestral lineage, and no effort was made by the Nationalist government to acquaint the common people with their new legal right, for the educated young who knew about the new law a legal instrument was available to facilitate a divorce should they choose to go to court. New urban developments meanwhile had opened increasing fields of employment for women, which reduced the economic difficulties of a divorce. Divorce and remarriage of divorcees became fairly common among the new intelligentsia in the cities, but the new conception of divorce, while threatening the organization of a small number of urban families in the upper and middle classes, left the families of the peasantry and the urban working class almost untouched. Such was the picture under Republican China.

When the Communists came to power in 1949, they inherited this development, and the new concept of divorce was fully written into Communist law. In fact, the subject of divorce received more elaborate attention than any other subject in the Marriage Law, taking up nine out of a total of twenty-five articles. These nine articles set forth the right of divorce for either of the matrimonial parties and seek to guard the economic interests of the divorced wife and the children, but the husband's parents and the family in general are excluded from any legal attention. As it was consideration for the solidarity of the patriarchal family as the dominant factor in traditional marriages which had formerly ruled out divorce, so it is consideration for the married individuals as the dominant factor in new marriages that now justifies divorce. Hence: "Divorce should be granted when husband and wife both desire it. In the event of either the husband or the wife insisting upon divorce, it may be granted only when mediation by the people's subdistrict government and the subdistrict judicial organ has failed to bring about a reconciliation" (Marriage Law, Article 17).

Divorce is facilitated for the wife by the new legal stipulations concerning the custody of and responsibility for the children, the settlement of family property, and support for the divorced wife. Custody of the children shall be decided "in accordance with the interests of the children" (Marriage Law, Article 20), which in the actual operation of the law means most frequently the granting of custody to the wife; and "after divorce, if the mother is given custody of a child, the father shall be responsible for the whole or part of the necessary cost of the maintenance and education of the child" (Article 21). The father's responsibility may be discharged by payment "made in cash, in kind, or by tilling the land allocated to the child" (Article 21). "In case of divorce, the wife shall retain such property as belonged to her prior to her marriage. The disposal of other family properties shall be subject to agreement between the two parties. In the case where an agreement cannot be reached, the people's court shall render a decision after taking into consideration the actual state of the family property, the interests of the wife and the child or children, and the principle of benefiting production" (Article 23). It may be mentioned here that since Communist land reform the wife's share of the family property may be written in her own name and may even be registered in a separate deed, thus assuring her a fair share in case of a divorce.

"After divorce, if one party has not remarried and has difficulties in maintenance, the other party should render assistance" (Article 25). The "other party" which has to render assistance means the husband in most cases. Later, the socialization of urban business and collectivization of agricultural land minimized the importance of property settlement in divorce.

The Consequence of Increased Family Instability

With political support for the assertion of individual rights against family "oppression," and with propaganda on the new concept of marriage and divorce penetrating into the working class and the peasantry, the influence of the family revolution has spread from a minority of the urban intelligentsia to a much larger segment of the population. There are visible signs that the stability of a large number of families has begun to waver and that divorces are on the increase. The Minister of Justice of the Communist Central Government, Shih Liang, a woman, reviewed the situation seventeen months after the promulgation of the Marriage Law in May 1950:

> Statistics from different localities show that after the promulgation of the Marriage Law the number of matrimonial suits received by judicial organs of different levels increased appreciably. In twenty-one large and medium-size cities, including Peking, the number of matrimonial suits received was 9,300 for the months from January to April 1950, and it was 17,763 for the months from May to August of the same year. In other words, there was an increase of 91 per cent in the four months following the promulgation of the Marriage Law in comparison with the preceding four months. In ten county-seat towns in Hopei, P'ingyuan, and other provinces the number of matrimonial suits received was 986 for the months from January to April 1950, and it was 1,982 for the months from May to August of the same year. The increase here has been 101 per cent. In Hupei Province the average number of matrimonial suits dealt with by each people's court was 13.7 for February of 1951, and it was 23.9 for July of the same year, showing a considerable increase.[8]

Some two years later, in March 1953, the municipal court of Canton handled about eight hundred matrimonial cases as compared to one thousand-odd cases of labor-capital conflict. Domestic disharmony came to rank with labor-capital struggle as the two numerically largest items of litigation during the early Communist rule.[9] Such was the situation in the major urban centers.

It is noteworthy that the rural communities, which remained so long in the tight grip of traditional conservatism, are also sharing in

the increase in matrimonial suits which reflect growing family instability. The beginning of serious rural reaction to the new concept of
divorce is shown in Ch'en Shao-yü's statement made in April 1950,
just before the promulgation of the Marriage Law: "According to
statistics from the eight cities of Peking, Shanghai, Tientsin, Harbin,
Sian, Kalgan, Shichiachuang, and Paoting, from 71 rural counties in
the old liberated areas of North China, from some places in the old
Shensi-Kansu-Ninghsia border area, and from eight rural counties of
Shansi Province 17.4 to 46.9 per cent of all urban civil litigation cases
are matrimonial cases, and 33.3 to 99.0 per cent of all rural litigation
cases are matrimonial cases." [10] "In the Central-South Region the
32,881 matrimonial cases constitute over 60 per cent of all civil suits
received by the People's Courts during the months from January to
May 1951." [11] Matrimonial cases accounted for 90 per cent of the 700
civil cases handled during the months from January to the end of
August 1952 by the People's Court of the rural county of Laipin,
Kwangsi Province of the Central-South Region.[12]

While these reports do not present the contents or nature of the
matrimonial suits, they do give a general indication of growing family
instability as the new agitation of the family revolution has made it
increasingly difficult for the traditional family institution to maintain
role harmony among members who have become exposed to the idea
of individual liberty as against family restriction. This is particularly
true of the role of the wife, as a very high proportion of the matrimonial cases are brought to court by women (see the discussion on
women's status in Chapter VI). Where the traditional family institution is operating effectively, family conflicts are very seldom brought
to court for settlement, sometimes not even when human life is involved.

Among the increasing number of matrimonial cases, divorce suits
constitute a high percentage. Of the 32,881 matrimonial cases of the
Central-South Region in 1950, 29,972, or 90 per cent, were divorce
suits. A year later "divorce suits constituted from 46.44 to 84.32 per
cent of all urban matrimonial cases, and from 54.1 to over 90 per cent
of all rural matrimonial cases according to statistics from the four
cities of Peking, Shanghai, Tientsin, and Harbin, from seventy-one
counties in the old liberated areas of North China, and from some
places in the old Shensi-Kansu-Ninghsia border area." [13]

The trend of the high proportion of divorce cases apparently persisted at least until 1953. In the month of March in that year 80 per
cent of all cases received by the municipal court of Canton were divorce

suits, and the percentage may have been higher in the subsequent months owing to the launching of the "enlarged propaganda campaign on the Marriage Law" to acquaint more people with their new rights in marriage and divorce.[14] The Communist authorities have published little further statistical information on marriage and divorce since 1953, possibly because of fear of the socially disturbing nature of the figures; but a hint of the general continuation of this trend is seen in the report made in July 1957 by Tung Pi-wei, Communist judicial leader, that domestic conflicts still constituted an increasing and prominent proportion among all cases handled by Communist courts throughout the nation.

Only a few facts are mentioned in the official reports regarding the contents of the divorce figures. First, there is the almost overwhelming proportion of divorce suits brought by women as compared to those brought by men, especially in the rural communities, where conservatism is strong and the suffering of women under the traditional institution has been deep. For example, in 1950 in the cities of Shanghai, Peking, and Tientsin, 546 of the 800 divorce suits, or about 68 per cent, were brought by women, 176, or about 22 per cent, by men, and 78, or about 10 per cent, by both husband and wife.[15] In the provincial town of Nanchang, in Kiangsi, from January to October 1951 it was stated that 84.3 per cent of all divorce cases received by the municipal people's court were brought by women.[16] Of the 21,433 divorce cases in 32 cities and 34 rural county-seat towns mentioned in the *Jen-min Jih-pao* (People's Daily) of September 29, 1951, 76.6 per cent were brought by women. The 1951 edition of the *Hun-yin Fa Chi Ch'i Yu-kuan Wen-chien* (The Marriage Law and Its Related Documents, p. 72) listed 763 divorce cases in three rural counties in Shansi Province; of this total, 705 cases, or 92.4 per cent, were initiated by women. Among 29,972 divorce cases in 1951 in the Central-South Region, including both urban and rural areas, "The vast majority of them were brought by women who have suffered the severest oppression from the unreasonable institution of traditional marriage." [17]

Without specifying time or locality, Ch'en Shao-yü, who led the drafting of the Marriage Law, gave an analysis of the age composition of the parties involved in divorce suits. According to him, "About 50 per cent of them were between the ages of 25 and 45, about 40 per cent youths under 25, and about 10 per cent were very young people married before their maturity and old couples." [18] Teng Yung-ch'ao, wife of Premier Chou En-lai and a leading figure in the Democratic Women's League, which was vitally concerned with the drafting and enforcement of the Marriage Law, surveyed the statistical information possessed by the government on marital conditions and stated that the "vast majority of those demanding divorce were young and middle-aged laboring people." [19]

Not much is said about the causes of divorce. Obsessed with attacking the "feudalistic" marriage institution, Communist leaders take for granted that the evils of the traditional institution form the fundamental cause of the present divorces, something too obvious to need any statistical proof. Thus,

> the first major cause of divorce is the lack of harmonious relationship between husband and wife resulting from the marriage institution of the old society based on compulsory arrangement and male dominance over the female. This constitutes the ground for divorce in the vast majority of the divorce cases received by the people's courts. From this it can be seen that under the present conditions in China freedom of divorce, like freedom of marriage, is an expression of the revolutionary struggle against the remnants of feudalism. The second cause of divorce is the result of particular conditions of the minority, such as prolonged parting between husband and wife, one party committing a crime, one party sexually impotent on account of physiological defects, one party having a loathsome and incurable disease, or one party being progressive while the other is backward in ideology.[20]

There is a little more detail in the official figures for the city of Canton.

> From May 1, 1950, to February 23, 1951, the People's Court of Canton dealt with 534 marital suits which may be classified into four types: (1) cancellation of engagements, 18 cases; (2) divorces, 319 cases; (3) cancellation of cohabitation relationship, 131 cases; (4) non-support of children, 66 cases. Among all the cases divorce suits constituted 59.7 per cent, cancellation of cohabitation relationship 24.5 per cent. Of these two types of cases, those brought by women constituted 78 per cent of the total and those by men 22 per cent. The causes of divorce may be listed as (1) dictated marriage, (2) polygamy, (3) mistreatment, (4) abandonment [majority of cases brought by women], (5) disharmony, (6) extramarital love affairs, (7) physiological defects, (8) spouse leading a decadent and corrupt life [including refusal to labor and unwillingness to stand poverty], (9) uncertainty of spouse being alive or dead.[21]

The large number of cancellations of cohabitation relationships, resulting chiefly from family separations during the anti-Japanese war, shows a weakening of the traditional concept of marriage and family in the cities. Under the traditional social order such a relationship was disapproved of as a threat against the orthodoxy of the family institution and was a clandestine affair. It was never an open relationship having semilegal status. Its widespread practice during World War II and the pre-Communist postwar period can be seen in the fact that almost one-fourth of all the matrimonial suits were cohabitation cases. The Communist Marriage Law extends no recognition to cohabitation except the possibly related provision holding the parents, especially the father, responsible for any children born out of legal wedlock. There is no information on the extent of such practice under Communist rule, but general observation suggests that it is not very common.

These fragmentary divorce figures are given in such a form that they cannot be compared to figures for periods preceding the Communist regime; therefore there is no statistical evidence whether or not this is a new phenomenon created by Communist rule. In the Nationalist period divorces were notably on the increase, especially after 1930, but they were largely limited to the big cities where the sanctity of the traditional marriage institution had been seriously undermined. The traditional kinship system, including the institution of marriage, had been strongly maintained in the countryside, and divorce in the modern sense was still repulsive to the peasantry. The sharp resistance to the injection of the divorce idea into rural communities even under Communist rule, to be considered later, attests to the newness of the divorce factor in the rural social situation. Hence, while it is not known how many urban divorces mentioned above represent a consequence of Communist reform, it may be taken with some degree of certainty that rural divorces constitute a new phenomenon in the hitherto vast redoubt of the traditional institutions.

Even in cities considerable legal expense was entailed under the Nationalist government to obtain a legal divorce, something only the upper and middle classes could afford, and only an educated few were acquainted with the law. But the use of lawyers is no longer part of the Communist legal system, and the people's court has abolished court fees. The propaganda campaigns on the Marriage Law are introducing legal knowledge to the common people. Hence the poor and even the illiterate can use the court to settle matrimonial disputes and to obtain divorces. The many cases of legal divorce among the urban working class [22] is a new phenomenon, then, and some increase in urban legal divorces since the establishment of the Communist regime seems quite possible.

Economic Support, Property, and Children in a Divorce

The possibility of a marked increase of divorces under the Communist regime draws support from other factors. Aside from the encouragement given by vast propaganda efforts and the increased accessibility of legal aid, divorce is facilitated by women's new legal privilege of being able to take along their share of property, to receive maintenance assistance, and to have custody of the children. The Nationalist marriage law gave some consideration to the woman's share of property but ruled that the husband's family should have the custody of the children, evidently out of respect for the traditional importance of perpetuating the ancestral lineage and because children were a security asset of the family. The Communist Marriage Law favors the interests of the divorced woman and the children.

There is some information on the actual operation of the Communist law in assisting women in a divorce to obtain economic support and property compensation. In a report entitled "Examples of Legal Decisions on Matrimonial Cases Rendered by the People's Court of Tientsin," [23] published in 1951, there is the case of a college graduate who married an illiterate girl by parental arrangement. When the incongruity of cultural levels between them led to divorce, the court ordered the husband to support the wife until her remarriage and to buy her a sewing machine to help make her self-supporting. In granting the divorce the Communist court advised: "The suffering (between the couple) is a product of the old society and a gift from the institution of arranged marriage . . . . Each day that the matrimonial relationship lasts will give the defendant an additional day of suffering and will reduce the wife's chance of remarriage. For the long term interest of the wife, a divorce should be granted . . . . She should actively take part in production and become self-supporting. She should choose a good companion in the process of her work, and this will give her a happy future." The report listed another case involving a working couple married by parental arrangement. While both husband and wife had agreed to a divorce, the husband refused to pay back the wages the wife had earned in a cotton mill for several years which had been handed over to the parents-in-law as a traditional practice. The court in granting the divorce ordered the husband's family to return the accumulated wages.

Another Communist document recounts a court decision in Shanghai granting a divorce to the owner of a photographic shop and his wife. The court ordered the husband to contribute to the support of the divorced wife from the income of the shop and to give her one half the proceeds should the shop be liquidated.[24] This legal decision was made in 1951 when private business was still in operation. Since the spring of 1956 the majority of businesses have been turned into joint ownership between private parties and the state. Presumably, under the new circumstances the economic interest of a divorced woman would have to be taken care of by the wage income of the husband.

Such court decisions, although totally contrary to tradition, would not necessarily seem strange to the urban population, which has lived in the midst of change. In the countryside, where the old family institution has been relatively insulated from modern influences, the implementation of the new economic benefits and property rights for the woman seeking a divorce has been more difficult, as reflected in the following Communist statement:

> Those still possessed of the old legal views often take the stand that "officials do not attend to cases which are not contested by the parties involved." As a consequence, they sacrifice the legal interests of the divorced women and the children and act against the official policy. Some women are still not acquainted with the Marriage Law, and they did not take the initiative to bring up property demands in connection with their divorce procedure. The property question of such cases has been completely ignored on the ground of "no court action without legal contention." But there have been cases of no court action even if legal contention of property rights was made. In such cases, the women were frequently told, "You already got a bargain by receiving a divorce, and you still want property on top of that?" or, "The other party already feels terrible about the divorce, and you still want to grab some property in addition?" In Ch'ien county of Shensi Province in 1951, ninety-three cases of divorce were handled by the court, and women were given property by the court in only thirteen of these cases. In the past two years [1951 and 1952] the court in Wuhsiang county of Shansi Province handled over two thousand divorce cases, among which over 33 per cent obtained no solution to the problem of women's property.[25]

The increasing number of divorce cases granting economic support and property rights to women serve as an important influence, one which has been reinforced by the successive campaigns from 1951 to 1955 to indoctrinate the political leaders and to acquaint the people with the new Marriage Law.

With regard to another major traditional obstacle against divorce, the custody of children, Communist courts have given dominant consideration to the interests of the children as individuals. Thus, in granting a divorce to a couple in Tientsin in 1951 the municipal court awarded the custody of a thirteen-year-old boy to the mother in addition to ordering the husband to give the wife a lump-sum financial settlement and contribute to the support and education of the child until he reached the age of eighteen. The court opinion clearly expressed the new principle in settling the problem of the custody of children:

> Because the marriage was an arranged one, there has always been domestic friction. The wife once attempted suicide by swallowing gold, and the situation also became unbearable for the husband, who is now asking for a divorce but insisting on the custody of the child. . . . This insistence upon keeping the child is motivated by the feudalistic thought of perpetuating the ancestral lineage, and not by sincere consideration for the welfare of the child. When the wife keeps the child, it does not prevent the husband from doing his duty for the child's upbringing and education.[26]

In awarding the custody of a five-year-old son to a wife who had been married as a child bride and suffered cruelty from the husband's family the Tientsin court struck a recurrent note: "The wife is a woman worker with a dependable income, and she has a mother to help care for the child. The husband shuns labor and only hawks black beans on the street, and his income is uncertain . . . . Comparing the situation on both sides, it is better to let the wife keep and raise the child. The husband should not be motivated by the feudalistic thought of perpetuating the ancestral lineage and ignore the interests of the child." [27]

The granting of economic benefits and the custody of children to women may discourage men from seeking divorce as a settlement of domestic discord, and it may serve to curb the traditional mistreatment of the wife in the family, thus altering the role relationship between husband and wife. In this sense, the new legal standard may to a certain extent have a stabilizing influence on the family while at the same time improving the status of the wife. This influence is, of course, much weaker than the traditional restrictions against divorce. Meanwhile, as large numbers of existing traditional marriages have irreconcilable tensions and conflicts, the dominant effect of the operation of this new legal principle has so far been to facilitate divorce and to increase the divorce rates.

Indiscriminate Granting of Divorce

That divorce is being established as a new factor in family relationships in Communist China and becoming an "important weapon in abolishing the feudalistic institution of marriage and in liberating the long oppressed women from their yoke" is further interestingly substantiated by charges that many local government organs have been indiscriminate in granting divorces. Such charges have been made not only by people unsympathetic to the Communist regime or its new Marriage Law but also by Communist government leaders. Thus Shih Liang, the woman Minister of Justice, charged some political workers with irresponsibly spreading the word that "divorce may be granted even when the spouse is not pleasing to the eye." [28] In Hang county of the southern province of Chekiang "some subdistrict political workers have been very thoughtless in their disposal of matrimonial cases. Less than half an hour was spent on each case, whether it was one of divorce or marriage registration. In some places the general attitude toward divorce cases is 'no wish will be denied.' Some couples just happened to quarrel and want a divorce, and the government would actually grant it to them, only to see them return soon, asking to restore the husband-wife relationship." [29]

Hsü Teh-hsing, a member of the Committee of Laws and Institutions, made the following statement:

> In some places local cadres have adopted an irresponsible and sloppy style of work. In propaganda they lay one-sided emphasis on the "freedom of divorce," and in legal procedure they unrestrictedly favor the party demanding divorce, consequently creating a situation of indiscriminate divorce in which everyone's wish [for divorce] is granted. For instance, the Special Office of Yungchow in Fukien Province followed the one-sided demand of those cadres who came down South to work and granted divorces to twenty-one couples without having given a hearing to the other party's story. It was said that this was done for the morale of the cadres. In Nank'ang (a rural county in Kiangsi Province) Hsiao Shih-hsiu and his wife had been a happy couple. Once they had a quarrel and decided to get a divorce, and the court actually granted it. In Sheh county of Hunan Province Kuo Ch'ou-nü and her husband divorced and reunited as often as three times in a single year.
>
> When divorces are granted as lightly as this, the result is bound to be an increase of abnormal phenomena such as getting a divorce one day and asking to be reunited the next, Some of the reasons presented by men for divorce even include "spouse not having a pretty face," "spouse having coarse skin," "spouse too small in stature," "spouse illiterate." Some

women have demanded a divorce on the grounds of "husband too poor,
livelihood not comfortable," or "husband unemployed." . . . All these
leave the masses with a very bad impression regarding the "court as an
office of divorce" or the "Marriage Law as a divorce law." [30]

It is notable that most of such occurrences were reported south of
the Yangtze River where, in the early years of Communist rule, both
the quality and quantity of local political workers were below the
level of those in the northern provinces. In the northern part of the
country, where political workers were more experienced and better
trained and the new order better established, the divorce problem
seems to have been handled more carefully, particularly in the cities.
Thus the Department of Justice of the Northeast Regional Government explained that "the People's Government is not promoting divorce, and the Marriage Law is not a divorce law. Those who take
'freedom of divorce' for 'divorce at will' are committing a grave
error." [31] It gave examples of court rejections of divorce requests based
on flimsy grounds. In the northern city of Tientsin many requests
for divorce on weak grounds have been rejected by the court. Among
such cases was a wife who wanted a divorce since she did not wish to
go back to the village to farm with her unemployed leather-worker
husband, and another concerned a man who wanted to get rid of his
wife to make room for another romance.[32] If a divorce involves a
Communist Party member serving in the revolutionary armed forces,
or if it involves a situation where a divorce would affect production,
the chance of obtaining a court grant is limited,[33] as the interests of
the armed forces and of production claim priority in the attention
of the Communist state.

One explanation for some of the cases involving reunion soon after
divorce is the possible ignorance of the serious meaning of the term
divorce among the common people. It may well have been mistaken
by some people for the same situation as when the wife decided to go
back to her parents' home as a consequence of a quarrel and then
would return to the husband when the heat of the moment had passed.
Divorce as a permanent legal separation in the modern sense remains
unfamiliar to most of the people.

Social Resistance against Divorce

It is important to note that even under communism strong social
resistance against divorce survives, particularly in rural communities,
which not only precludes the possibility of rapid spreading of indiscriminate divorce but also limits legitimate divorces.

To the many people who feared that marriage by free choice of partner and romantic love would lead to promiscuity, the idea of freedom of divorce and political support for it was an even more unthinkable evil. Local sentiment in many places ran strongly against the Marriage Law for its sponsoring freedom of divorce and regarded it as a step that would "plunge the family and social relations into general chaos," that would "break up the family," that would "wipe out moral obligations." [34] In East China "the people regarded freedom of divorce as a step that would lead men to 'lose both person [wife] and wealth,' and regarded the right of 'child brides' to cancel their marriage contracts as being against moral conscience." [35]

Such attitudes survived among Communist party workers also, who, ironically enough, used their new revolutionary power to enforce traditional moral standards. This situation is best summarized by the following significant statement by a Communist writer in 1951:

Remnants of the feudalistic marriage institution are still persisting in serious proportions in the vast countryside. . . . Many cadres of subdistricts and villages are still deeply imbued with feudalistic ideology and are following a bad style of work, thus directly and indirectly protecting remnants of the feudalistic marriage institution and hindering thorough enforcement of the Marriage Law.

The feudalistic ideology of the subdistrict and village cadres is based mainly on the following points:

They fear that the Marriage Law will lead the world into chaos. After the promulgation of the Marriage Law, in the provinces of Liaotung and Heilungchiang of the Northeast, in the provinces of Hopei and Pingyuan in North China, in the provinces of Shantung and Chekiang in East China, and in many other places, subdistrict and village cadres are generally afraid to disseminate knowledge of the Marriage Law. In Pingyuan Province, some village cadres locked up the Marriage Law in their desk after receiving it. One village cadre in Chekiang Province even said, "Whoever makes propaganda on the Marriage Law in my village, I'll break his leg!" This gives law-breaking landlords and certain bad elements a chance to attack the Marriage Law as a divorce law, and to accuse the government of mobilizing the masses for divorce. This arouses fear among a part of the masses regarding the Marriage Law in some places. When propaganda meetings are held for the Marriage Law, younger women are often not allowed to take part lest they become emboldened to demand divorce.

Many subdistrict and village cadres are straightforward, fearless fighters in the struggle against the feudalistic land system, in the sharp class struggle between the peasants and the landlords. But when it comes to the struggle against the old marriage institution, it is different. It is a struggle between backward thought and progressive thought within the peasant himself. They realize that, if the Marriage Law is thoroughly enforced, the relationship between the sexes will radically change, the old family institution will gradually alter. But they are accustomed to the feudalistic institution and the old relationship between the sexes. Therefore, they are unwilling to accept the Marriage Law; they even resist it. . . .

Another factor is the policy of the "supremacy of men" in handling divorce cases. They [rural cadres] regard divorce as putting men in a disadvantageous position, costing them both "person [wife] and wealth." Hence, they set up a variety of conditions for divorce by women, or even make open, unreasonable interference. In Liuchia village of Hsienyang county, Hupei Province, when Su Chin-chun demanded a divorce from her husband, her husband colluded with the village cadres, locked her up in a room, tortured her, and forced her to accept four conditions. (1) She was not to get a divorce, and for three years she was not to visit her own parents' home. (2) She must report to and obtain permission from the parents-in-law every time she went to the toilet. (3) She was not to talk to anyone from her parents' village. (4) She must report to the village council of women if she travelled away from the village. Many subdistrict and village cadres, and even the cadres of some county people's courts, hold that in a divorce, the woman should take as little property along as possible, and that it is best not to let her take any property at all. The people's government in several subdistricts of Yutz'u county in Shansi Province even illegally set up a rule governing the settlement of property in a divorce: "When the woman initiates the divorce, she cannot take any property; when a man initiates a divorce, the woman may take along property." As a result, after a divorce, many a woman is forced by hunger to seek reunion with her husband, thus returning to a life of torture.

Still another factor is the use of old moral concepts in the settlement of divorce troubles. Divorce is taken as an "immoral affair," as a "loss of face," as "breaking up the family." Hence, many subdistrict and village cadres in handling divorce cases always attempt reconciliation and do not permit divorce as a solution.[36]

In another Communist official report some subdistrict and village cadres were pictured as adopting a policy of open suppression against divorce demands by women. Women demanding divorce were imprisoned for "forced reconciliation." They were treated with "reform by education." They were locked up in granary buildings as a measure of suppression. In Mienyang county of Hupei Province a woman was removed from her position as delegate to the people's representatives council because she demanded a divorce. In Chun county the secretary of propaganda of the Chaotien subdistrict government encouraged his uncle to beat the aunt who had succeeded in obtaining a divorce, and forced her to kowtow to apologize for her mistake and to restore the husband-wife relationship. Such local leaders regarded divorce as spreading an "unfavorable influence" and as a "disreputable affair." [37]

In Yihsing county in the southern part of Kiangsu Province a peasant woman, Yang Mei-hua, twenty-one years old, could not bear the cruelty of her husband and mother-in-law. She ran away in the traditional style and wished to marry another man. She was caught by the village workers and given a severe beating. In the end she hanged herself.[38] In the Central-South Region "many women said, 'To get a divorce, there are three obstacles to overcome: the obstacle of the husband, the obstacle of the mother-in-law, and the obstacle of the cadres. The obstacle of the cadres is the hardest to overcome.' " [39] The large number of resulting tragedies is partly recounted in the following report:

> Those of the old legal view make freedom of divorce a target of attack. They think: "Good women should hang themselves (as a result of family discord), only bad women seek divorce." They either reject women's demands for divorce by misinterpreting the new law regarding the requirements of reconciliation, or they lay one-sided emphasis upon the wifely obligation toward the family and reject women's demands for divorce regardless of mistreatment suffered by the women. In Ninghsia county of Kansu Province a woman named Li could no longer bear the mistreatment of her husband and repeatedly demanded a divorce. In her last attempt she pleaded with the court: "If my request for divorce is rejected, my only alternative is to die." But the judge named Tien, who was retained from the Kuomintang government, replied: "You may die if you wish, but you cannot have a divorce." Li returned home and hanged herself. The number of women who have committed suicide or have been killed in various parts of the country has reached alarming proportions recently. The vast majority of these deaths were results of the lack of legal support for their struggle for freedom of divorce because of unreasonable matrimony and domestic mistreatment. In eight special districts in Shantung Province 504 women committed suicide or were killed during the period from January to June of 1952. In eight counties in the southern part of Szechuen Province 116 women met similar deaths in the first half of 1952. In Liaoch'eng, a special district of P'ingyuan Province, 56 women met similar deaths in the months from January to April of 1952.[40]

It is interesting to note that peasant leaders who have been able to fight hard to overthrow the traditional institution of property ownership cling to the traditional institution of family and marriage although changes in the system of property ownership eventually bring about a change in the family system. They exemplify the difficulty of attempting to change a social institution by decree without the necessary political leaders who understand and accept the new idea. Many modern laws attempting to introduce new institutions in the Nationalist period died on paper because of the same situation. The Communists are trying to meet the situation created by the Marriage Law not only with extensive propaganda and indoctrination of the local leaders but also by coordinating these efforts with the change of other social, economic, and political institutions.

The suppressive action of the local leaders and the bitter struggle in numerous divorce cases show that the idea of divorce is spreading extensively; and the terror with which local leaders have regarded the idea, as well as some of the ruthless measures they have used to combat it, suggest the potential strength of the development of the divorce factor. Hence, while the actual number of divorces in China may still be few when viewed by Western standards, the function of these cases as living examples of a new idea of improving personal welfare cannot be ignored, particularly when the idea is supported by a revolutionary political power and dramatized by women's new privileges of taking children and property along in a divorce. When bold women lead off and break the thick ice of ancient tradition against divorce, others are likely to follow their example. In the village of Tunghua in Lushan county of Honan Province a child bride, Li Hsiu-yuan, demanded a divorce, but the local officials were against it, and for three months, the case hung fire. Seeing this trouble, other women who wanted divorces did not dare to bring their demands to court. However, after the "democratic reform campaign" was concluded in the village Li Hsiu-yuan was granted her divorce, and immediately following this, seventeen women obtained divorces or annulments of betrothal contracts. Simultaneously, there was an increase in marriages based upon free choice of partners in the village.[41]

Significance of Freedom of Marriage and Divorce

Since freedom of marriage and divorce may be viewed as the most significant factors in the disorganization of the traditional Chinese family system and the development of a new one to supersede it, it seems worthwhile to summarize their effects.

First, the generational composition of the family has been affected. With marriage focused on the couple to the exclusion of interference by parental and family authority, the husband-wife relationship be-

comes the center of the new family, and the married son's parents occupy only a peripheral position. The traditional arrangement of the
parents-children relationship taking precedent over the husband-wife
relation is now reversed. In the husband-wife-centered family the married son's parents are no longer *ipso facto* members holding a controlling position. Should conflict arise between the parents and the
daughter-in-law, the parents' position is no longer protected by institutional authority or law, and they may have to leave the son's
family. Even in the 1920's, when freedom of marriage first became a
strong demand by the young urban intellectuals, modern women had
already raised the question of setting up separate households from the
parents-in-law, and many of them succeeded in doing so. In such
cases a two-generation family replaces the traditional three-generation
system.

Even if the parents continue to live with the married son's family,
they no longer enjoy a controlling position in the family. Should they
have several married sons, they no longer possess the authority to hold
them together in a closely organized unit or integrate them into a
single household. They can live only with one of the married sons at
a time. Thus their continued living with the married sons no longer
has the same significance as before, for the traditional primary importance of the parents in the family is now being superseded by the
primacy of the husband-wife relation. The parents in the new family
are an adjunct, not a controlling authority; their continued presence
depends a great deal on the pleasure of the daughter-in-law. This new
situation nullifies the ability of the traditional family to expand into
a large, multi-generational structure.

Second, the size of the family has been affected. While the average
of four to six persons per family for the majority of the population will
remain unless altered by a change in birth rates, the size of the middle
and upper classes will be reduced, for the old large family composed
of parents and married sons, so common in the wealthier classes, is
no longer possible when marriage is no longer an affair designed for
family expansion. As the generational composition of the family
changes, there is a corresponding reduction in size.

Third, the solidarity of the family organization has been affected
in various ways. The relation between parents and married sons and
daughters-in-law is weakened by the modern affirmation of the husband-
wife relation as the closest tie. The solidarity of the traditional family,
based on the primacy of the parents-children relation, is thus diminished. The new conjugal family gains solidarity by a closer husband-

wife relation not morally subjected to alienation by parental interference, but this new solidarity has the effect of restricting the strong
family tie to the small circle of the married couple and their unmarried
children.

The new right of remarriage for widows, with the related privilege
of taking children and property to their new home, has obvious disorganizing effects on the solidarity of the traditional family, which
treated a widow as a member permanently related to the family as a
whole and not to the husband alone. The new marriage would be
similarly centered on the husband-wife relation and not on her relation
to the new parents-in-law.

The new trend against institutionalized polygamy affects various
aspects of the family differently. The discontinuation of polygamy
means the loss of its formal function in helping to insure continuity
to the ancestral lineage and a large membership to the traditional
family. On the other hand, the informal function of providing men
with romantic experience or additional sexual pleasure has always
been a disruptive influence on domestic harmony. Thus the abandon-
ment of polygamy would increase the solidarity of the family organization. The suppression of open prostitution as institutionally condoned
behavior has a similar effect.

Fourth, by emphasizing the couple's mutual interest, modern marriage by free choice of partners assigns no importance to the continuation of the family lineage. Belief in the necessity of continuing the
family lineage made marriage a religious act in ancestor worship
which, among other functions, served to expand the membership of
the kinship system and to generate solidarity among them by translating
biological relatedness from common descent into a social bond. The
longer the family lineage continued, the larger the number of descendants. But a large number of descendants from a distant ancestor
would not know each other or recognize any social ties and obligations
among themselves if ancestor worship did not translate biological
relatedness into a living social bond. The traditional identification of
marriage with the sacred function of perpetuating the ancestral lineage
had the purpose of insuring both size and solidarity for the kinship
organization. Now that the main purpose of modern marriage is to
fulfill only the romantic or other requirements of the couple, the result
is the weakening of the relationship between the couple and other
kinship members, especially collateral relatives, thus reducing the
organized kinship circle to a small group of lineal male descendants
and their wives.

The reduction in size and solidarity of the family and its extended kinship organization is of major significance. A small family without support from a large kinship organization cannot perform the multiplicity of socio-economic functions and retain its traditional position as the core of the Chinese social system.

CHAPTER V

Crumbling of the Age Hierarchy

THE STRUGGLE for freedom of marriage and divorce represented a rebellion of the young against parental authority over the arrangement of the children's marriage and their married life, but the ascendance of the young and the retreat of the old resulting from this rebellion concerned more than parental authority over children's marriage. These influences undermined the structure of traditional family authority in general. If the change in the form of marriage mainly affected the roles of the married sons in relation to the roles of the parents and other family members, the undermining of family authority by the rise of the young affected the general structure of the entire traditional family organization, for it altered the role of practically every member in the family and changed the mode of family integration. There is hardly a more significant aspect of the Communist revolution than the attempt to shift the foci of power from the old to the young in the family as well as in society in general.

The Traditional Age Hierarchy and the System of Family Status and Authority

In the traditional structure of family status and authority age was a leading factor. The Five Cardinal Relations, the basic principles of family organization, taught that family members should be arranged into "proper order by their age." The importance of age was clearly pointed out by Mencius' statement: "In the Kingdom there are three things that command universal respect. Nobility is one of them; age is one of them; virtue is one of them. In courts nobility is first of the three; in local communities age is first; but for helping one's generation and presiding over the people the other two are not equal to virtue." [1] The organization of the local community was centered upon the kinship group, hence the supremacy of age. Elsewhere in Confucian teachings, upon which generations of Chinese down through the centuries have been reared, the importance of age as a factor in family status and authority was elaborated and emphasized with tireless repetition. A modern middle-aged Chinese today still retains vivid childhood memories of being ceaselessly reprimanded for not having observed the age line and for showing disrespect to those senior to him. Such reprimands were so much a part of an individual's upbringing that he finds it difficult later in life to address even older friends and senior colleagues by their first name, preferring to call them by their surnames with the prefix of *sen sheng* (the English equivalent of mister), literally meaning "born earlier," or *hsiung*, meaning elder brother.

This "proper order by age" formed the foundation for the hierarchy of status and authority in the traditional Chinese family. In its kinship connotation age implied two factors, generation and chronological age. The generational structuring of Chinese kinship members has been analyzed by H. Y. Feng in his *Chinese Kinship System*. He says, "The architectonic structure of the Chinese kinship system is based upon two principles: lineal and collateral differentiation, and generation stratification. The former is a vertical and the latter a horizontal segmentation. Through the interlocking of these two principles every relative is rigidly fixed in the structure of the whole system." [2]

The status and authority of family members were defined first by the stratified successive generational layers as shown in Feng's chart, reproduced below, and, second, by chronological age. Thus all members in a senior generation enjoyed higher status and authority than those in a junior generation, and, among members in each differentiated group of relatives of the same generational level (as represented by each square in the chart), older members took precedence over younger ones. A third factor in the situation was the proximity of biological relatedness or kinship. This was what Feng calls vertical segmentation based on lineal and collateral differentiation. Feng's chart shows that Ego was under heavier pressure from the status and authority of members closer to him in kinship and senior to him in both generation and physical age than with members of the same generational and age seniority but more distant to him in kinship. Ego's status and authority over members junior to him in generation and chronological age was also graduated by the proximity or distance of kinship. Thus Ego's relation to lineal relatives was closer than to collateral relatives, and the closeness of Ego's relation to collaterals was in inverse proportion to the number of collateral degrees. Ego's relation to a patrilineal relative was closer than to a corresponding matrilineal relative. It was an

The Chinese Kinship System

	Descended from females through males			LINEAL	Descended from males through males				
4th Collateral	**3rd Collateral**	**2nd Collateral**	**1st Collateral**		**1st Collateral**	**2nd Collateral**	**3rd Collateral**	**4th Collateral**	
				Kao tsu fu, Kao tsu mu,					**IV**
			Tsèng tsu ku fu, Tsèng tsu ku mu,	Tsèng tsu fu, Tsèng tsu mu,	Tsèng po tsu fu, Tsèng shu tsu mu,				**III**
		Piao tsu fu, Piao tsu mu,	Ku tsù fu, Ku tsu mu,	Tsu fu, Tsu mu,	Po tsu fu, Po tsu mu, Shu tsu fu, Shu tsu mu,	T'ang po tsu fu, T'ang shu tsu fu, *T'ang ku tsu mu,*			**II**
	T'ang piao po fu, T'ang piao shu fu, *T'ang piao ku mu,*	Piao po fu, Piao shu fu, *Piao ku mu,*	Ku fu, Ku mu,	Fu, Mu,	Po fu, Po mu, Shu fu, Shu mu,	T'ang po fu, T'ang shu fu, T'ang ku mu,	Tsai ts'ung po fu, Tsai ts'ung shu fu, *Tsai ts'ung ku mu,*		**I**
Tsai ts'ung piao haiung, ti, *Tsai ts'ung piao tzŭ, mei,*	T'ang piao hsiung, ti, *T'ang piao tzŭ, mei,*	Piao hsiung, Piao ti, *Piao tzŭ, Piao mei,*	Tzŭ, Tzŭ fu, Mei, Mei fu,	**EGO**	Hsiung, Sao, Ti, Ti fu,	T'ang hsiung, T'ang ti, *T'ang tzŭ, T'ang mei,*	Tsai ts'ung hsiung, ti, *Tsai ts'ung tzŭ, mei,*	Tsu hsiung, Tsu ti, *Tsu tzŭ, Tsu mei,*	
	T'ang piao chih, *T'ang piao chih nü,*	Piao chih, *Piao chih nü*	Wai shèng, *Wai shèng nü,*	Tzŭ, *Nü,*	Chih, *Chih nü,*	T'ang chih, *T'ang chih nü,*	Tsai ts'ung chih, *Tsai ts'ung chih nü,*		**I**
		Piao chih sun,	Wai shèng sun,	Sun, *Sun nü,*	Chih sun, *Chih sun nü,*	T'ang chih sun, *T'ang chih sun nü,*			**II**
			Wai shèng tsèng sun,	Tsèng sun, *Tsèng sun nü,*	Tsèng chih sun, *Tsèng chih sun nü,*				**III**
				Hsüan sun, *Hsüan sun nü,*					**IV**

The heavy squares represent the nuclear group of relatives. Those in italics, indicate their descendants have not been carried over into the next generation, e. g., the children of *nü* are *wai sun* and *wai sun nü* but not given in the following square. The Roman numerals represent ascending and descending generations.

important part of a child's education to learn to recognize and distinguish the degree of *ch'in* (closeness) and *su* (distance) in his contacts with his kinsmen as a basis for the proper amount of deference or obedience to be shown to them. In this respect, kinship relations take on the form of a series of concentric circles with Ego as the center — hence the foremost place for parents-children and sibling relationships in the Confucian system of family ethics.

The interlocking operation of these three factors, generation, age, and proximity of kinship, resulted in a system of status and authority that assigned to every person in the kinship group a fixed position identified by a complex nomenclature system.[3] The identification of status for distant relatives was facilitated by giving the same middle name to all sons born into the same generational level so that the kinship position of a person could be readily identified by the generational name whenever distant members met. An important feature of this system was that it could fit a kinship group of any size, from a small conjugal family to a vastly extended family like a clan with ten thousand or more members, thus giving the small family a ready organizational framework for expansion whenever economic conditions permitted.

This hierarchy of status and authority imposed strong compulsion on the individual to observe his own place in the group through, among other factors, the operation of the mores of filial piety and veneration of age. Filial piety demanded absolute obedience and complete devotion to the parents, thus establishing the generational subordination of the children. In traditional society an individual from childhood to the end of his life was completely immersed in an atmosphere which compelled the observation of filial piety. The lesson of filial piety was carried in nursery stories, in daily exhortations and reprimands, in tales and novels, in textbooks from the first primer to the most profound philosophical discourse, in the numerous "temples of filial sons and chaste women" (*chieh hsiao tz'u*) which studded the land, in dramatized living examples of extremely filial children.

The requirement of obedience to parents, fully supported by formal law in the Ching dynasty before 1912,[4] is still supported by the informal coercive instrument of clan regulations in the rural communities and even by "unregenerated" local officials in the Communist government, whose judgment of civil cases is frequently based more on social institution than on the already changed formal law. Under traditional social order it took exceptional courage and imagination to be an unfilial son.

To be sure, coercion was not the only means by which filial piety was instilled into the individual's mind. Equally important was the emphasis upon parental affection, parent-children interdependence, the children's moral obligation to repay parental care and affection by observing filial piety. Parental affection and feelings of gratitude were very active factors, for Chinese parental affection toward the children is traditionally both genuine and strong. In the old family institution the parents depended upon the children for their old-age security; hence their deep devotion to the care and upbringing of the children. Where the parents belonged to a humble station, they pinned their hopes of social and economic advancement on the future development of the children, particularly the son, another basis for the strong traditional affection toward children. Consequently, the old family structure and ethics did not permit a son to leave his parents in a humble social position when he himself had gained social and economic advancement, the basis for the automatic granting of honorific titles by the imperial government to parents of sons who had won social distinction by passing the traditional civil service examinations.

Dependence upon the children, especially the sons, was particularly strong with the mother. Since her status in the family depended upon the bearing of male heirs, it was not uncommon in traditional society for a mother to sacrifice her health, at times even her life, for the benefit of the children, especially the sons. The writer was told in his boyhood that an aunt contracted tuberculosis and finally died from it on account of her sacrifice for and worry over her son. It matters little whether that was the real cause of her illness and death; what is important was the significance the story had for inducing a feeling of filial piety among the young. The poor family selling property and undergoing extreme sacrifice to give the son an education reflected the same principle.

In recent decades, the once strong parent-children interdependence has been steadily diminished by the increasingly individualistic development of children, the elevation of the social and economic status of the young, the separation of married sons from the parental household through the new form of marriage, the decreasing significance of the family as a basic unit of economic production, and the gradual shifting of the individual's center of loyalty away from the family. These factors, which have an adverse effect on the value of children as an asset to the parents, plainly tend to dilute traditional parental devotion. In addition, the rise of democratic and individualistic trends in the Republican period resulted in widespread resentment against the oppressive features of filial piety which required absolute obedience, devotion, and sacrifice on the part of children. Thus filial piety, once the most emphatically stressed value in the traditional social order for over two thousand years, was subjected to open challenge in the 1920's, gradually lost its sacred and binding character among the modern intellectuals by the 1930's, and, by the time the Communists became the ruling power, was publicly discredited by them as feudalistic, designed for the exploitation of the young.

While the functioning of filial piety was limited to relationships between parents and children, the veneration of age was traditionally a means of inspiring respect and obedience by the young toward all the other senior members of the family and society as a whole. To demonstrate the glory and prestige of age, an individual's sixtieth birthday and every subsequent tenth birthday were celebrated with a feast and ceremony as elaborate and impressive as the family and close relatives could possibly afford. This ritualistic glorification symbolized increased respect for the person's status and authority and implied a greater consideration of his personal needs by others.[5] In vital matters of the family and community his advice was heeded, although he might no longer have the heavy family responsibilities or the actual compelling power of his younger days. The old grandfather and, to a lesser degree, the old grandmother were frequently the only ones in the family who could restrain a despotic or wayward father, relying upon the support of the mores and law for their authority. The seat of honor on family and community occasions was for the old man. Not only did the family try to give him the best material benefits in food and clothing; the clan also accorded him honor. In the southern provinces of Kwangtung and Kwangsi, where the distribution of pork to male clan members was a token of clan membership and status, he was given a double share. He was at the pinnacle of the age hierarchy.

The social logic for this practice was the consideration of old people as a symbol of wisdom. In a society of empirical knowledge and predominant illiteracy the old person had the advantage of experience. He had traversed the greater part of a life cycle and so had seen the operation of major crises in life from routine matters of birth, marriage, and death to other happenings such as major clashes between family members, devastation of wars, visits of natural calamities such as flood and droughts, or the appearance of a portentous star in the skies. When younger people were stunned by a happening, an older person remained calm and knew what to do. He knew the procedure for handling the birth of a baby, the marriage of the young, the burial of the dead, the settlement of a dispute in accordance with the traditional sense of justice, and the safe direction in which to flee when calamity struck. His stock of common sense even included the administration of medicine to the sick. An "old man of worldly affairs" was the guiding hand of the family and the community. His "I have lived longer than you" was the ready and effective reminder to the occasionally disrespectful young.

Where empiricism and illiteracy prevailed, age was also an asset in technical fields. In every traditional craft, the "old master" was most respected, not the brilliant and vigorous young worker. In agriculture his experience was similarly valued by the community. In 1949 the writer tried to introduce into a village an improved weeder which worked much more effectively than hand weeding or hoeing. The younger peasants tried it and liked it very much, but a few days later nobody wanted to use the new instrument because "the old people concluded that it will hurt the root system of the plant." The writer challenged the younger peasants to experiment with the instrument by offering to pay for any damage resulting from it, but to no avail. Confucius' advice of learning to farm from an "old farmer" still stood firm.[6] From handicraft to farming, the "old master" was the model of skill and knowledge. There were few books and no school of technical training in traditional society. The old master taught and advised and laid down rules for the young to follow. He led the family and the community in economic matters.

Thus old people in traditional society were far from being decrepit seniles living off the kindness of society on empty prestige, for age had very practical significance for both the family and the community. The veneration of age not only compelled respect for the aged but also lent prestige to all senior members in the hierarchy of age.

Functioning through the strength of filial piety and veneration of age, the hierarchy of age served to provide a status system for the operation of family authority, to firmly initiate the young into the institution of family life until they reached full maturity, to establish security for the old, and to impress upon the individual the dominance of the family as a corporate body. The long stability of the traditional family institution was due in no small measure to the successful operation of this factor.

But such stability was achieved at the price of strenuous repression of the young and was weakened when it came under fire from modern ideologies and social movements that advocated equality and freedom, particularly freedom for the young. Under the weight of the age hierarchy, the status of the young was indeed low, at times helpless. The authority of parents over the child was absolute. Infanticide, approved by the community, was an expression of it; and even as the child grew older, the parents' threat against his life was by no means completely eliminated. The proverb "The son must die if so demanded by the father" was a means of compelling obedience from the young in traditional China, especially in rural communities, although the carrying out of the threat was extremely rare. A childhood that passed without frequent physical punishment was an exception rather than the rule. When a child reached his mid-teens, his increased physical strength and his ability to run away bolstered his security, but the requirement of filial piety kept a tight rein on him. The necessity of observing this moral code was not merely impressed upon him in the operation of the family institution and group pressure of the community; it was also enforced by formal law. In the Ch'ing period sons were flogged or banished by the court merely on the charge of disobedience brought by the father.[7]

In the Republican period few such cases came to public attention, but the rigid enforcement of filial piety by the clans was not much relaxed in places where the clan organization was strong, such as in rural communities in the Central-South provinces. It is interesting to note that P'eng Teh-huai, a prominent Communist general, was once close to being condemned to death by his clan on the charge of being unfilial to his stepmother.[8] In the writer's own boyhood in the 1920's there was still the frequent verbal threat of being taken back to the ancestral village "to be drowned in a pig's cage by the clan elders" in case of gross disobedience to the parents — although he lived in the city, where the clan wielded no direct influence. Such legal and social pressures drove fear and a feeling of rigid subordination deep into the mind of the young individual.

Although less absolute and rigid than parental dominance over the children, the pressure of status and authority of senior members over junior members in the age hierarchy was by no means light. This was especially so with members of one's own superior generation having a close degree of kinship tie, such as one's grandparents and older uncles. Before them one behaved only with great respect, and one did not argue with or talk back to them. In material rights and privileges their share undisputably came first. On ceremonial occasions one stood or sat in an inferior position to them. They were the "respected elders" even though some of them might not actually be chronologically older. They were held up to the young as models of good conduct, as masters of arts and skills. Before a person reached the age of thirty his words had little weight; his conduct and his work were under constant criticism by senior kinsmen around him. Not until the fourth decade in one's life would one begin to gain serious consideration from senior members in the age hierarchy.

Rise of the Young under the Republic

The practical value of age as a major basis for the great respect of the age hierarchy began to be challenged with the impact of revolutionary currents early in this century. The dominant note of the modern times has been the acquisition of Western knowledge and technological skills and the development of new institutions to implement Western-inspired ideas in an effort to save China in the struggle for national existence; and these could not be acquired simply by experience in the traditional social environment. The only means of acquiring them were through learning and training in schools and through new sources of information; and the required method of developing them, in China as elsewhere, was through science, not empiricism enriched by age.

In the acquisition of new knowledge, new skills, and new ideas the young (those from families capable of affording a modern education) had a distinct advantage over the old. The young had plasticity of mind, eagerness for the new and the adventurous, fewer obstacles in the consciousness of vested interests and entrenched traditional social relationships. Above all, rigid repression of the young by the hierarchy of age gave them an eagerness to alter their old status by acquiring new knowledge and skills and by promoting the adoption of new institutions. Hence, the modern educated young Chinese formed a nucleus from which new influences germinated and gradually developed into leading forces in political, economic, and social trends. The young were no longer bowing to the old at every turn, and age was no longer always a mark of personal prestige and social authority.

Over the past half century every political revolution and social development has acted as a new force in expanding the number and influence of the modern educated young. In the course of its limited success in encouraging revolutionary ideas championed by the young the Republican revolution of 1911 put a larger number of young elements into prominent political positions than there ever had been under the old imperial government. In the turbulent years of 1917 to 1919 the young were presented to the nation as a distinctive age group under the term "new youth" by the rising crescendo of the youth movement, culminating in the May 4th Movement of 1919, which placed the educated young in a position of new importance in political and cultural fields. Led by the historic periodical, *Hsin Ch'ing-nien* (The New Youth), tons of literature in the form of magazines, press articles, and pamphlets poured forth on the subject of the new youth and its problems, forcing the new age group to the nation's attention. Political and economic crises of the period, the necessity of new means for their solution, together with the impotent traditionalism of the old and the general illiteracy of the common people, created a new role for the modern educated youth and led them to demand revision of the subordinate status of the young. For the first time a powerful social and political movement put up a young group in opposition to the old and the institutions the latter stood for.

When the Second Revolution swept the country in the mid-1920's, the exaltation of the young was carried to new heights. The revolutionary regime based in Canton was marked by the youthfulness of the personnel that staffed it. Every branch of the new political machine that baffled and at times frustrated the old was led and manned mainly by young men and colored by the outlook of youth. The occasional presence of an old man over sixty in their midst was a spectacle, for here was "an old dog that had learned new tricks." When the seat of political power, the center of formal social control, was captured by the young, the sanctity of the age hierarchy could not be expected to remain intact.

In the cultural field the "Renaissance" of the May 4th Movement was a product of the young, and by the mid-1920's it had made deep inroads into the educational system of the country, particularly in the storm center of the South. The quantity of "New Culture" publications in all fields had by that time distinctly pushed Confucian classical works to the side, at least in the cities. The new literature, particularly in works of fiction, clearly steered away from the traditional motif of fairy tales and from Confucian themes and drew its inspiration from Western ideas that concerned the special problems of the young. Its undisputed literary dominance together with its modern theme of romantic love led the educated young and indirectly the younger generation in general, toward an outlook of life and love which retained little respect for the age hierarchy and frequently held little consideration at all for the old.

In the economic field accelerated industrial development after World War I gave increasingly responsible positions to the young, who alone commanded modern technical qualifications. Technical dreams of the young set the blueprints for the nation's economic development. The "old master's" prestige declined with the diminishing importance of the traditional crafts under the crushing superiority of modern technology. The old master still held sway in the vast pre-industrial sector of the country's economic structure, but his technical competence no longer commanded the moral respect of the educated young, and his outmoded technical role could no longer support the age hierarchy in that modernized segment of the population which was leading the trend of economic development. The social and economic plight of the growing army of unemployed old craft masters was hardly conducive to the effective maintenance of age as a criterion of technical competence.

The older generation watched in bewilderment the making and unmaking of governments, the waging of the unending civil wars, the ever-rising prestige of new commodities and new economic organizations, the unfamiliar events that occupied increasing space in the newspapers and in the people's daily conversations, the untraditional ways of training and educating the young — all these changes staged by a group that had hitherto been in an inferior position in the age hierarchy forced society to grant more consideration to the young. In the family, if the young still paid a measure of respect to parents and senior members in the age hierarchy, it was done with a tinge of begrudging formality and seldom with the spontaneous sincerity and voluntary devotion formerly developed by filial piety and veneration of age.

The vital change of attitude toward age was limited largely to the modern educated young, the new youth, but the new youth were an articulate group playing a strategic role in the shaping of social trends. The facilities of modern education were rapidly expanding, with its middle and primary levels steadily extending to members of the lower middle class, and the mass education movement which started after the May 4th Movement of 1919 served as another vehicle for the diffusion of the new attitude into a small part of the working class and the peasantry. Largely centered in urban areas, the change affected also the young elements of the richer portion of the rural population as they took to the cities for better educational facilities, where their attitude toward the traditional age hierarchy was altered by absorbing new ideas and by insulation from the immediate pressure of parents and senior kinsmen at home.

When the great upheaval of the 1920's settled down to a divided course in the 1930's, with the Kuomintang dominating the nation and the Communist Party setting up red areas in the South, the traditional Chinese attitude toward the age hierarchy had already been substantially diluted. The two decades that followed saw the continued extension of the new influence to growing numbers of the young, aided by the increased absence of the young of all social classes from home in a period of increasing population mobility, which freed the younger generation from the immediate pressure of the age hierarchy in the kinship system. In the early 1930's such mobility was mainly a consequence of the accelerated development of urbanism, which set many of the young on the move away from home for jobs or educational opportunities. After 1937 the Japanese invasion drove millions far from their local communities, and the young were left free to develop the new attitude toward age with a minimum of immediate interference from older kinsmen. Thus, long before 1949 the ground had been prepared for the developments under communism.

Status of the Young under the Communist Regime

The triumph of the Communist revolution carried the exaltation of the young to a new height. If youth furnished the vital force of China's previous revolutions, it certainly did so even more emphatically with the Communist revolution. Its radical ideological departure from tradition first found acceptance only in the more plastic young minds, and the Communists possessed great skill in organizing the young for the service of the revolution.

The elevation of the status of the young under the Communist regime has been, first of all, a highly organized movement, not a spontaneous development. Secondly, that movement has spread from the hitherto confined circle of upper- and middle-class young intelligentsia to the numerically large group of young workers and peasants. For some three decades before Communist accession to power youth organizations had had a steady growth, but they were comparatively small in membership and poorly integrated. Under the Communist regime youth organizations have been vastly expanded in membership, centrally directed, and well-disciplined.

The New Democratic Youth League is an example. According to statistics of September 1951, its national membership had reached 5,180,000 — twenty-seven times the membership figure of 190,000 of April 1949. There were 24,200 branches in various parts of the country. Classification of the membership was as follows: workers, 33.88 per cent; peasants, 51.18 per cent; students, 11.44 per cent; others, 2.5 per cent. Females accounted for about 30 per cent of the total. By 1957 the

League membership had leaped to 23,000,000, "accounting for 19.17 per cent of the total number of young people in China." [9]

It is notable that students who monopolized the youth movement in the pre-Communist period now comprise only a little over one-tenth of the membership of the most important organization of the young under the Communist regime. In this respect, the Democratic Women's League, with its vast network of affiliated organizations, also has a fast expanding membership, the majority of whom are now women peasants and workers, not intellectuals. Above all, the Chinese Communist Party itself, which has experienced a phenomenal growth in membership since 1949, is dominated numerically by the young, who are drawn mainly from the peasantry and the workers, only a minority coming from the urban intelligentsia.

Youth organizations and other organizations containing a majority of young members serve a variety of purposes, among which is the conscious and unconscious function of advancing the power and status of the young. In this sense, these organizations have the significance of representing a formally organized struggle, aided by political power, to alter the status of the young in the traditional age hierarchy.

Organized struggle for status by the young is actively advanced by the publication of literature on the subject of youth in unprecedented quantity. Let us consider the publishing activities of the New Democratic Youth League in 1951 alone: "For the purpose of propaganda and education, the Youth League publishes 61 newspapers and periodicals for its general membership throughout the nation. The Youth Publication Company under the Central Committee of the Youth League, which was established in 1950, has published 14 categories and 260 kinds of book series and periodicals, which total 8,800,000 copies. *Chung-kuo Ch'ing-nien pao* (Chinese Youth), the daily newspaper serving as the official organ of the Central Committee of the Youth League, will be published on April 27 of this year [1951]. (*Chung-kuo Ch'ing-nien Shuang-chou-k'an* (Chinese Youth Biweekly), also an organ of the Youth League's Central Committee, is among the most widely circulated periodicals in the country." [10]

If the youthfulness of the personnel of the Southern revolutionary regime in the mid-1920's had the effect of elevating the status of the young, the same is even more true of the present Communist regime. Although the top leaders of this regime are generally older than their counterparts in the mid-1920's, Mao Tse-tung and the majority of the leading party figures started their political career in close connection with youth organizations.[11] The three decades of struggle for power advanced their age, but it did not lessen their identification with the cause of youth.

As for the middle- and lower-ranking party members who form the lower echelon of the Communist regime, the average age level is lower than that of corresponding personnel in any previous Chinese government. A government announcement on the recruitment of young men and women for training to be junior officers in police work listed an age limit of eighteen to twenty-three.[12] Similar age limits for other types of political work can be seen in other recruiting announcements. Young men in their twenties and thirties head local government departments that concern the vital interests of tens of thousands of people. In urban neighborhood and village indoctrination and propaganda meetings it is the young leaders who do the talking and lay down the line, and it is the older people who have to do the listening and following. In enforcing policies, be it a bond sales campaign, suppression of counterrevolutionaries, mass trial of landlords and local bullies and the redistribution of land, the Five-Anti movement against businessmen committing bribery, evasion of taxes, theft of state property, cheating on state contracts and theft of confidential state economic information, or a score of other major and minor movements that have disorganized the traditional pattern of life under Communist rule, it is the young leaders, ranging in age from the teens to the thirties, who have been running the show.

The amount of political power and responsibility vested in the hands of young local leaders is certainly without precedent in China's history; and it is shared by young men and women belonging to public organizations which are regularly mobilized to participate in current movements and to help enforce government policies. Members of the Youth League, the Democratic Women's League, the student union, and many other organizations work side by side with party officers in carrying out major government policies.

The young have come to possess not only coercive power but also social prestige under the new standards set up by the regime. To the young go the large proportion of awards for "model workers," "model farmers," winners in production emulations; they are the recipients of many other honors symbolizing new values [13] that are foreign to the old generation. The leading "model workers" held up as examples of production efficiency for the rest of the workers, from Ma Heng-chang in mining to Nan Chien-hsiu in the textile industry, the counterparts of Stakhanovites in the Soviet Union, are young men and women, most of them in their twenties. The influence of youth begins to invade even the old empirical field of agriculture wherever improvements of agricultural methods are being vigorously introduced:

> In the patriotic production movement in the villages, members of the Youth League are vigorous shock brigades. They not only participate in agricultural production but also actively propagandize the agricultural policy of the People's Government among the people. They lead in organizing mutual-aid teams, in popularizing new agricultural methods. For example, Kuo Yu-lan in Heilungkiang Province and Wang Ching-mei in Hopei Province, both female members of the Youth League, have won the title of model agricultural workers. They both have popularized seed-selection, the soaking of seeds before sowing, and other new agricultural methods in their own communities, and the yields from their fields are higher than the average of other farmers. In the irrigation project of controlling the Huai River, members of the Youth League inhabiting the banks of the river mobilized large numbers of young people to participate in the work. Last winter [1951], in the northern part of Anhwei Province alone, one-third of the 600,000 labor conscripts were young people. Among these young workers were 16,000 members of the Youth League who formed the leading force of the labor conscripts. In the county of Pu-yang, Youth League members accounted for 30 per cent of the model irrigation workers.[14]

If it was the young technical men of the modern bourgeois intelligentsia who dimmed the prestige of the traditional "old craft masters" in the pre-Communist period, now the progressive young workers and peasants are doing the same thing on a more extensive scale. In traditional days a brilliant and successful young man might be held up as an example for members of his own generation, but never for his senior members in the age hierarchy or the old masters of the trade, who might regard him with benign approval but always considered him immature, with more to learn from older people. Now in every factory, every neighborhood, and in the villages young models of production and revolutionary conduct are glorified with fanfare and honored with material rewards. Ended is the sanctity of the time-honored rule that the old teach and the young learn, the old lead and the young follow. A student leader told his professor in 1951: "You and your generation are too beset with considerations and worries for decisive action, so we young ones should lead in changing the nation's way of life."

Change of Status of the Old in the Family

It is clear that the traditional older generation with its conservatism is regarded as an obstacle to progress. Even though there is no substantiation to rumors of summary gross mistreatment of all old people as an age group, such rumors reflect the general decline in status and power of the older generation. This change has inevitable effects on the status of the older generation within the family organization.

The political struggle in which the young are playing a leading part is carried into the family. From the time the Communists took control of the nation, and through the successive crises of the suppression of counter-revolutionaries, the Five-Anti and the Three-Anti movements, and the "thought reform" of the intellectuals, every progressive young person has been increasingly under group pressure to disregard kinship ties and the prestige of age and ferret out dissenters and recalcitrants for correction and, at times, even for elimination.* Since parents and uncles and elder brothers have been openly accused or secretly reported by junior members in the age hierarchy for offenses leading to police surveillance, fines, labor correction, imprisonment, or even death, the progressive young person is as much feared at home as in public. It is common to find older people suddenly stop talking about public matters, particularly political affairs, as soon as a progressive young family member comes home, especially if he comes home from school, where ideological indoctrination has been vigorously carried on. While the exact proportion of progressives among the young will remain unknown for some time, there is little doubt of the widespread effect of the new ideology on young minds and the rapid extension of this effect from the bourgeois intelligentsia to the much wider circle of young workers and peasants, as seen in the membership growth of the Youth League. Sharp is the contrast between this situation and the traditional order when family mores were in complete harmony with the nation's political ideology, when a successful and prominent son paid homage to his socially humble parents and other senior kinsmen.

Communist law and political principles no longer provide any support for the superiority and rights of an individual over another based on age. On the contrary, they tend to limit traditional authority and the rights of the old over the young. The prohibition of mistreatment of children limits what the parents can do with the young.[15] Elaborate legal stipulations on the protection of children's interests in the family have the same effect.[16] The single legal requirement of children is that they must support the parents and must not mistreat or abandon

---

* The Five-Anti movement, aimed at the business class, has been explained before. The Three-Anti movement is aimed at correcting corruption, wastefulness, and bureaucratism among government officials and employees.

them.[17] In stipulations of the Marriage Law responsibilities of parents are much heavier than their rights over children — a reversal of the requirements of traditional filial piety which compelled almost one-sided devotion by the children.

There are no stipulations in Communist law governing the relationship of the older generation to the young aside from that of parents to children. However, since the parent-child relationship is stronger than the relationship between other members in the age hierarchy, when the parents' position is greatly weakened the position of other senior members in the family over the young deteriorates more rapidly. For a young progressive the traditional authority of an uncle or an aunt carries little weight, and that of more distant seniors in the age hierarchy means even less. Published documents show more political accusations by the young against other relatives than against parents.[18]

If the older generation finds no protection for their traditional status from politics and law in the revolution, it finds the safeguards also weak in other directions. Wherever modern economic development prevails, older people are finding it difficult to retain positions of leadership in family production. The replacement of numerous family businesses in trade and industry by state enterprises and the development of collectivized agriculture have had serious effects in this respect. The tendency of increasing economic qualifications and rights of the younger family member and the growing system of free education lessen the dependence of the young and reduce the economic authority of the older generation as a factor in maintaining its traditional status in the age hierarchy.

The development of centers of activity outside the home for the young adds another difficulty to the maintenance of the age hierarchy as a system of family status and authority, both because of the lack of time to teach the traditional ideas to the young at home and because of the conflicting ideology being instilled into the minds of the young in outside centers of activity. The development of modern schools during the past half century and the rapid growth of membership of youth organizations under the Communist regime are examples of this development. Under the Communists young men and women are recruited in large numbers as paid workers or volunteers for a great variety of public activities which take them away from home part time or full time at an age from the early teens to the twenties, an age in which they would have remained very close to home in the traditional system. The following is illustrative of the increasing separation of the young from family influence.

> In Feng Ch'i village near the city of Canton over forty young men and women, led by some twenty Youth League members, cultivated an acre of "tabooed" land [land that the villagers would not till for superstitious fear of bringing misfortune]. They sold the rice yielded from it, bought lumber with the money, built a house, and called it "The Home of Youth." They used the house for ideological classes, meetings, and activities. It has become the youth center in the village.[19]

The establishment of a center of organized activities exclusively for the young as an age group in the rural community is a new phenomenon, for all activity of the young except school was traditionally centered in the home. It is interesting to note the name of the center, "The Home of Youth," still using the word "home" which has a connotation of strong social affinity for the Chinese. At this "home" the older generation can no longer exercise discipline and control over the young.

With the superiority of age being seriously undermined, with the young tending to move out of the range of family education and discipline, with the legal support of filial piety gone, with the basic concept of the marriage of the children being changed, the welfare and security of the old becomes a weighty consideration in this transitional period. True, Communist law requires children to support their parents. In Shanghai, for example, an old woman abandoned by her son obtained support from him by order of the "people's court." [20] But the law does not prosecute such cases unless brought to court. In spite of increased accessibility to the law, there is a question whether every neglected or abandoned parent will bring the case to court in a situation where rule by law is still unfamiliar to common people. There is little doubt that such legal support is incomparably weaker than the guarantee provided by the traditional family for the welfare and security of the old.

The spectacular rise of the young and the decline of the old in power and prestige are plainly products of that stage of revolution which needs plastic young minds to accept the novel ideology, to practice the new standards, and to effect a drastic break with the traditional past. As the revolutionary situation settles down to an established order, with its new institutions and tradition sufficiently developed, age as a factor affecting the status and authority of individuals will undoubtedly resume some degree of importance, and accumulated knowledge and experience through age will again bear weight in the social evaluation of an individual. But it is doubtful whether age will ever resume the former traditional importance which summarily subjected the young to an inferior position in disregard of his other qualifications. The development of industrialization, which emphasizes technical competence, not age, and the popularization of science, which discounts empiricism, are both major goals of the present Communist revolution. Should the revolution successfully set up its institutions and traditions, these two factors among others will preclude a full return to the former Chinese consideration for age.

CHAPTER VI

The Ascendancy of the Status of Women in the Family

DIFFERENCE IN SEX, as in age, was a factor in the stratification of status and allocation of authority, which in traditional China meant the subordination of women in the dichotomy of family membership based on sex difference. This was partly a result of the patrilineal and patrilocal nature of the Chinese family structure, in which the definition of membership of the patrilineal kinship system and the distribution of rights and duties in it called for a male-dominant system of status and authority so as to prevent interference and disruption from maternal kinship ties. Subordination of female members, like subordination of the young, in the traditional family always constituted a point of tension which was kept under control by various authoritarian features of the old family institution.

In the modern period the liberal humanistic values and socio-economic developments of industrial urbanism seriously weakened the features which forced women into a subordinate position, and there was a general movement toward the emancipation of women. The alteration of women's status both in the family and in society became a major theme of the family revolution. Since the Communist revolution from its beginning advocated equality between the sexes even more emphatically than other social movements, it was inevitable that a change in the role of women should become an ever important factor in the reshaping of the family institution under Communist rule.

The Status of Women in the Traditional Family

The traditional status of women may not have been so low in China as in some of the contemporary cultures, the Islamic and the Japanese for example. The status of a Chinese woman improved with age and the bearing of children, and she could become the head of a household. Socially, women achieved distinction in various fields of endeavor, including art and scholarship, and they occasionally occupied the throne, as exemplified by the powerful nineteenth-century Empress Dowager. Among the common people, especially in the South, women's active part in economic production bolstered their position in the family and mitigated the general social discrimination against them. Nevertheless, the low status of Chinese women whether in the family or in society is proverbial. In traditional Chinese fiction the female character was frequently introduced by the line "unfortunately [she] was born a woman." K'ang Yu-wei, the precursor of modern reformers at the end of the last century, listed being born a woman as one of the calamities of life.[1]

The status of the female in the traditional Chinese family changed in different stages of her life. Her status in childhood and girlhood was not particularly low compared to that of her brothers or male cousins in the same household. In spite of her low evalution as a family asset, she enjoyed a fair share of parental affection and material family benefits. The first serious discrimination came in the matter of educational opportunity, which went first to the son even when the idea of education for women had started to be accepted in modern cities, for educational investment in a girl was considered irrecoverable owing to her eventual departure from the family. Her most trying period began with her marriage into another family.[2] She was a stranger in a new family, under relentless intimate surveillance and discipline from the parents-in-law, unprotected by the supposedly intimate husband, and left to fate by custom and law. Before she gave birth to a son, she was considered only a half-qualified member of the family. With the birth of a son, she fulfilled her duty in perpetuating the ancestral lineage and found protection and security in the future of the son. Motherhood of a male descendant always lessened family discrimination against her and from then on, her lot improved as the children grew older. When she became a grandmother, she was usually the supreme woman in the household, ranking in status next to her husband should he still be living.

In each stage of her life she held an inferior position to the male members of the family of the same generational level in vital matters, and to those in the generation above hers in all matters. This inferiority of status, mitigated by parental and general family affection while she was still at home, explains the harsh situation of the bride trying to adjust to the intimate ways of the superiors who were strangers to her, including the husband whom she had married by parental arrangement and not by personal choice. With marriage began the most personally humiliating and emotionally disturbing stage of a woman's life, generally covering the age from sixteen or eighteen to the thirties, after which the mother-in-law would either have died or retired and the children would be grown. In this stage one saw the raw subjugation of an individual, for the most relentless measures were sometimes taken by the family against the young female who tended to reject subordination.

The young wife was subordinated not only to the males of the family but also to the mother-in-law and, to a lesser degree, to other females in the superior generation. It could be argued that the mother-in-law, in order to exercise discipline upon the daughter-in-law, must enlist the approval and cooperation of her own husband and her married son, and that her authority was delegated by the male. This seems to be only academic. What really mattered was that only the young wife's submission made it possible for the traditional family to assimilate a new female member into its intimate life and thus prevented the breaking off by the young wife and her husband into an independent family.

Loss of Women's Lives in the Traditional Family

The process of subordination and adjustment of the wife was so painful, and the traditional family institution, recognizing no right of divorce, left so little possibility of escape, that it sometimes resulted in the loss of her life by suicide or by murder. The long history of family conflicts ending in the death of the wife was echoed in the slogan of the May 4th Movement: "Down with the human-devouring ritualistic tradition."

In 1935, when statistics were grossly incomplete, 1,353 suicides were reported in 244 counties and in 22 provinces. Of this total, 351, or 26.0 per cent, were caused by domestic discord or matrimonial difficulties, which constituted the largest single item among all causes of suicide in China (economic difficulties caused 341 cases, or 25.2 per cent, of all suicides). Among the 351 cases of suicide caused by family conflict 253, or 72 per cent, were women.[3]

In the Communist period a greater amount of information on this subject is published, although figures are still fragmentary in character. The following are excerpts from reports in the Communist press:

> According to incomplete statistics, women who committed suicide or who were killed on account of . . . family mistreatment numbered over

10,000 in the Central-South Region, and 1,245 in Shantung Province, both in the past year [1950], and 119 in the nine counties of the Huaiyin Special District in the northern part of Kiangsu Province during the months of May to August, 1950.[4]

In the special district of Changsha, Hunan Province, during the period from May to August 1950 incomplete statistics show that 99 women lost their lives on account of family mistreatment, and among them 68 were forced to commit suicide, and 31 were killed or died from inflicted injuries. In the county of Huangan of Hupei Province during the two months of July and August 1950, 14 women died from the same cause. In Shangshui county of Honan Province during a period of three months in 1950, 90 women were driven to death by family mistreatment. In Ningyuan county of Hunan Province in the period of two months 17 women committed suicide for the same reason.[5]

In Tsuiyang county of Honan Province during the period of not quite a year in 1950, 212 women were killed or committed suicide. In Shangch'iu county of the same province during the months from January to April 1951 over 30 women committed suicide on account of matrimonial problems . . . . In Tsang-hsien Special District during the first half of 1951, 47 women were forced into suicide or killed by family situations. [Among these cases] in the village of Chaohsiamatou in Chiaoho county, the woman Han Kuo-chen was axed to death by her husband when she threatened to get a divorce.[6]

During the past year [1950] among the 936 cases involving the loss of human lives handled by the people's courts of various levels in the province of Shansi somewhat over 600 cases, or about 66 per cent, were women who were either tortured to death or forced into suicide.[7]

Available Communist literature published after 1952 contains no further statistical information on the subject, possibly because of the socially disturbing nature of such figures at a time when the Communists wanted to consolidate their political power by stabilizing the social order. The significant point is that these statistics do not represent the entire number of women who lost their lives but only those incidents which came to the attention of the authorities. In T'eng-hsien Special District of Shantung Province it was only as a consequence of the court making an issue out of the case of P'an Shi, a wife who was tortured to death by her husband and mother-in-law, that 103 other cases of women who had been killed or committed suicide in that district came to the attention of the authorities.[8]

The lack of basic population data for the territories for which the above fragmentary statistics are given makes it impossible to compute rates. One can get an idea of the situation in the following statement by a woman leader made in 1951: "My mother was so mistreated by my father that she hanged herself. My father sent me into the Wang family as a child bride when I was only nine. I know well the suffering of women. Later, in the struggle against local bullies, I joined the Communist Party. The people elected me chairman of the peasants association of the Shawangtien subdistrict [of Mingchuan county in Honan Province]. . . . Since the promulgation of the Marriage Law, women have become organized, and people do not dare to oppress women as before. Some mothers-in-law and husbands still try to mistreat wives. This problem has to be solved, otherwise a small incident can develop into a big tragedy. We are trying hard on this point. . . . And in this subdistrict, which comprises twelve villages with a total population over 2,200, not one woman has been forced into suicide or beaten to death since the Liberation [the fall of 1949]." [9] It is significant that this woman leader was proud that no women's lives had been lost in a small community of 2,200 people inside of two years. It suggests the possibility that in a community of some 2,200 people over a period of two years, people would expect one or more cases of the killing or suicide of women.

Lacking comparable statistics on deaths of women from domestic discord in the pre-Communist period, it is not known to what extent such deaths in the foregoing figures are a part of the traditional situation and to what extent they are a result of new conflict arising from the introduction of the family revolution into rural communities hitherto isolated from modern influences. Commenting on the rise of such deaths in all parts of the country during 1951 and 1952, a Communist writer, Ch'en Yu-tung, stated that those women who met death "were mostly progressive in thought, militant in spirit, strong in their capacity for work, and young in age," enthusiastic about the new rights of marriage and divorce, and active in the struggle against the old family institution.[10] From this characterization, these women were so-called activists in the Communist movement.

This statement from a writer who had access to Communist official data suggests that the alarming figures of suicides and killing were not so much a part of the pre-Communist situation as a result of the increase and sharpening of domestic conflict stimulated by extension of the women's emancipation movement and the family revolution into the rural countryside, the stronghold of traditional conservatism. Moreover, the years covered by these statistical figures, 1950–1952, were years when the new Communist regime carried its revolutionary fury into rural communities to liquidate the landlord class and to uproot the "feudalistic system." Executions, tortures, and other forms of physical punishment were liberally used in this struggle; and in the general flare of violence men employed their new political power to defend their traditional authority over rebellious women, as we have noted in Chapter IV. In such a situation it is fully possible that the number of suicides and the killing of women would increase noticeably. But even if the figures do not represent the normal traditional situation, they reveal the rigidity of the old family institutions, its intolerance toward deviation, and the lack of any channel of personal readjustment for women who might dare to violate the ancient mores by raising new demands and showing rebelliousness.

Factors in the Traditional Subordination of Women

To hold women in general, and young and middle-aged wives in particular, to an inferior status where mistreatment abounded and even death lurked, the authority of the family was supported by all the repressive features of the traditional institution of arranged marriage. We have noted that this institution minimized the roles of the marrying couple, reducing the significance of the bride as an individual. The practice of the husband's family in paying a symbolic or realistic price for her, the "buying and selling marriage" as it is called by modern youth, was a particularly influential factor in giving her a subordinate status. That it continued to exist widely as late as 1951 and 1952, the early years of Communist rule, is shown in the following reports:

> In Ts'ang county of Hopei Province the "buying and selling marriage" is still the rule. There is a common saying in that locality, "In a betrothal, when a daughter goes out, an ox comes in." The meaning of this saying is that the money obtained from selling the daughter is sufficient to buy an ox. In Yinch'iu county of the same province the man's family has to pay the girl's family one hundred feet of cloth, and some even pay a thousand catties of grain.[11]
>
> In Yungnien county of Hopei Province when a girl is betrothed the man's family has to pay the girl's family a certain amount of cotton or the equivalent in cash. The girl's family will not give up the girl in case the promised amount is not fully paid. In Szu village in P'inglo county of Ninghsia Province the village head, May Yu, for the marriage of his son paid the girl's family forty silver dollars, thirty-eight feet of cloth, and 800 catties of wheat. To pay this, Ma Yu sold seventeen mow of his land and some other property. After the marriage the entire family suffered from hunger, for the family was financially bankrupt.[12]
>
> In the rural district of Shaohsing county in Chekiang Province the

common practice of figuring the price for a bride is by her age, paying one picul [133 pounds] of rice for each year. In Kiashan county of Chekiang Province the ritual cash for a bride is from twenty to thirty-piculs of rice, aside from the price for the go-between.[13]

And the consequence of this practice? In Changnan village, in Kiashan county of Chekiang Province, Ch'en Chin-lao beat his wife. When a leader of the land reform program came up to stop him, Ch'en snapped back: "I bought her for 1,200 catties of rice. What does it matter if I give her a little beating?" [14] And wife beating was not limited to the peasantry. Thus ran a Communist report from the modern city of Shanghai in 1950: "Among the most serious problems brought forth by women workers is the common practice of beating and mistreating wives. Some husbands beat their wives until they bleed from their wounds. Even the chairman of a labor union beats up his wife." [15]

We have also noted that in traditional marriage the woman belonged to the husband's family for life. The traditional wedding ceremony was attended only by the relatives of the husband's family, the girl's family held its own celebration separately without participation from members of the husband's family, and there was no occasion during the whole process of the wedding when the two families met together. This had the effect of serving notice on the girl's family not to meddle in the affairs of the husband's family concerning the treatment of the bride. And since, except on ceremonial occasions, frequent visits by the wife to her own parents' home were discouraged, the wife was deprived of her own family's support in case of mistreatment.

In addition to concubinage, which posed a constant threat against the wife, and the absence of freedom of divorce, which served to block the wife from a peaceful means of escape from an unpleasant situation, there were three other traditional limitations which applied not only in marriage but to the general status of women in Chinese society: loss of her name, seclusion, and lack of education.

After marriage a woman discarded her own given name and was known to the community only by her surname prefixed with the surname of her husband's family. In the home she was addressed by a kinship term denoting her position in the family organization which omitted both her surname and given name. In effect, her individual existence in society was effaced.

Women were generally secluded. They were not only prevented

from contact with men outside the family, thus forestalling romantic love as a basis for marriage, but also, after marriage, cut off from opportunities for independence in political, economic, and social activities. Even in the early years of Communist rule traditional Chinese still insisted on this practice of secluding women, especially when such seclusion was being threatened:

> Restricting and interfering with women's participation in social activities is a form of mistreatment. After the victory of the Chinese people's revolution, due to the growth of political awakening, the broad masses of women have begun to participate in social activities, but they face a great deal of resistance. Some women who participated in the women's association, in literacy classes, or in newspaper-reading groups, have come home to confront the long faces of a husband and mother-in-law. Some women have returned from a meeting and the family would not give them food to eat, and some have even been locked out of the house. Some husbands and mothers-in-law summarily forbid women from participating in any social activity. Still other women are beaten up or even tortured to death by their husbands and mothers-in-law because of participation in social activities. Such conditions occur not only among peasants and workers, but also among urban bourgeoisie, and even among the intelligentsia.[16]

Lastly, women were not only generally denied the benefits of formal education but also discouraged from developing any ability or talent useful for a career outside the home. "A woman's lack of talent is in itself a virtue" was a frequently used proverb to check any worldly ambitions of a woman, especially in recent decades when a daughter demanded to go to school like her brothers. The result was the general lack of professional skills among women and the incomparably higher percentage of illiteracy among women than among men. In a village in South China surveyed in 1950, 65 per cent of the men but only 8 per cent of the women of ten years of age and over were literate. In the sample census of nine counties in Szechwan Province in 1942 and 1943, 48 per cent of the men but only 19 per cent of the women were literate.[17]

Forced seclusion and imposed ignorance, lack of occupational opportunities, general discrimination against working women, and repressive marriage customs inevitably resulted also in women's economic dependency in traditional society. And, since that dependency was accompanied by the lack of family property rights for women, the simple threat of hunger forced them to submit to the inferior status assigned them by the male-dominant family institution.

Change in the Subordination Factors Under the Communist Regime

The foregoing factors have been among the most responsible influences in shaping the traditional status of women, particularly that of the young and middle-aged wife. In the past half century of family revolution such influences have been progressively weakened, at least among the bourgeois intelligentsia, by the reformation of the marriage institution, the development of modern urban economy giving rise to more occupational opportunities for women, the development of women's education, and the general social movement for equality. This trend toward elevating the status of women was well marked prior to the rise of Communist power; it has been accelerated since the Communists took over national control. Much of this aspect of change in the family has been discussed previously, but some leading points will be reviewed here.

The principle of sex equality as one of the causes espoused by the Communist revolution is clearly written in the regime's Marriage Law (Article 1). In a legal opinion rendered by the municipal court of Tientsin on the case of mistreatment of a wife, we find the following statement: "The attitude of belittling women still widely exists among a part of the people in the city of Tientsin. Some say, 'Women cannot possibly be the equal of men in any way'; 'If women do not listen to men in the family, to whom should they listen?' and 'Beating her is to discipline and teach her for her own good.' Such attitudes must be seriously corrected." [18] The Communist government and party organizations have encouraged people to bring in cases of mistreatment of women for public correction by law or by group pressure. In Hsiangt'an county of Hunan Province during the month of June 1950 there were 180 cases of mistreatment of women, but only 40 cases were brought into the court by the parties involved. "We must make ceaseless efforts to bring such cases to public attention," [19] exhorted Hsü Teh-hsing, a member of the Committee on Laws and Institutions in the central Communist government. In the province of Shantung, after the court in T'eng Hsien Special District had made a big case out of the murder of P'an Shi by using it as an example, 119 cases of mistreatment of women were brought to court by the people in the neighboring Linyi Special District.[20]

It may be noted that no similar efforts to execute the principle of sex equality had been made by previous governments in modern China, and that up to the time of Communist accession to power the cause had been carried forward only by the slow and spontaneous process of social movement.

Cases of murder and suicide of women resulting from family conflict, once they come to the attention of superior Communist authorities, bring drastic punishment, and such cases are used widely as examples for propaganda and indoctrination purposes. The murder of P'an Shi in Shantung Province and the killing of Kao Ch'uen-wa in Shansi Province are examples. Nevertheless, it seems that for some time to come the persistence of traditional social attitudes and the old family institution among a considerable proportion of local junior party leaders will prevent legal action in large numbers of similar cases by concealing them from superior authorities who have more understanding and firmer convictions on the new concept of women's status.

Plainly, the alteration in the form of marriage under communism, the effort to prohibit "buying-and-selling" marriages, and the serious attempt to prohibit polygamy by the Communist Marriage Law all operate to elevate woman's status. Moreover, the traditional mode of appellation for a woman after marriage is also being changed.

Echoing the call of the Western feminine movement, this issue was raised during the early years of the Republic. As the women's movement developed, and as a small number of women trained in modern education came out to take up independent occupations in the cities, married women began using their own surnames and given names, usually with the husband's surname prefixed to the maiden surname, thus showing her marital status by a double surname. As the young generation of modern intellectuals advanced in age and moved into positions of responsibility and as the old generation receded into social and economic positions of lesser importance, the new manner of appellation increased steadily until it became a part of the normal order of urban social life. The Nationalist law, reflecting the factual development, stipulated that a married woman might use her own surname and given name, but prefixed with the husband's surname to show her marital status, and that for a man marrying into a woman's family (which occurs only very rarely) the man's given name should be headed by the wife's surname so as to show equality of treatment.

The Communist Marriage Law stipulates that "husband and wife each have the right to use his or her own surname and given name." [21] This does not prevent husband or wife from prefixing the spouse's surname in front of his or her own surname, making a double surname, which is the current practice with middle and upper-class educated women. Neither does it prevent the continued use of Mrs. for the women. After the Communist assumption of power a large number of maiden names appeared in newspapers and publications, belonging to women holding important political positions. Reading them, one did not know whether their owners were married, or, if married, to whom they were married, and sometimes one was surprised to learn that so-and-so was the wife of an important official.

The individualization of appellation for married women, besides reflecting their greater independence, naturally weakens the social significance of the family as an organized unit of common action, symbolized by presenting the wife to the public by the prefix of the husband's surname; and it tends to reduce the importance of the patriarchal lineage as the backbone of the family organization.

Of particular interest is the vigorous Communist campaign on literacy and technical education for women, a nation-wide movement covering not merely cities but also penetrating into rural areas, extending a pre-Communist trend from the upper and middle classes into the large numerical base of workers and peasants. Under the Communist regime every city is buzzing with literacy classes for women as well as for men. In 1950 in the Shanghai textile factories alone, where women employees form the majority of the working force, there were 170 literacy groups organized into classes, with the total membership of 9,000.[22] That number in proportion to the total of illiterate women workers in the textile industry may not have been great, but it signified the beginning of a growing phenomenon. In 1951 in the cities of "Darien and Port Arthur, of the 9,115 illiterate women workers, 8,640, or about 94.5 per cent, participated in a literacy program." [23] Technical training classes for the improvement of workers' skills and evening trade classes in the cities were opened to women students. In July 1952 in the northern city of Tientsin there were 7,247 literacy classes with about 300,000 students, among whom more than 100,000 were women. Attached to these literacy classes were 81 nursery stations where mothers attending classes could leave their children.[24] In one district in Peking women accounted for 85 per cent of the members of literacy classes.[25]

The literacy campaign is also waged actively in rural communities. Thus, "in six counties including Hsingning and Mei in the eastern part of Kwangtung Province there are 3,000 evening schools, and women account for over 60 per cent of the students." [26] "In the coastal counties of Shantung Province, there were 597 literacy classes for women in 1949, but these increased to 1,687 classes by the spring of 1950, with a total enrollment of 40,000 women. In Chunan county alone in 1950 there were 450 classes, with 14,300 women students. In the rural town of Huiming, 15 of the 16 street neighborhoods set up literacy classes. . . . In the village of Houku in Poshan county, Shantung Province, a literacy class for women was established in March 1949, with an initial enrollment of 22. One year later the enrollment had grown to 74." [27]

Since 1952 Communist publications have been comparatively silent about the family problem, and they no longer single out women as a special object for literacy and universal education campaigns. Presumably, since the principle of equality between the sexes has been fully established and illiteracy is widespread for both sexes in China, any present educational campaign aims equally at men and women. On this assumption, women are reaping their share of benefit from the ever-quickening pace of Communist efforts in mass education. If the southern city of Canton was representative, 80 per cent of all school-age children in 1956 were in schools, and the Communist authorities planned to have the entire school-age population in schools in another year.[28] As to adults, the Communist plan in 1956 was to completely "sweep away" illiteracy in cities as well as in the rural areas within seven years.[29]

The accelerating development of education for women, which will be reflected in the social and economic status of women and in turn further the alteration of the Chinese family organization, has been powerful indeed. A discussion of the comprehensive influence of the women's movement over the course of the past half century and its acquisition of political power under the Communist regime is now in order.

CHAPTER VII

The Ascendancy of Women's Status Through the Women's Movement

THE CHINESE women's movement, like its counterpart in the West, has been an organized collective effort to attain status equality with men in all major sectors of social life, including the family. Although much of this massive drama is enacted outside the home, women's role in the family is but a structural segment of their general status in the entire institutional system of society, especially in the economic and political institutions. In this sense, the development of the women's movement forms an integral part of the process by which the traditional family institution is transformed.

The Pre-Communist Setting

The history of the Chinese women's movement is as long as that of China's modern revolutions. The participation of a large number of armed women in the Taiping Rebellion in the early 1850's still remains an intriguing historical riddle. One ramification of the abortive 100-day Reform of 1898 was the advocacy of giving women a modern education and the unbinding of their feet. Subsequent revolutionary activities to overthrow the monarchy attracted many women. An example was Chiu Chin, who published the first "Women's Journal," organized the "Restoration Army" in Shaohsing of Chekiang Province, and was finally executed in 1907, a martyr of the revolution. Battalions of women were organized in many parts of China in the Republican revolution of 1911, a revolution which promoted women's rights to education, "to make friends," to marry by free choice of partners, and to participate in government. A Republican parliament in 1913 was stormed by a mob of women demanding implementation of women's suffrage as fulfillment of the revolution's promise. Police dispersed the mob, and the men parliamentarians laughed off the episode.

Like China's revolutions, the women's movement ran a course of ebb and flow. After the disillusionment of 1913 the movement settled back to a more staid course, mainly promoting modern education for women, unbinding of the feet, and modern training in order to become a "virtuous mother and good wife." Then came the thunderous New Culture Movement of 1917 and the May 4th Movement of 1919, which injected renewed social and political consciousness into the women's movement. All the social, political, and economic demands which modern womanhood had made in the Western world became their inspiration and guidance. Publications on the subject of modern womanhood were vastly expanded in volume and were eagerly read by the increasing number of literate women in the middle and upper classes in the cities. Women's organizations began to appear in large cities under a variety of labels, such as *Fu-nü Hsieh-chin Hui* (Association for Collective Advancement of Women) and *Fu-nü Chiao-yü Ch'u-chin Hui* (Association for the Promotion of Women's Education). What had been mainly a rising tide of opinion and individual action was now being crystallized into an organized collective movement.

The Second Revolution in the mid-1920's carried the women's movement to new heights. The political character of the movement was greatly sharpened by the tenet that feminist rebellion against traditional restrictions could not be successful without women's full participation in political power; and many women donned uniforms and became political workers in the Kuomintang and the Communist Party as members of the propaganda corps, as organizers, even as soldiers in the Northern Expedition of 1926. The 1924 declaration of the first plenary session of the Kuomintang Party recognized sex equality in law, in economic matters, in education, and in society. "Women's emancipation" associations sprang up in the path of the Northern Expedition. A few women sat in the high councils in the early coalition regime of the Kuomintang and Communist Party. Women's occupations developed steadily in urban areas during this period.

The split between the two parties led to divergent courses in the development of the women's movement in the Kuomintang area and in the "red areas" after the late 1920's. In the red areas the women's movement continued to develop as a part of the Communist political movement, as will be discussed later, but in the Kuomintang area the political aspect of the movement was checked whenever the leadership turned too much to the left. Otherwise the women's movement in general continued almost unhindered; from the late 1920's on, at least the principle of sex equality was generally accepted by the urban intelligentsia, and the voicing of this principle was widely heard by the urban population as a whole, particularly by those in the middle and upper classes. There was an accelerated pace in the development of women's educational and economic opportunities in the cities, and women's appearance on the social scene was fast becoming an accepted fact.

While these developments continued during the period of the war against the Japanese invasion (1937–1945), there was also a resurgence of the political aspect of the women's movement in the Kuomintang area. Women's extensive participation in the war effort provided the motivation for a reawakened political interest among feminist leaders. The ravages of war and the growing unsatisfactory conditions of the Kuomintang regime, coupled with the strong propaganda and organizing efforts of the Communists, increasingly drove a number of feminists towards the left, many of whom became directly or indirectly affiliated with Communist efforts in the political scene. The Kuomintang's rein over the political energies of the women's movement was weak; for, in spite of party control of the leadership of many major women's organizations, members in these organizations as well as women in general had not been organized to participate actively in political work. Meanwhile, the Communists emphasized political action as the leading instrument for attaining the goals of the women's movement.

Predominance of the Political Character of the Women's Movement Under Communist Leadership

In Chinese traditional society, despite the occasional rise of women rulers such as Empress Wu Tse-tien in the T'ang dynasty and the Empress Dowager in the Ch'ing period, women occupied no recognized routine position in the political world, and political activity was neither encouraged nor approved of by the traditional code of conduct for women. Infringement of social and political restrictions in the Ch'ing period was punishable by law. Hence the feminist leaders' enthusiastic participation in China's revolutions, and the fact that, despite the many recessions of political interest in the women's movement during its half century of development, this interest always swept up to new heights in every resurging wave of modern Chinese revolutions.

The Communists from the beginning recognized the potential political strength of the women's movement, and during the thirty years of their struggle for power consistently nursed its development to augment their political force. Taken under Communist wings, the women's movement became a branch of the Communist political movement, the influence of the Communist Party being evident as early as Women's Day of March 8, 1924, when a rally was held under Communist leadership in the First Park of Canton. Above the din of the city rose the shouted slogans of a small band of women, mostly students and workers: "Down with imperialism," "Down with warlords," "Same work, same pay," "Protection for child labor and pregnant mothers," "Equal education," "Abolish child brides and polygamy," "Prohibit the buying of slave girls and the taking of concubines," "Formulate a child protection law." A demonstration parade followed the rally. Thus began a new page in the women's movement, and for a quarter of a century thereafter these slogans continued to echo throughout the nation, and women were increasingly pitched into the political battle that eventually led to the triumph of Communist power.

Communist decisions in 1926 on the women's movement perhaps marked the beginning of a major Chinese party making a political arm out of the women's movement by working out systematic tactics for recruiting and organizing its members and by expanding the movement from the modern urban intelligentsia to women workers and peasants.* In "red areas" during the late 1920's and early 1930's political mobilization of women peasants, and to a lesser extent women workers, was an important feature of the nascent Communist political power. The setting up of a large number of representatives' conferences of women peasants and workers in this period was an expression of this. Another expression of Communist policy on the women's movement was the promulgation in 1931 of Marriage Regulations which

---

* In the third enlarged meeting of the central committee of the Chinese Communist Party decisions on the women's movement contained the following points: 1. In party work among women emphasis must be laid on carrying the activities to the common people. 2. Though women workers constitute the backbone of the women's movement, women students are also important, for they are the bridge between the party and women workers, and they are an important influence in breaking up the thought and habits of the traditional familistic society. 3. Peasant women occupy a very important position in the Chinese women's movement, and it is necessary to train leaders for this branch of work. 4. Women's publications must be in simple and popular style, emphasizing the intimate experience of women's own suffering and practical needs. 5. Efforts must be made to increase women party members and to develop leaders for the women's movement. (Lo Ch'iung, "The Principles of Development of the Chinese Women's Movement," *Hsin Chung-kuo Fu-nü* (New Chinese Women), January 1953, pp. 29–30.)

placed only light restrictions on marriage and divorce. In the subsequent two decades, through the period of the Japanese invasion, mobilization of women for political and military struggle remained the main theme of Communist leadership in the women's movement as well as a major instrument in the attainment of the movement's goal of sex equality in social, economic, and political status. From 1930 on, many professionally prominent women, especially writers, became active Communist leaders, and women constituted an important component in the Communist political force.

On Women's Day of March 8, 1951, a little over a year after inauguration of the Communist government, an editorial in the official New China News Agency acclaimed the contributions of the women's movement: "In the anti-Japanese war, in the people's liberation war, under the leadership of the Communist Party, large groups of women workers and revolutionary intellectual women joined the great struggle for the liberation of the nation. They actively participated in military mobilization and in the work in the rear. They took part in the land reform movement and the production movement. China's women have formed a powerful, integral part of the people's revolutionary ranks, and have made great contributions to the victory of the national revolution."

The first charter of the Communist regime, the Common Program, stated: "The People's Republic abolishes the feudalistic institutions which hold women in bondage. In political, economic, cultural, educational, and social aspects of life women possess equal rights and privileges with men. Freedom of marriage is adopted for both men and women." The new Marriage Law was formulated in accordance with this principle. When the Communist constitution replaced the Common Program as the basic law, the same principle was reaffirmed.[1] On Women's Day of March 8, 1951, when Communist participation in the Korean War and land reform were raging simultaneously, women were being exhorted by the New China News Agency editorial: "The duty of Chinese women is to join the people of the nation to develop the 'Resist America, Aid Korea' patriotic movement, support Korea's People's Army and China's Volunteer Army, oppose America's rearmament of Japan, enforce land reform, struggle for a good harvest this year, develop the patriotic emulation of production, suppress counter-revolutionary elements, strengthen the learning of patriotism, and let the 'Resist America, Aid Korea' patriotic movement pervade the daily activities in production work, political study [indoctrination], and general living."

These editorial exhortations set the pattern for local activities of the women's movement throughout Communist China. Thus, in the district consisting of sixteen counties in the northern part of Kwangtung Province, party cadres issued a directive on Women's Day of March 8, 1951, outlining the work of the women's movement:

> Review the strength and line up the organizations of women in the locality; use action to set the masses of village women in motion; lead them to join in the work of mopping up bandits, fighting local despots, reducing land rent, and refunding land rent deposit; strengthen the suppression of counterrevolutionary elements; develop various types of [class] struggles in the land reform movement; answer the government's call to help in repairing highways and bridges, in building up the people's militia, and in developing water control work. For the cities, the missions of women are to join the patriotic emulation of production, improve the quality of production, save raw materials, reduce the cost and increase the quantity of production.[2]

To put the Communist political program into practice, women go through rigid indoctrination. In schools, women students, like men students, must take full part in the process of political study through the "big class" and the "small unit" discussions, the endless political and propaganda gatherings, group study of newspapers and discussions of current events, and, on special occasions, participate in demonstrations, in speechmaking and in posting slogans, in group visits to government propaganda exhibitions, such as the exhibition on the reconstruction of the U.S.S.R. or the exhibition of criminal evidences of counterrevolutionists. Women students must take leaves of absence from school from time to time to participate in land reform work, to copy documents for the government, and to launch special political campaigns when the government is short-handed. Recreation such as dancing, singing, movies, plays, and parties are thoroughly permeated with political implications; newspapers and radios blare out political tunes continuously. Throughout the waking hours, the plastic young individual is imbued with the new political atmosphere.

Mothers watched in amazement as their daughters went through the political mill during the earlier days of the Communist regime. Now they have found themselves forced to go through a similar program. Street and neighborhood meetings lay claim to their time and energy. Care of children and household duties must be put off so that they may attend meetings from one to three times a week. They are told:

> We must remold ourselves in order that we may survive in and not

be washed away by the current of this great age. To meet the demands of the social situation, we must learn to make progress and overcome our own weaknesses. . . . Most of us do not have interest or confidence in political study; we even let household duties prevent us from thinking and learning, confining our views only to our husbands and children to the exclusion of everything else. We must have determination to overcome such weaknesses.[3]

At one neighborhood indoctrination meeting held in Canton in the summer of 1951 in a small, hot room crowded with over one hundred people, mostly women, the bawling of a baby rose above the voice of a speaker who was yelling himself hoarse on the "Resist America, Aid Korea" movement. The speaker stopped, inquired, found that a mother had brought her two young children to the meeting for lack of someone to care for them at home, ordered the mother to lock up the two children in another room for the duration of the lengthy meeting, and went on with the lecture.

Women may not close their minds and just sit through the meetings. Many such classes have quizzes besides compulsory attendance (at least one person from each house, frequently the wife), and the lecturer, usually a young student in the late teens or early twenties, asks questions. One woman in Canton, the wife of a medicine store owner, was asked to repeat the reasons why America was China's enemy. She stood up and talked irrelevantly. Punishment for her was compulsory attendance at ten extra meetings, one every night for ten consecutive nights. Women who have failed in such tests and who can read and write have been made to copy a hundred times some political articles from indoctrination pamphlets so that "they will remember."

We can be sure that many women have resented such forced indoctrination but it is impossible to ignore such evidence as the following propaganda story.

> In the northern part of Shanghai city lives Mrs. Ts'ao, a woman of fifty-eight. She lives with only a young granddaughter, and her life has been a lonely one.
>
> She started to work in a Shanghai silk factory at the age of nine. But she worked only half a day, and the other half of the day was devoted to schooling; so she was able to read and write. When she grew up, she continued to work in the same silk factory until 1932, when the Japanese invasion destroyed it. . . .
>
> Ten years ago Mrs. Ts'ao felt that, after working so hard, all that she had was loneliness and bitterness. She became a pessimist and took to Buddhism as a solace. She refitted her living room into a shrine chamber

and put an idol of the Goddess of Mercy on the altar, hoping that in so doing she would be spared further suffering. Old ladies in the neighborhood came to join her in burning incense, praying, and chanting. Seven or eight years of pious worship seemed to do little good, for the Japanese invasion and the worst part of the Nationalist rule came in succession. The painted surface of a whole side of the sounding-box for chanting had been knocked off by rhythmic beating and yet the good days in her dream were still nowhere near.

Then the Communists came to Shanghai. What she saw and heard gave her the impression that the world was very different. After the campaign to suppress the counterrevolutionists started, many characters long known to be bad men in the neighborhood had been arrested, and this pleased Mrs. Ts'ao very much.

Soon the neighborhood set up a local committee for the purge of counterrevolutionists and took over her shrine chamber for an office. Later the neighborhood's Inhabitants Committee and the Family Women's League [a subsidiary of the Democratic Women's League] also set up office in her shrine chamber. From then on, great changes began to take place in her mind.

The Family Women's League held frequent meetings in her place. At first, during a meeting, she hid behind the door, peeping out in curiosity. As time went on, sister Li in the League said to her, "Old lady, why don't you join in and listen?" She was happy at the invitation. From then on, at every meeting, she would sit down and listen. Gradually the terms "liberation," "changing place" [changing one's social status by revolution], and "Resist America, Aid Korea movement" began to make sense to her. She said to sister Li of the League, "Meetings make more sense than worshipping Buddha, for the meetings have helped me to understand a number of things I didn't understand before. From now on, when the old ladies in the neighborhood come again to burn incense and worship Buddha, I am going to ask them to worship chairman Mao and give the incense money to the government to buy airplanes and artillery. This includes myself." She severed her relationship with Buddha. . . .

When the Family Women's League moved its office to new quarters, she was sorry to see the League people go. She took out a piece of red silk which she had kept for years and gave it to sister Li and said, "There must be a picture of chairman Mao in your new office. Please drape this over the picture. Should there be any material left, please make a big bunting out of it and put it in front of the picture."

Sister Li asked her to invite some of her old ladies who used to worship Buddha with her to a meeting. At the first meeting over twenty old ladies came, and sister Li helped her to chair the meeting. At the meetings, they talked about family affairs, the Communist Party, and the world situation, and they agreed to visit twice a month families of soldiers and those who had died for the revolution. . . .

At a mass rally at the railway station to welcome the Korean delegation, people pushed her to the platform to make a speech. She said, "In the past, I only knew that the Goddess of Mercy saved people from suffering, but now I realize that the one who really saves people from suffering is chairman Mao."

She is now doubling her efforts at "learning" and is reading pamphlets all the time. She is getting ready to help the old ladies use their spare time to make match boxes and do bookbinding in order to contribute the proceeds to the purchase of airplanes and artillery.[4]

Pressure from the general political atmosphere and the influence of the group is clearly marked in the case of this old woman, especially in view of her loneliness and the consequent desire for company. If her case represents a relatively uneducated woman, the following is that of a young woman student told in an article of self-confession:

In the past the goal of my life was to please my future husband and raise my future children, to manage a household, to serve as a model for a "kind mother and a good wife." Mother taught me the "three obediences and four virtues" and other ethical rules of good womanhood. I was a good girl of the traditional type who never ventured out the door. I remember at the age of ten I still had to have the maid dress me, and at twelve I still had to have the maid accompany me to school. I was such a weak, helpless, temperamental burden on others.

At seventeen I stepped out of the family to go to school and began to take my first breath of freedom. Throughout my middle school period, though I was able to get out of the control of the feudalistic family authority, my life was so decadent. I fell into the abyss of love. I pursued happiness. Hypnotized in the clutch of love, I was wasting my youth away.

The gongs and drums of the "liberation" woke me up like thunder in spring, and I began to crawl out of the dirt. In September of 1950, still with dirt on my body, I entered the university [not named]. The school was like a big family of revolutionists, making me feel strange at every turn. I was groping about and made some trials. I wished to wipe the dirt off my clothes, but my hands were so weak and tired.

One after another, the high tides of social and political movements passed before my eyes, marching columns paraded beside me, and the soaring notes of group singing rang in my ears. I felt alone, I felt the pressure of solitude. I was perplexed, sometimes so terribly perplexed. Sometimes I sat alone on the lawn and cried, and sometimes I cried under the covers in bed. When schoolmates asked me why my eyes were so red, I failed to answer.

As the days flew by, the "old" and the "new" were battling in my mind. In that battle, time and again, the "new" fell down and the "old" stood up with renewed arrogance. I was spiritually tortured. In such days suffering wore down my spirit and the "old" things corroded my soul.

I will eternally remember my roommate, little Wei. She was younger than I and called me Big Sister. I was very grateful for her help, but she also put me to shame. She could take hardship and was a person of action. She was very progressive, good at revolutionary doctrine, and lived very actively and happily. When she did things, she was as systematic as a mature adult. I often laughed at her for resembling a boy, and she always answered proudly, "In the age of Mao Tse-tung women will never trail behind men." She surely had a deep effect on me. She was a member of the Young Communist League. Her every act and her work made me so ashamed of myself and made me feel like a weakling.

Last November [1950] I began to change. I made a resolution not to imagine things and not to linger with the "old" any longer. I started out to catch up with little Wei, retracing her past footsteps. I took action. I came to hate my bird-nest-like coiffure [permanent] and I cut it off. Now my short and straight hair looks as beautiful as that of Wei. I tore up my once-fashionable cowboy pants [dungarees]; humans do not wear dog's clothing. Now I wear the cotton clothes and cotton shoes of the laboring people, and when I walk side by side with Wei people say, "You two look like sisters, so thrifty and solid." This pleases me so.

That was my first victory in the new direction.

Then came the movement to join the armed forces under the "Resist America, Aid Korea" movement. I pushed aside my mother's objections. I wanted to offer my life to the fatherland, to the people. Big red paper flowers were pinned on me. They symbolized the redness of my heart. I felt so honored and proud. When the students threw me up into the air, I was so very happy. That was the second victory in my battle of thought.

Now I have gone one step further and joined the New Democratic Youth League. Through education by the League I have come to recognize clearly the two divergent roads. One leads to decadence and decline, filled with lifeless atmosphere, darkness, and death. The other leads to happiness, activity, hope, light, and new life. . . .

I anticipate Women's Day this year with enthusiasm. I have prepared my uniform. I am going to throw myself into the human current and follow the flag and march forward bravely. I want to shout with millions of sisters and let the shouting become a strong current.

We want to be masters of the new society. We are the nurses of mankind. We bear the mission of mankind's prosperity. We have to break the chains on our hands and create the garden of happiness for humanity.[5]

This story of the making of a young convert as a result of group pressure, youth, and idealism is typical of numerous confessions made by young students at political meetings. It has been estimated that from 10 to 30 per cent of all girl students in colleges and universities were members of the Youth League by the end of 1951, and there seems to have been continuous increase in League membership. These are the girls who become leaders for women's organizations and who help push the vast multitudes of common women into the political line.

Although we do not find such detailed stories about peasant women, short reports show substantially the same emphasis on political action in the women's movement in the countryside under Communist rule. The Communist press stated that during the battle for Hainan Island [1950] in the southern part of Kwangtung Province numerous women were organized into carrier, food transportation, and service corps, helping tens of thousands of troops passing through that part of the country. In two villages in Suich'i county (Kwangtung Province) alone, over twenty thousand mosquito nets were laundered for the army, not counting the innumerable clothes washed. When the Communist army was in urgent need of food, one peasant woman carried over a thousand catties of rice in one night to the fighting men. Many wives were said to have encouraged their fisherman husbands to join the battle of crossing the sea, and many women directly participated in the crossing.[6]

According to reports, in other rural areas of Kwangtung Province political activities by women claimed attention from a public that had not seen women playing a similar role before. In Shihsing county a peasant woman with only a kitchen knife in hand captured alive a counterrevolutionary "bandit." In Shunteh county peasant women organized an espionage corps and captured a counterrevolutionary leader and a long-hidden Japanese spy. In another village in Shunteh county peasant woman Chang Shu-fen, a production and anti-bandit heroine, helped local troops to wipe out over ten counterrevolutionary "bandits" and capture many pieces of fire arms.[7]

Since 1953 there has been a noticeable tendency to tone down the political mission of women and increase the emphasis on their devotion to economic production and family duties, the Communist government having turned to the task of consolidating its power through stabilizing the economic and social order, but the political responsibility of women is by no means overlooked. In 1955 a woman in the northern city of Tientsin was commended for her discovery of a "spy" among her neighbors, leading to his arrest and eventual execution,[8] and similar reports continue to appear in the Communist press.

The Organization of Women

In pre-Communist days activities of the women's movement consisted mainly of publishing promotional literature, shouting slogans, and, on occasion, of women students speaking to street crowds, group meetings for charity, and agitating for women's welfare legislation. An occasional woman intellectual broke away from home or committed suicide to dramatize the demand for freedom of marriage; a woman intellectual might create a social sensation by insisting upon being addressed as Mr. instead of Miss or Mrs.; and, with expanding literacy and education among women, a few women leaders reached high political and social positions in either the Kuomintang or the Communist Party. But women's activities were mostly unorganized, and such organized activities as women's participation in politics were rather sporadic except among women Communists. Moreover, they were almost entirely limited to urban educated women, who belonged mostly to the middle and upper classes; the working class and peasant women remained little touched by the movement.

Assumption of power by the Communist Party changed this picture. Organizational efforts became persistent, systematic, and extensive, affecting an increasing proportion of the female population. For the celebration of Women's Day of March 8, 1951, for example, Communist leaders in Shanghai started their organizational work early. The Family Women's Leagues in various parts of the city organized mobilization units, visiting from house to house in each neighborhood, asking women to sign up for the demonstration parade. The mobilization units also held "accusation meetings" in every neighborhood for the women to recall their experiences of rape or insults under Japanese rule so as to arouse the anger of the women and draw them out to the demonstration. As a result, 300,000 women of Shanghai turned out on that day's demonstration.[9] No doubt a majority of the 300,000 were not voluntary or willing participants but acted under direct or indirect pressure. Nevertheless, the mobilization of a third of a million women for an occasion was unprecedented in China even in a large city like Shanghai.

The women's movement is no longer confined to the educated elements of the urban middle and upper classes. The objective of broadening the Communist women's movement to embrace the entire female population of the country is clearly set forth in the "General Principles for the Organization of the Council of Women Representatives" passed in September of 1950 by the third meeting of the executive committee of the All-China Democratic Women's League, which is the highest directing body of the women's movement. According to the resolution, the Council of Women's Representatives is to be the chief instrument by which the Democratic Women's League directs the "broad masses of women" of the country, and any woman with citizenship rights who supports the principles of the Democratic Women's League has the privilege to elect or be elected to the Council. The goal is to expand the "women's organization to the masses." Hence, every province, county, subdistrict, city, town, and village has a Council; so has every profession and occupation, every large scale enterprise employing women, every organization and every school with women members.[10] The Communist system of organization permeates every territory and occupational unit in the country primarily to serve political purposes, namely, to help transmit and execute government orders and policies, and to bring women's demands and opinions to the attention of the government.[11]

To insure that the organizational system does not serve any other purpose and is not controlled by dissenting elements, leaders of the Democratic Women's League are given a prominent position in the Council at every level and in every occupation.[12] Again, to insure the desired political orientation, the Democratic Women's Leagues in many localities specify that the core of the branch organizations must be founded upon the proletarian section of the population. "In cities women laborers should be the core around which all patriotic and democratic women will be united; in the villages poor peasant women and hired women farm laborers should be the core around which the women of middle peasants will be united." [13]

The extent to which women are becoming politically organized has been indicated in numerous official reports. In 1951, in the four administrative regions of Central-South, East, Southwest, and Northwest, women already accounted for about 30 per cent of the 88,000,000 members of the peasants' associations, and in places where the organizational work had been well done women accounted for as high as 50 per cent of such membership. Women occupied from 10 to 15 per cent of the positions of committee members, chairmen, or vice-chairmen of the peasants' associations; and large numbers of them had been mobilized to take part in the village defense corps, and to cooperate with the local militia in the surveillance of "law-breaking landlords" and local bullies. It was stated that the number of organized women doubled after land reform and in some places increased four- or five-fold; that in Kwangsi Province organized women numbered about

490,000 before land reform but increased to 1,300,000 after land reform, and that in Tsinkiang Special District of Fukien Province the number of organized women grew from 48,000 before land reform to 220,000 after land reform.[14]

A large number of local reports show that peasant women everywhere in the country are coming under an organizational network dominated by the peasants' association and the Democratic Women's League. There are no figures for a nation-wide urban picture, but reports on individual cities show the same trend, women taking to organizations outside the home on an increasing scale. For example, in Shanghai:

> The number of organized women in 1951 was 301,412. Among them were 162,563 women workers in various occupations, 70,000 peasant women in suburban villages, 32,030 women students, 8,240 women teachers, 4,266 women employees in the government, 20,578 family women, and 3,753 members of different democratic women's groups. It is estimated that there are about 1,500,000 adult women in Shanghai, and 22 per cent of them are now organized. It can be observed from these figures that women workers form the mainstay of the organized women in Shanghai. Among all the organized women workers, over 2,000 of them have joined the All-Shanghai Labor Union and have participated in the leadership of the basic labor union organizations.[15]

Women's Political Power

We have noted that occasional political power for women on a very high level is not new in China, and that there have been women members both in the Kuomintang high councils, such as the party's central committee and other government organs, and in the Communist Party and in its government. But such women, besides belonging exclusively to the modern educated upper-class, were exceptions in a man-dominated system of power. That common women such as laborers and peasants now hold responsible positions as a regular part of the political system is striking evidence of the new situation brought about by the changed social status of women under Communist rule.

Identification and selection of activists from among the general population is an important step in the Communist effort to build a new local leadership for the revolutionary regime, and women supply a considerable number of such activists. In thirteen rural counties and one city of Hunan Province 16,507 activists were selected and trained from the beginning of 1950 to the end of 1952, of whom 2,907, or about 17.6 per cent, were women.[16]

In localities where the people's representative councils have been set up there are considerable numbers of women representatives. In twenty-three counties of Heilungchiang Province of the Northeast, 12,000 women representatives were sent in 1951 to the people's representative councils, accounting for twenty per cent of all representatives sitting in such councils.[17] In the village and subdistrict councils of peasant representatives in Hsingning and Mei counties, Kwangtung Province, women accounted for 30 to 40 per cent of all the representatives. In the county councils of peasant representatives in Hsingning, Pingyuan, Chaoling, and Mei counties there were 204 women representatives in 1951, accounting for 28 per cent of all the representatives. In the First Kwangtung Provincial Council of People's Representatives in 1951 women representatives accounted for about 13 per cent of the total number of representatives.[18] By 1952 it was officially reported that women constituted an average of 15 per cent of all representatives in such conferences throughout China,[19] representing an increase of 5 per cent over 1950. In the city of Peking 48 per cent of the representatives were women, scoring a gain of 26 per cent over 1950.[20] The main actual function of such representative councils is only to transmit government policies and to discuss ways and means of implementing them, since only the Communist Party makes policy decisions. Nevertheless, since a position as representative carries political prestige and influence in the home community, the membership of women in such councils may be regarded as a sign of women's new political power and influence.

A more direct expression of women's new political importance is their position in village governments and in peasant associations, which are the center of influence in local politics under the Communist regime. In Hsingning county women members in peasant association committees numbered 3,827 in 1951, comprising a majority of the committee membership. In Ta Pu county, Hsiao Siu-ying became the head of her village and was regarded by the party officials as a model village head. In Mei county there were three women heads of peasant associations, in Chaoling county there was one, and in Pingyuen county, there were two.[21] Both village heads and peasant association chiefs wield considerable power, especially over certain people such as landlords and those accused as local despots.

Social class origin constitutes an important factor in qualifying for local political power in the Communist regime, particularly in rural areas. No member of the landlord or rich peasant class may hold political positions. Hence, those women newly become important in the rural power structure are almost all poor peasant women. In Shantung Province a university professor interviewed a woman village head who was of poor peasant class origin and formerly illiterate. After being the village head for over a year, she had learned to read and write, and she kept a diary of her executive work. In that diary, statements such as "This proposal has the fault of levelism" revealed a fairly complex and firmly indoctrinated mind. Another example is found in a woman representative in the village government council of Nanpu village of Panyü county, Kwangtung Province:

> In a visit to my home village after a prolonged absence the most un-imaginable thing I found is how progressive the women folk have become in this old, culturally a-century-behind place. When I first arrived I heard the woman representative for the village was none other than the female sorcerer, the "spirit-worshiping Ti." Immediately, an ugly, laughable, and contemptible face appeared in my memory of things ten years ago. In the past this poverty-stricken female feigned the incarnation of gods and spirits, talked of mysticism to the ignorant women in the village. She threatened, she bluffed, she swindled, she aroused excitement. She used every trick to gain money. I thought, "It couldn't be a fact!" If such a person could become the village's woman representative, the appointment of public officers would be too indiscriminate. But she was no longer the picture in my memory; she has become a vanguard of the new age. When she spoke before the women audience of the village, she talked fluently and systematically on the new political line.[22]

Female sorcery was an occupation for the poverty stricken when there was no other alternative to make a living. Here again, in conformity with Communist stated policy, the poor are being brought in as the core of the new local government. In this case, the skill in human relations and facility of speech so necessary in her former trade became invaluable assets for this woman in her present position of power. New local leaders are uncovered and promoted usually through the process of "visiting the poor and questioning the victims of suffering," which has been a preliminary step to conducting local Communist programs. The ability of the prospective leader is tested through his or her performance in the class struggle when a program such as land reform unfolds. The new leader is confirmed or approved if he or she shows courage, organizing ability, and an uncompromising spirit toward the landowning class and "feudalistic" influences.

Another component of the power structure in local government is the militia, now called "people's soldiers." In pre-Communist days the militia was a bone of contention between conflicting factions in local politics. Under Communist rule it has been made into the armed support for the new political leadership against any possible counter-revolution from old vested interests, particularly from uprooted land-lords. Hence the presence of women in the local militia is a new factor of possible significance, for the participation of women in local militia is not a fortuitous fact but a regular phenomenon in many localities under the new regime.

In Chungshan county, Kwangtung Province, when 648 local militia were mobilized in 1950 to fight anti-Communist guerillas in the mountains, 440 of them were women, constituting the majority.[23] After land reform, in 1951, Hsingning county of eastern Kwangtung Province had 8,136 women militia under arms. Before land reform the village of Ningsiu in the same county had four women militia, but after land reform the number increased to 204, almost half of the total of 421 militia members of the village.[24] Participation of women in the militia in rural communities is found not only in the province of Kwangtung but also in other parts of the country, particularly in the South and Southwest regions, where women are robust and used to outdoor work. The participation of women in the Korean war and in the training programs for military cadres is also a notable fact.

To summarize, after fifty years, during which it advanced and re-treated alternately, the major scenes of battle being the cities and the main engaging force the bourgeois intelligentsia, the Chinese women's movement now embraces the urban working class and the peasants in the countryside; and the engaging force, besides growing immeasur-ably, is increasingly better organized for a systematic attack on the traditional status of women in the family as well as in society. Whether the gains already made can be consolidated and exploited further de-pends, among other factors, on the development of industrialization, which can give occupational opportunities to women to sustain their new independent status, and on the success of agricultural collectiviza-tion which recasts women's role in production and redefines their share of income.

Stages of Development in the Women's Movement

In reviewing the Chinese women's movement, several stages of de-velopment are discernible. The initial stage, lasting from the last decade of the nineteenth century to the Republican revolution of 1911, consisted of the early introduction of Western ideas on equality be-tween the sexes and on human rights and freedom and the resulting individual action by a few pioneering women and sporadic, short-lived organized adventures. Occurring at a time when the subordination of women was a part of the institutional framework of society firmly enforced by mores and law, such early actions were of spectacular excitement to the public; but there was little change in social institutions which might have given the required coordinated support to these actions. Many of the pioneers died as martyrs, and group activities had no sustained organized existence. Nevertheless, this initial development performed the function of presenting the first open challenge against the age-old institutionalized subordination of women, which had previously been held as a principle of social life as unalterable as heaven and earth. Doubt regarding an established tradition had been planted in the public mind.

The second stage covered the first half-dozen years of the Republic, during which there was a general retrenchment of the women's movement. The excitement of early action had cooled down considerably. But the movement made a steady gain in women's education, which trained leaders for the continued development of the movement and disseminated its basic ideas to an ever-increasing number of women students. Alongside this was the development of a literature as a medium to propagate the movement and to expand its following among both men and women. The course was staid and unspectacular, but the advance was steady.

The third stage began with the New Culture Movement of 1917 and the May 4th Movement of 1919 and lasted until the early part of the Second Revolution, 1921–1924. In this period the movement was no longer a current isolated from changes in other social institutions but received its support from the two momentous movements that marked the beginning of this stage, movements that supplied the major ideological orientation for subsequent social and political developments. Women's occupational opportunities began to develop, though slowly, providing a livelihood for women who were inspired by the movement to leave their traditional dependent status. This was an important step forward, for previously such women were mostly forced back to traditional subordination by economic necessity. Above all, by this time a new generation of feminine leaders had arisen from the increasing number of women's and co-educational schools, and an ever-growing following for the movement was created by the literature of the movement. Growth in leadership and in following resulted in the crystallization of the movement into local and national organizations, and in its organized form it became an important influence in the rapidly changing social setting of the times. The family revolution, already a powerful force, was a result of and at the same time an assistance to the women's movement.

The movement was marked by increasing identification with revolutionary political movements in the fourth stage, which began when the Second Revolution was in full swing in the mid-1920's and ended with Communist conquest of the China mainland in 1949. Coordinated support now came from changes in the political as well as the educational, economic, and family institutions. There developed an interdependence between the women's movement and the revolutionary political movement. On the one hand, the women's movement could expand its following and materialize its demands through the universal and coercive nature of a political power which professed full sympathy for the women's cause and encouraged the development of the women's movement in order to win its following as a part of the working force for the revolution. In this stage the women's movement began to extend beyond the urban intellectuals to include peasants and workers, a process developed most effectively under Communist leadership.

The fifth stage of development came with the success of the Communist political movement, its installation as the national ruling power, and incorporation of the basic objectives of the women's movement into law. The principles of the women's movement are now in harmony with the ideology of the new governing power. Through the universal and compulsory force of law, women's new status, long demanded by the movement, is being extended to an ever-increasing number of women in both urban and rural communities in all sections of the country.

We would point out that the present stage does not signify the complete and universal triumph of the movement's objectives throughout China. In a country with such a huge population, vast area, widespread illiteracy, and backward communications, it will take much longer than a half-dozen years to turn the new law into a universally effective standard and to translate the movement's principles into a stabilized institution.

Moreover, the status of women is most intimately related to the structure of the family, and the family still has basic significance for economic production in spite of the rapid nationalization and collectivization of production by the Communist government. As the majority of families stemming from traditional marriages continue to operate on traditional principles in most respects, the sudden change in women's status, which has disruptive influences on family unity and harmony and therefore adverse effects on economic production, is a development which could pose a serious threat to the economic programs of the Communist government.

Now in the stage of consolidating its new power, Communist leadership feels the need for general social harmony in order to make its plans materialize, and a rebellious women's movement operating on its previous militant pattern would be a disruptive influence. In the latter part of 1955 there appeared a new Communist line stressing the "building of a democratic and harmonious new family, united for production and devoted to the cause of socialist reconstruction" as the main responsibility of women. The new line significantly states: "The new Constitution has guaranteed women's equality with men in political, economic, cultural, social, and family interests, and the state has come to protect women's rights in marriage, in the family, in motherhood, and in the welfare of children. Henceforth, women no longer need to initiate a militant struggle for such things." [25] While previously the Communists had made great efforts in mobilizing "bourgeois women" to participate actively in social and political struggles under the women's movement, in 1956 they were told that their responsibility lay in homemaking and encouraging their husbands and relatives to accept the socialization of commercial and industrial enterprises.[26] But with the development of people's communes in 1958, the policy is again the mobilization of women for production. Under strict Communist direction, the women's movement is no longer an independent militant movement battling exclusively for the interests of women; it has become mainly a tool of the general Communist cause.

The degree of human dignity and the share of material benefits that women will gain from the new social order as compared with the old is a matter that concerns the nature of the authoritarian structure of the new social order and its relationship to the intrinsic interests of the individual regardless of sex. The question has been raised whether women emancipated from one form of social bondage are not falling into another. What is discernible from present observable facts is that the tendency toward greater sex equality in the social, political, and economic status for women is definitely destructive to the traditional family institution and tends to help develop a new family system more in harmony with the changed social status of women.

CHAPTER VIII

Changing Family Economic Structure

Modern change in the family owing to economic influence theoretically begins with the alteration of the economic institution, as would be true with Western society, where the modern economic order was originally developed. But in China, where a new economic pattern was being introduced from the West, it was the ideological promotion of a modern economy that formed the first step; and changes in some of the economic aspects of the family system stemmed from ideological agitation rather than from the immediate pressure of a new economic environment. Thus economic relations among the family members concerning property rights and women's participation in traditional occupations started to change before the actual development of an industrial economic order. But ideological agitation and new economic development were not mutually exclusive influences on the family; the two forces were operating side by side, with sometimes one and sometimes the other playing the leading role. And when a drastic change in the general economic institution finally came, socio-economic environmental pressure became the major factor in altering the basic economic position of the family and in forcing a change in the family economic structure. This historical sequence provides the framework for analyzing change in the economic aspects of the family.

Economic Position and Structure of the Traditional Family

Related to the present discussion are several well-known characteristics of the economic structure of the traditional Chinese family, the most outstanding of them being the predominance of the family as a unit of production: a unit of organization of labor, capital, and land for the acquisition of goods and services to meet the needs of the members of the household. This condition more than any other compelled the individual to center his loyalty in the family and placed the family in the central position in the traditional pattern of social organization.

In agriculture, partnerships and other forms of organization were numerically negligible in comparison with the vast majority of China's traditional family farms. In commerce and industry the family as a unit of organization was equally dominant. When a boy reached working age, he worked in the family business. Should the family business be too small to employ him, he would be apprenticed if possible to a firm owned by relatives. Should a village boy wish to make a living in the city, he would be given an apprenticeship or a job in a relative's firm. City stores and handicraft shops were mostly family businesses in which the working force consisted mostly of kinsmen, and the kinship system was the most important network of employment. In the southern city of Canton a Communist survey in 1950 showed that, of the 20,000-odd industrial and commercial enterprises large and small, about 94 per cent were family businesses.

The dominance of the family as an organizational unit of production led to the development of another prominent characteristic of the Chinese family, namely, the provision of collective security for its immediate members and the extension of economic aid to more distant kinsmen. It was the function of the traditional family not only to care for the aged within its financial means but also to support the sick, the disabled, and the unemployed. Even a distant relative meeting economic misfortune had a moral claim on the family for assistance. (Hence the often-mentioned absence of Chinese relief cases in the United States during the great depression.) Such functions were basic factors in the strength of the traditional family organization and the extended kinship ties.

A high degree of economic self-sufficiency was another vital characteristic of the traditional family. Only those necessities that could not be fashioned at home or grown from the soil were purchased from outside. In agriculture the degree of family self-sufficiency is indicated by the fact that some 80 per cent of the family's needs were supplied by the family itself.[1] Although city families were much less self-sufficient, family labor was utilized to the maximum to process materials purchased from outside to supply the needs of the family members. Economic self-sufficiency, together with the family as the leading organizational unit of production and economic security, gave the family overwhelming dominance over the individual, exacting from him undivided loyalty and forcing him to submit to the authority of the family.

Internally, the economic organization of the traditional family was structured with reference to age and sex differentiation. The acquisition of goods and income was predominantly the responsibility and right of the male, and the processing of materials for consumption at home was mainly the duty of the female members. This division of labor was enforced by many institutional devices, such as superstitious taboos against employment of women in many types of work and social customs and guild rules that would admit only males into certain occupations. J. L. Buck's survey showed that women supplied only 16.4 per cent of all the farming labor,[2] mostly in the form of helping with the harvest during busy seasons, weeding, and other secondary chores. With some local exceptions, only in home industry did women generally occupy a significant place in income-acquiring activities. For instance, women in the northern part of China participated less in main production work than women in the South, where women were more accepted in both agricultural and urban occupations.

Age as a structuring factor in production was uniform throughout the country. The average family started training a child for production by the age of from eight to ten, having him perform minor tasks and acquainting him with the scene of labor. From early teen age a child began to take a fairly active part in production if the family was financially unable to send him to school. Children supplied 10.9 per cent of the agricultural labor on a traditional Chinese farm.[3] By fifteen or sixteen a boy was considered a full-fledged worker in agriculture and in many other fields of production, and he assumed his full share of labor or contributed his share of income to the family if he worked outside. In family production he worked under the direction of his father, who remained the leading organizer and income provider for the family. The father's age signified both prestige and technical competence, and he gradually retired into the position of advisor and supervisor as he neared the age of sixty, performing a decreasing amount of physical labor, the amount of which was determined by the economic circumstances of the family. From twenty to thirty years of age, the son's position in the economic organization grew in importance in proportion to the aging of the father until he took full leadership upon his father's death or upon the father's retirement into a supervisory capacity. For a woman a full share of labor in the household economy began at fourteen or fifteen, and her share was particularly heavy immediately following her marriage into the husband's family, where she worked under the direction of the mother-in-law, who was the chief organizer of the household and who would surrender her leadership only upon her retirement into a supervisory capacity or at her death.

In the scale of values, only the labor of acquisition of goods and services or income from primary production was rated high. Household labor, whether in processing food or clothing for consumption, in sanitary activities like washing and cleaning, or in child care, was rated so low that no man would perform it without feeling some sense of inferiority. The difference of value assigned to various types of labor contributed toward the stratification of status and authority of the members of the family.

Property ownership and management of income as a factor in the economic structure of the family was again based on sex and age differentiation. The right of property management belonged to the leader of the family's economic organization, the head of the household; when the head of the house died, it passed down the line of male inheritance.* On this ground, the head of the house also dictated the disposal of income brought into the family by various members should they work outside; minor members in the status system, the young and the women, did not have complete control over the disposal of their own income.

Although management was dominated by the head of the household, family property was collectively owned, with other family members retaining their share. Under the collective principle family property was often legally registered in a form of corporate ownership known as t'ang (hall) under the direction and management of the head of the house and could not be disposed of without common consent of all the male members, each of whom held a share. A son might not have his share without the father's consent or until the death of the father. Female descendants had no claim on family property. A woman might own family property on the death of her husband, but she could not dispose of it without consent of the son if she had male children. As already pointed out, no divorced woman was permitted to take any part of the husband's family property into a new marriage or back to her own parents' family. Even without further details on the complex subject of family property ownership, it can be seen that it gen-

---

* Should there be no male heir after the death of both husband and wife, an unmarried daughter might have some claim to the family property, but she could not take the property into her husband's family upon her marriage should there be claims on it by male collateral descendants of the extended family. In the absence of both male and female descendants, male collateral descendants would claim the property.

erally discriminated against the female and junior members of the family.

The Chinese system of collective ownership of family property was largely a result of the earthbound peasant economy, which required the organized labor of the entire family to till a plot of land; and the traditional distribution of property rights within the family was developed mainly from the male-dominated structure of the family as a unit of economic production. The strong organization of the family proved itself equally effective for traditional commercial and handicraft production, the vast majority of which was on a small scale as it was limited in its development by a confining localized economy.*

Change in the Right of Ownership of Family Property

Objection to the discriminatory features in the traditional system of family property ownership has long been a feature of the Chinese family revolution, especially from modern educated women; and when equality was accepted as a general principle by the educated young, sex equality in property ownership rights became a logical demand. When the Kuomintang government promulgated its marriage and kinship law, considerable concession was made to women, giving conditional equality of inheritance to sons and daughters.[4] When the Communists wrote their new Marriage Law, the matter of property rights was redefined more unequivocally to the advantage of women and children. Article 10 of the Communist Marriage Law stipulates that "husband and wife have equal rights of ownership and disposal of family property," and the following interpretation of that Article was given by the Communist government:

Family property falls into the following three categories:
1. Property belonging to husband and wife before their marriage.
2. Property acquired by husband and wife during their common living. This again may be subdivided into three types:
   a. Property acquired by the common labor of husband and wife. The wife's labor in housekeeping and raising children should be regarded as having the same value as the husband's labor in earning a livelihood. Hence, property acquired by the husband's labor should be regarded as acquired by the common labor of husband and wife.
   b. Property inherited by either or both parties while married.
   c. Gifts received by either or both parties while married.

* When the unit of organization grew large in certain commercial and industrial enterprises, the family organization often proved inadequate and the partnership organization came into operation.

3. Property of children who have not reached maturity, such as land and other kinds of property acquired by children in the process of land reform.

With the principles of equal rights between men and women and equal status between husband and wife in the family established, husband and wife have equal rights of ownership and disposal of family property in the first and second categories, and equal rights of administration of the family property in the third category. On the other hand, with the same principles as a base, husband and wife may make mutual voluntary agreements regarding ownership, disposal, and administration of any kind of family property.[5]

Under land reform, which was completed in all the major regions of China by 1953, both women and children have a clear share of the land distributed to the family by the government. Separate deeds could be issued to the wife and each of the children on request.[6]

On the matter of inheritance the Marriage Law stipulates that "both husband and wife have the right to inherit each other's property" (Article 12), and that "parents and children have the right to inherit one another's property" (Article 14). In the latter, the word "children" in the Chinese text is actually "sons and daughters."

The new system of family ownership of property under Communist law is thus radically different from the traditional practice. How far this new arrangement is being accepted by the people is not known, but several facts should be considered. Since equality in family property rights was long a part of pre-Communist agitation in the family revolution, it may be assumed that the new arrangement gains ready acceptance among the modern educated generation of urban upper and middle classes. As for the working class and the peasantry, propaganda and indoctrination of the Marriage Law and the efforts of the women's movement no doubt popularize the new idea; and in an age of revolution in which an individual is alerted to review his own interest in a different light the chance of its acceptance is high. That legal decisions support the new system can be seen in a large number of cases published in the Communist press during the early years of the regime. One such case in 1951 concerned a woman, Ma Ts'ui-yü, in Shanghai. Ma married into a "big family" where her husband and his married brothers lived together under the authority of the mother-in-law. In 1950 Ma's husband died, and soon afterward his brothers proceeded to dissolve the big family by dividing up the family property. The mother-in-law and the brothers decided not to give Ma her deceased husband's share of the property on the traditional ground that she had born no son. When Ma brought the case to the Communist court it upheld her claim for the deceased husband's share, citing the law that "husband and wife have the right to inherit each other's property." Another typical case involved the property rights of a peasant girl in Lulung county of Hopei Province. The girl, stimulated by the propaganda of the Communist Marriage Law, fell in love with a young Communist Party member and wanted to marry him, but her parents regarded the untraditional love affair as a humiliation to the family and forbade her to leave the house. In 1951 she brought the case to court, which not only recognized her freedom to marry but also permitted her to take her share of land from her parents' family to her new family.[7] Thus she not merely brought no "ritual wealth" or "body price" into the family when she married, but actually took away property that traditionally belonged to her parents.

A last and interesting point for consideration is the recognition of household services as a part of productive labor contributing to the acquisition of family property. Under Communist law such services furnish legal ground for women's claim to family property, but apparently this new valuation of household labor is far from gaining popular acceptance despite a vigorous propaganda campaign to popularize it.

In this connection it must be noted that the weight of private property rights as a factor in elevating the status of women and young family members is being drastically reduced by the socialization of the Chinese economy. By 1957 China's farms had been collectivized into the agricultural producers' cooperatives, and urban private businesses had been socialized into joint state-private concerns controlled by the state. By the end of 1958, the more thoroughly collectivized people's communes replaced the agricultural producers' cooperatives as the national form of rural production. The individual or the family no longer owns land, business enterprise, or any other significant means of production, and private property is reduced mainly to personal articles, with private ownership of houses in serious doubt.

It is obvious that as private property ceases to be a major factor in status stratification, redistribution of property rights can serve only in a limited way in the alteration of the status of the family members. It is the equalizing right to work outside the family, not property rights, that will serve that function. The reduction of family property to an insignificant position has another important meaning, namely the removal of the means of production (in the form of land or business enterprises) from family control, thereby depriving the family of the hitherto most basic factor in integrating its members into a strongly organized group.

Women's Participation in Production

An important factor which is changing the economic status of women in the family as well as in society is the increasing participation of women in production and the development of occupational opportunities for women. This is a new and disruptive factor in the economic structure of the traditional family.

The relation between traditional women's status and their formerly limited role in production is vividly illustrated in the case of Chou Po-lin in Yenchi county of Kirin Province. Chou was a farmer tilling four mow of land. After promulgation of the new Marriage Law, when Chou's wife claimed sex equality during a family squabble, Chou said to his wife: "Now that men and women are equal, let us also be equal in labor." Subsequently Chou tilled only two mow of land, leaving the other two mow for his wife to till. As a consequence, the other two mow of land were left to waste, since his wife could not farm.[8] Chou knew that she could not farm that two mow of land! There was no possibility that she could, as tradition had kept women from participating in productive labor, particularly in the northern section of China.

In the traditional social order it was an informal taboo for upper- and middle-class women to work at income-earning jobs if the family could support them, as it would seriously damage the social dignity of the family. With poor families in which the husband's earnings could not keep the family going, such as with peddlers, laborers, and poor peasants, it was common to find, particularly in the South, women taking up an occupation or working alongside the husband in a small business or in the fields, all in addition to heavy household duties. But all traditional occupations admitting women as independent workers were poorly paid and offered no prospect of a woman's becoming prosperous or gaining social respect. As soon as a husband could support the family, the wife followed the upper- and middle-class practice and ceased to work. Even the idea of women receiving an education to prepare for a profession or occupation met strong resistance from upper-class families.

During the Republican period the increasing influence of modern education, the agitation of the women's movement, and the development of a modern urban economy gradually broke down the disapproval of working women. In a sense, from the day when women were emancipated from their crippling bound feet, which had been a heated issue in the earlier part of the century, the course was set for women to walk with "liberated" feet to the outside world and to work. Within two decades the idea of women participating in income-earning work as a normal part of life and not merely because of dire economic necessity gained general acceptance among the urban intelligentsia. Urban occupational fields with better social and economic prospects opened up for women: factory work, sales work, many kinds of personal services such as those provided by barbers and waitresses, medicine, teaching, scientific research, stage arts, clerical positions, government jobs, and even a few high-level political posts. But in rural communities, particularly in the North, the traditional restriction stood firm in the pre-Communist period.

When the Communists assumed national power, the right of women to participate in productive labor was written into the statute: "Both husband and wife shall have the right of free choice of occupation and free participation in work and in social activities" (Marriage Law, Article 9). Promotional efforts have been made to put this legal stipulation into practice, and the mobilization of women into production has become a leading policy of the government in order to meet the labor requirement of the Communist program of increasing agricultural and industrial production in the modernization of China's economy.

Thus, in 1950 elaborate propaganda fanfare heralded the first group of women tractor drivers and locomotive engineers in the Northeast. All-women-operated railroad trains in Tientsin and Shanghai in 1951 were Communist showpieces demonstrating sex equality of work.[9] In the same year in the Northeast, the bastion of modern Chinese industrial development, a substantial number of women were engaged in a variety of technical and skilled occupations as a result of Communist encouragement. In the cities of Darien and Port Arthur 1,196 women were in 35 kinds of technical and skilled jobs in heavy industry including operating lathes, repairing ships, and metal casting; and 6,183 women were in 14 kinds of light industry jobs. Among these women workers were one factory manager, seven technical assistants, 81 foremen, and 1,178 sub-foremen. In 1950 in Mukden 1,100 women workers were promoted to positions of factory administration and leaders in labor unions. In the field of mining, 814 women were found in 39 kinds of skilled jobs in the Fushun Coal Mining Company.[10]

Since then there has been steady increase in the variety of skilled and unskilled occupations open to women as the tempo of Chinese economic development has quickened. In 1954 a woman worker made news by mastering high-temperature welding at perilous heights on construction projects. From 1949 to 1954 the number of women employed in industrial, commercial, and political jobs increased from 420,000 to 1,900,000 throughout the country.[11] By the end of 1955 women accounted for 14 per cent of workers and staff members in all state enterprises, including 2,500 in administrative positions and 16,000 technicians. In professional fields during the same year there were 65,000 women medical and public health workers and 33,000 women educators, including 7,500 teaching in higher educational institutions.[12] There has also been a steady increase in the number of women in political and military services in the government. Ts'ai Ch'iang, a prominent Communist feminist leader, declared that there were 500,000 women officers in 1951 as compared to 764,000 in 1955, an increase from 8 per cent of all officers to 14.5 per cent.[13] It is now normal to find women mingling with men officers in Communist government offices. In the early years of Communist rule in 1950 and 1951 women police were a common sight in many cities, and they eyed in a prejudiced way bourgeois members of their sex who did not work, led a "parasitic" life, and had a low degree of political consciousness.

While the foregoing data leave many statistical problems unanswered, they nevertheless serve to indicate the trend away from the days when the only occupations for women were low-paying jobs such as embroidery and needle work, domestic service, and hard labor like carrying dirt or crushing rocks for construction projects — jobs which reinforced women's servitude. No doubt sizeable numbers of women under the Communist regime are still engaged in such jobs, but the new situation differs from the old in that, in addition to these jobs, women are now being admitted to a large variety of occupational fields offering possibilities of status advancement, fields that had been traditionally closed to their sex.

Since the widening of occupational opportunities for women had been going on for more than three decades previous to the inauguration of Communist power, Communist figures on the employment of women in some fields contain contributions from pre-Communist development. An example is the Communist figure of 70 per cent of all textile industry workers in the country being women.[14] The fact is that women were numerically important in the textile industry even in pre-Communist days. The proportion of women workers has also always been high in many light industries such as the manufacturing of matches.

However, even after taking previous developments into consideration, the situation of women's employment under the Communists still presents two new features. One is the opening of administrative and supervisory positions to women in places where members of both sexes work together, which means that men may be taking orders from a woman superior, something unusual if not intolerable in traditional public life. Secondly, a whole class of women formerly sheltered by a favored economic position from having to work are now being compelled by new circumstances to join society's working force. These are the upper- and middle-class women whose husbands belong mainly to two groups, businessmen and intellectuals who include educational, technical, and government workers. Since, except for some high-ranking technicians and officials, salaries for intellectuals are generally insufficient to support a family, a large number of wives from this group have had to seek work if possible. In fact, it has been a general rule that when the Communist authorities assign work for a man, they also try to find a placement for the wife. To the Communists, the non-working wife is almost as unthinkable as the traditional bound feet; and the low salary arrangement for men serves the function of obtaining a maximum working force from the population by compelling women to work. Having the same effect was the widespread unemployment of intellectuals during the first half-dozen years of Communist rule, a situation that forced women to look for work whenever possible. In spite of the rosy picture the Communists painted of the economic growth of the country, over 6,800 intellectuals alone registered for employment in Shanghai in September 1956.[15] As to women belonging to businessmen's families, the Communists' steady liquidation of private business through a variety of means has made it necessary for women to leave their sheltered position and seek employment.

Thus, ideological promotion, financial pressure from the collapse of an old economic institution, and increasing employment opportunities in a new economic order jointly bring into the nation's working force large numbers of women who never had to work before. From this it appears that growing female participation in production outside the family is inevitable.

This new situation is largely confined to urban occupations, except for isolated cases such as tractor driving. In the agricultural sector of the economy the development of new occupational opportunities differs according to geographical regions. In the northern section of the country, where women were traditionally kept from main agricultural production tasks and confined to minor jobs such as weeding and processing grain, a new field of economic activity is opened through Communist ideological promotion and pressure from the collectivization of agricultural production. Realizing the predominant importance of agriculture to the country's economy at the present stage, the Communist government from its very start has put efforts into promoting women's labor in farming. As early as 1950, when land reform was being carried out in the Northeast and North China, women who received their own share of land for the first time were stated to have participated increasingly in major agricultural tasks such as plowing, sowing, and harvesting. In many localities in these two regions women taking part in such tasks accounted for 50 to 75 per cent of all able-bodied women.[16] In the Northeast, where the Communists had established their power earlier than in many other regions, it was stated that in Kirin Province women participating in year-round agricultural production numbered over 857,000 in 1951, constituting about 83 per cent of all adult women; and in Jehol Province over 400,000 women were said to have taken part in major farming jobs.[17] Another report stated that in 1951, in the three Northeastern provinces of Jehol, Heilungkiang, and Kirin, 40 to 50 per cent of all adult women participated in spring planting, 70 to 80 per cent in summer cultivation, and over 90 per cent in autumn harvesting.[18]

In South China there has been a similar drive for women to participate in all aspects of agricultural production. In Ch'ao-an county of Kwangtung Province, for example, it was claimed that in 1951, 3,000 peasant women cleared 3,000 mow (about 460 acres) of new land, and that elsewhere in the same province women were active in major agricultural work.[19] Even if the relative reliability of these statements is taken for granted the extent of women's contribution to agricultural production as a result of Communist efforts is not clear, for women in South China have always taken part in most aspects of agricultural work, at times including plowing. This is especially true with districts like Ch'ao-an and the "four counties" of Kwangtung, where wholesale emigration of men to foreign lands had left women the responsibility for tilling the soil.

But even in South China women were traditionally kept from certain types of agricultural work. For instance, for women to labor on dike work was a religious taboo, as it was believed the presence of women on a dike might cause it to collapse. It is significant, then, that in many instances during 1951 Communist cadres mobilized whole villages, including women, for emergency repair work on dikes that were being threatened by rising rivers. In the southern province of Kwangtung, in Chungshan county, it was a group of peasant women who led the emergency repair of a dike breakage, rescuing some 32,000 mow of paddy fields from flood. In Panyü county women supplied two-fifths of the workers in a major job of repairing a 38,000-foot dike. An age-old superstition has thus been broken, and peasant women have entered into another aspect of agricultural work which had traditionally been closed to them.[20]

A standard Communist technique in stimulating enthusiasm for production is the use of emulation contests to glorify and reward "model workers," a technique applied to encourage agricultural as well as industrial production. Women in agricultural production have produced a large number of "model workers." In 29 counties of Liaotung Province in the Northeast 3,096 women were made model agricultural workers, and in six counties of the Chuangho district in the same province women supplied 17.9 per cent of the 835 model agricultural workers during 1951.[21] In the southern province of Kwangsi in 1953, 53 or 15.6 per cent of 339 model agricultural workers were women.[22]

The most effective pressure to increase the participation of women in agricultural work in the North as well as in the South, has been exerted by the collectivization of the farm economy, which will be discussed later. Here we would note that women supplied one-third of all the work-days in the agricultural producers' cooperatives throughout the country in 1954,[23] and that in 1955, in Ch'angteh district of Hunan Province in the South, women accounted for 1,100,000 of the 2,500,000 labor units used in accumulating fertilizer.[24]

Development of Child Care for Working Mothers

The Department of Women's Labor of the All-Shanghai Labor Union noted in one of its early reports:

> State Cotton Mill of Shanghai No. 1 employs a large number of women. Almost 80 per cent of these women workers are married and 70 per cent of the married women workers have children. These mothers, even those returning home from night shift, have to cook, care for the children, wash clothes, and can sleep only three or four hours a day. This is the average picture of the female textile worker in other places. Some of them even have to wait on their husbands and parents-in-law when they go home from work and suffer from beating and malnutrition.[25]

The northern city of Tientsin presented a similar picture. A survey of two industrial districts there in 1952 showed that 1,104 out of 4,310 working women were married, and that there was an average of one child to every two working married women. Household chores and child care were causing low efficiency among these women and compelling many of them to leave work.[26] Other reports indicate that such conditions were typical for city factories in the country as a whole.

The problem of working mothers, not entirely a new product of Communist rule, was generally ignored in pre-Communist days. A working mother added the burden of work to her regular domestic duties, still retaining her traditional role in the family. In the traditional three-generation or multi-generation family grand- or great-grandparents too old to work could care for the child while the mother worked, but in the cities a large proportion of families were conjugal families with no aged grandparents — due to economic reasons and the relatively short life-span. Thus the working mother was an exception, since she generally had to place her children outside the family. The Communist regime, having chosen to mobilize women, including mothers, for production, has met the problem of working mothers by setting up nurseries in both urban and rural communities — an institutional innovation with obvious potential effects on the structure of the family.

The development of nurseries in urban centers had an early start. By the end of 1951, a little over two years after the inauguration of the Communist regime, "there were over 15,700 nurseries, kindergartens, and other types of child-care agencies in different cities, caring for some 520,000 children, the number of such agencies representing a nine-fold increase over the pre-Liberation period." [27] Most of them were nursery stations or rooms attached to large manufacturing and mining enterprises, schools, and public offices where large numbers of mothers worked.[28] Of neighborhood nurseries open to the public, there were 4,300 in all cities in the country in 1952.[29]

Such early reports seemed impressive but the development of nurseries has apparently fallen far short of meeting the needs of a society in which it is official policy to promote women's labor. "In Peking there were only eleven nurseries before the Liberation, and these have increased to sixty-five [February 1951], forty-seven of which have been attached to public offices. Recently four nursing rooms have been added. But in Peking there are over four hundred government offices, over eight hundred schools, and over thirty comparatively large factories. Because of the absence of nurseries and nursing rooms in the vast majority of the government offices, women cadres cannot work with ease of mind, and some of them have even stopped working. Some unmarried women comrades, seeing the burden of motherhood, are unwilling to get married, and those already married resort to contraception." [30]

Lack of finances and shortage of trained personnel have proved serious obstacles to expansion. Obviously, a large proportion of the early nurseries were temporary affairs hastily set up without adequate organization, equipment, personnel, or operating expenditures. Unofficial reports disclosed high sickness and death rates among children entrusted to such agencies, which undoubtedly deterred many working mothers from using them. By 1955 there were only 4,000 nurseries among manufacturing and mining enterprises throughout the country, caring for 127,000 children, and 687 public neighborhood nurseries in 60 cities caring for some 38,000 children.[31] Those figures registered a decrease from 1951–1952. By the fall of 1956 only 6,000 nurseries were reported for industrial and commercial enterprises and government and educational institutions.[32]

Other difficulties developed to impede the transference of women from the home to urban occupational fields. By 1956 many reports noted a tendency among Communist administrators to discriminate against employing women in a large variety of jobs even though they had adequate qualifications. The reasons given were the "trouble involved" in employing women; that nurseries had to be set up; and that pregnant mothers had to be granted leave with pay, thus increasing the operating cost of the enterprise or office. The Department of Agriculture and Forestry of the Kwangtung provincial government refused to employ a twenty-year-old girl graduate from a school of accounting on the ground that she had a fiance and would soon be married and have children, thus bringing "all incidental troubles" to the department.[33] Such reports agree with statements from Communist leaders. Ts'ai Ch'iang, a feminist leader, raised objections at the Eighth Communist Party Congress to the discrimination against employing women by the Communist government.[34] Yang Chih-hua attacked the unfavorable attitude which regarded the employment of women as "being uneconomical and presenting too many problems."[35] Recent complaints by Communist leaders about early marriages of industrial workers, especially women, are related to the question of young working mothers being hampered by children.[36]

These difficulties, however, caused only temporary interruptions in the long-term growth of employment of urban women outside the home. The leap-forward campaign in 1958 brought a renewed increase of the country's women industrial and office workers to seven and a half million from about three million in 1957.[37] In Shanghai 460,000 women worked at industrial jobs in 1958 as compared with 190,000 in 1949.[38] In Peking women workers in industrial, commercial, and cultural fields numbered 210,000, a gain of 50 per cent over 1957, and the Peking Tramcar Company in 1958 hired three times as many female employees as in the previous eight years.[39] Even the interior city of Sian saw a gain of 23 per cent of women industrial workers in 1958 as compared with 1957, and 80 per cent of the city's commercial service occupations were said to be staffed by women.[40]

The mobilization of peasant women for agricultural production also brought active efforts to set up nurseries in rural communities when mutual-aid teams were started as the first step toward collectivization. "Many villages have begun to establish seasonal nursery units during busy seasons for mutual-aid teams. There are over 10,000 such organizations throughout the country [1951]. In rural communities where the problem of child care is solved, much of women's labor that used to be buried in the home begins to emerge in production activities. For instance, in Honan Province during the busy farm season 3,582 child-care teams and 76 nurseries have been organized for the mutual-aid teams in agricultural production. This makes it possible for 27,359 mothers to participate in agricultural production." [41] Another local example was the village of Hsushichen in Chienyang county of Fukien Province. "The mutual-aid team for farming in that village mobilized 8 old women to take care of 12 children so that the younger able-bodied women could work." [42]

The campaign of organizing seasonal nursery units among women agricultural workers apparently made progress in 1952, for it was claimed that the number of temporary nursery teams during busy farming seasons increased that year to 148,000, caring for about 800,000 children throughout the country. In six "special districts" of Anhwei Province 30,696 mutual-aid child-care units were organized in the spring and summer of 1952, caring for 157,575 children. In the southern part of the same province establishment of nursery organizations relieved 141,969 women for agricultural production, including "many women who previously did very little labor or did not know how to labor." Such nursery organizations were mostly staffed by women too old for active agricultural labor but glad to earn some "labor points." An old woman caring for four children earned from

3 to 4.55 labor points a day, depending on the number and ages of the children being cared for, as compared with the average of 10 labor points earned by a regular agricultural worker per day. These "labor points" were paid for by the agricultural mutual-aid teams of which the working mothers were members, the cost of child care becoming a part of the cost of agricultural production in such cases.[43]

Acceptance of the cost of nursery organizations as part of the cost of mutual-aid teams and later of agricultural producers' cooperatives and the utilization of otherwise idle old people for public child care were among the reasons for the early success of nursery work in some localities, but, as has been the case with the urban nursery movement, there seems to have been little progress after 1953. No further statistical figures on rural nursery work are seen in the available Communist press or literature after that year. On the other hand, reports continue regarding the conflict between the new burden of labor production and the old duties of child care and household chores for peasant women. During 1954 and 1955 there were many reports of children being injured or drowned in ponds and rivers owing to the absence of the mothers who were working in the fields.[44] In the pre-Communist period, there were occasional injuries or deaths of children caused by the absence of mothers who were working during busy farming seasons, but such cases "increased precipitously after the rapid growth in the number of agricultural producers' cooperatives" in 1955.[45]

In 1956 the problem of child care and domestic duties continued to plague Communist staff members who tried to mobilize peasant women for full agricultural production work. The head of an agricultural producers' cooperative in Chien-shih county of Hupei Province lectured his peasant wife: "To gain emancipation, women must do production work just like men." But the wife had to care for the children, cook, gather firewood, carry water, make shoes, sew and mend, collect feed for the pigs, and tend the vegetable garden, with the result that she earned only a small number of "labor points." The husband scolded her for not going out to work more often, for "living on the exploitation of men," and the wife in turn accused him of not helping out with the domestic work. In T'ung-shan county of Kiangsu Province an agricultural producers' cooperative set down a regulation that in order to receive a full worker's remuneration a woman had to work 270 workdays of the year. But a survey showed that a peasant mother spends a total of 131 days a year in child care and domestic chores, and that, at the maximum, she can work only 170 full work-days and 60 half workdays. A quota of 270 full workdays is obviously impractical.[46]

Whereas in urban occupations the employment of women, particularly mothers, seems to be slowing down somewhat because of difficulties in providing nurseries and childbirth benefits, there has been little letup in the drive for getting peasant women to take part in full agricultural production duties. In 1955 Communist propaganda still stressed woman's participation in collective agriculture as the only road to emancipation from man's domination and family oppression. The Communist press publicized many stories of peasant women who had previously suffered mistreatment from husbands and parents-in-law but were now respected by the latter because they brought income home by working on the cooperative farms.[47]

The sweeping transformation of the cooperatives into people's com-munes throughout China in the latter part of 1958 brought a system-atic effort at resolving the contradiction between the burden of domestic chores and the Communist policy of the full mobilization of women for agricultural production. On International Women's Day, March 8, 1959, the *Jen-min jih-pao* (People's Daily) claimed that the drive of "socializing household work" has set up in China 3,600,000 public mess halls and 4,980,000 nurseries and kindergartens staffed by some 7,000,000 women child-care workers. Thus freed from cooking, child care, and many other domestic chores now collectively performed, nearly "100 per cent" of all rural women have joined productive labor in the communes. But since the commune system as a socio-economic order is still in the experimental stage, its eventual success or failure will determine whether this drastic alteration of women's position in the role structure of the family can become institutionalized, or if it is just another transitional phenomenon in a revolutionary process.

Transformation of the Economic Institution

Functionally the most potent development affecting the family sys-tem has been the transformation of the general economic institution, a transformation which operates to replace the family as the dominant organizational unit of production. In the pre-Communist period the rise of large commercial and industrial enterprises in the limited modernization of the urban economy had disorganizing effects on the traditional family, but that influence was not extensive, as attested by the fact that 94 per cent of all commercial and industrial firms in the city of Canton were still family enterprises in 1950. Above all, the agricultural sector of the economy that employed over 80 per cent of the population remained in the firm grip of the family organization. Extensive change of the general economic institution came only after the Communists had started to enforce their socialist economic program at a rapid pace. Leading aspects of this change are the socialization of commerce and industry, the collectivization of agriculture, and the program of industrialization.

The economic importance of the family was founded upon private ownership of the means of production and free enterprise. When the Communists took power in 1949, they declared toleration of private business in a "relatively long transitional period of new democracy" during which a mixed economy of private and state enterprises was to be maintained. But this period of mixed economy proved to be quite short. Less than a year after the inauguration of the Communist government a warning was issued to the effect that the development of private business would not be allowed to "pursue its own natural course" but must be guided by state plans so as not to delay the coming of the socialist economy.[48]

From the day the Communists became the nation's governing power an atmosphere of doom descended upon private business. The high-living upper and upper-middle class either fled Communist rule or faced impending bankruptcy, thus depriving urban business of the bulk of its luxury consumers. The year 1950 saw a nation-wide decline of private businesses in all cities. A slight recovery in 1951 was followed by the scorching Five-Anti movement (against tax evasion, theft of state economic information, bribery of officials, cheating on government contracts, and theft of state property), which imposed ruinous fines on a large proportion of urban businessmen in 1952. At the same time, constant financial drain from taxes, forced subscriptions to a variety of bonds and loans, increased wages, and benefits to workers that were not based on a rise in productivity drove private businesses into insolvency. But a financially insolvent business was not permitted to close down without government permission, which was generally not granted. As large numbers of financially bankrupt businesses were compelled to stay open (so as to avert sudden widespread unemployment and economic chaos), businessmen had no alternative but to turn to the Communist government bank for loans to continue operation. In most cases the loan became the government's share in the business, and the firm was turned into a joint state-private enterprise, with the state's representative dictating its operation.

State enterprises and their ramifying system of control over private business developed rapidly after 1952. In 1949, 36.7 per cent of the nation's industrial products in terms of value were turned out by state enterprises, cooperatives, and state-private firms, and 63.3 per cent came from private enterprises. In 1952 the respective figures were 61.0 and 39.0 per cent.[49] From 1952 to 1955 state ownership took over almost all heavy industries, a substantial percentage of light industries, almost all of the wholesale, and a considerable proportion of the retail trade. Businesses remaining in private hands had come to operate as subsidiaries to the system of state enterprises which also effectively controlled the rapidly extending system of cooperatives.[50] Private industries relied mainly on orders or processing contracts from government agencies and state enterprises, and depended on state organizations for the supply of raw materials. Private trade similarly depended on state-owned wholesale agencies for the distribution of goods, and faced increasing competition from state stores and marketing and consumers' cooperatives in addition to the difficulties of a shrunken urban market. In spite of a moderate revival of private retail trade in 1954, it became clear that the days of independent operators were gone.

In 1955, the movement for socialist transformation of business enterprise was accelerated, and in January of 1956 it was announced that all of the remaining private enterprises in industry and commerce in the nation's leading cities, (Shanghai, Peking, Tientsin, Sian, Mukden, Nanking, Canton, and Chungking) had become private-state operations.[51] Later, Communist premier Chou En-lai stated: "By the end of June 1956, 99 per cent of capitalist industrial enterprises in terms of output value and 98 per cent in terms of number of workers and employees have come under joint state-private operation. Of the private commercial and catering establishments, 68 per cent in terms of the number of shops and 74 per cent in number of personnel have been transformed into joint state-private shops, cooperative shops, or cooperative groups. The conversion of capitalist industry and commerce into joint state-private enterprises trade by trade and the carrying out of the fixed interest system in these enterprises have prepared the way for nationalization of capitalist means of production." [52] The last part of the statement referred to the fact that, under joint state-private operation, the private share of capital was being given a flat 5 per cent interest rate regardless of the profit or loss of the business, but that in the future the private share would be turned over to the state. In view of the rapid conversion of private businesses into the state-private system, the day of complete nationalization is not distant — possibly during the period of the second five-year plan (1957–1962).

The above data omit the multitudes of handicraftsmen, small traders, and peddlers. Although there are no statistics on the total number of handicraftsmen in the country, it was announced that by September 1956, 4.7 million of them had been organized into producer cooperatives, and that only a small number of them were still working on a private basis.[53] In Peking all of the city's 53,000 craftsmen had been "cooperativized" in January of the same year. The organization of small traders and peddlers into cooperative stores has also developed steadily in the cities and towns,[54] but recent Communist policy has been to permit the continued existence of some small craftsmen, service establishments, traders, and peddlers instead of forcing them all into state-directed organizations such as cooperatives.[55]

In spite of reservations in the new policy about small handicraftsmen and traders, it is obvious that the family has been displaced as a unit of production and employment. No longer are the members of the family the basic components of the organization of production; nor do individuals look toward the family as the most important center of economic support or economic opportunities. Instead, state enterprises operating outside of the kinship system have become the basic unit of industrial and commercial organization, and individuals must look toward them for employment and economic opportunities.

The nationalization of an industrial and commercial system that contains close to ten million small businesses and individual operators will require huge numbers of technically trained personnel and solutions to a complex of problems. As Communist leadership is as yet unable to meet either of these two conditions, it is inevitable that mismanagement and dislocation will occur in both the industrial and the distributional system, as has been admitted in Communist reports.[56]

In the agricultural sector of the economy the family has also lost its significance as the dominant organizational unit in production. The first Communist measure for changing the agrarian economic system was the land reform completed in 1952, which redistributed land to landless peasants and those having insufficient land.* But

* See Liao Lu-yen, "The Great Victory of Three Years of Land Reform Movement," *Hua Ch'iao jih-pao*, New York, October 22–24, 1952. The percentages of land redistributed and peasants benefited in the land reform are revealed in sample investigations conducted by the Communist government. In the Central-South Region about 40 per cent of all the land had been confiscated and redistributed to about 60 per cent of all the peasants, with each landless or poor peasant gaining 1/6 to 1/3 of an acre. The corresponding figures for the East China Region are close to those for the Central-South Region. In the Southwest Region, where land ownership was more concen-

new land for the poor peasants did not remain in their private possession for long. Even in the pre-Communist period, efforts to modernize Chinese agriculture had found almost insurmountable obstacles in the "small farm economy" consisting of, among other things, diminutive farm units and widely scattered tiny plots of land belonging to the same farm. For the Communist regime, which is dedicated to large-scale mechanized production techniques and follows the Leninist line of changing farms into "agricultural factories" with mechanization and rationalized management as a means of elevating the peasants to economic parity with industrial workers, the collectivization of agriculture is as inevitable as the nationalization of business enterprise. And hastening the collectivization drive is the pressing need for capital for the industrialization program, capital which can be obtained more easily from 750,000 government-controlled collective farms or 26,000 communes than from some 120,-000,000 independent peasant farms.

The Communist program of collectivization is divided into four stages: the development of (1) mutual-aid teams, (2) the elementary type of agricultural producers' cooperatives, (3) the advanced type of agricultural producers' cooperatives, and (4) the people's communes.

Mutual-aid teams are groups consisting of half a dozen to twenty or thirty peasant families who pool their labor and equipment to work on the land possessed by the families. Essentially it is a labor pool. The individual worker, not the family, is the basic unit of the organization, and remuneration is based on the number of "labor points" earned by each worker, the average for a full-time worker being 10 points per day. Land ownership, work animals, and farm implements used by the team receive separate compensation. By the end of 1952, 60 to 80 per cent of all peasant households in the Northeast and the "old liberated areas" of North China had been organized into mutual-aid teams, and in the southern part of the country 25 to 40 per cent of peasant households belonged to a total of some six million teams.[57] While continued increase in the number of mutual-aid teams has been reported after 1952, national statistical figures have not been available. Even at this elementary step of collectivization, the peasant family retains a certain degree of economic significance chiefly in the ownership

---

trated than other regions, 60 per cent of all the land had been redistributed to over 70 per cent of all the peasants. In the Kuanchung area of the Northwest Region, where land ownership was rather dispersed, 20.3 per cent of all the land had been distributed to about 30 per cent of the peasants. See also *Shih-chieh Nien-chien* (World Year Book), Peking, 1952, pp. 336–339.

of land and not as a dominant organizational unit of agricultural production.

The so-called elementary type of agricultural producers' cooperative is essentially a land pool, with certain heavy farm implements and work animals also thrown into common use. The remuneration system is basically the same as in mutual-aid teams, but the difference lies in the development of a unified management concerning the type of crops to be planted, capital investment, distribution and organization of the labor force, marketing of farm products and distribution of earnings. In the advanced type of agricultural producers' cooperatives land ownership is no longer recognized as a factor for remuneration, it being taken for granted that after the land reform average peasants own a relatively equal amount of land. Work animal and heavy implements are taken into common ownership by the cooperative with compensation. With the peasant becoming chiefly a wage earner, the advanced cooperative has all the fundamental features of the collective farm in the Soviet Union.[58]

The development of agricultural producers' cooperatives made slow progress in the first few years of the Communist regime. There were 300 agricultural producers' cooperatives (types unspecified) throughout China in 1951, about 4,000 in 1952, 14,000 in 1953, 670,000 in 1954. There was some increase in 1955, but during the year many small cooperatives were combined into larger ones, reducing the actual number of cooperatives to 650,000 but with 16,900,000 peasant households as members, accounting for about 15 per cent of China's 120,-000,000 peasant households.[59] Toward the end of 1955 the drive for "cooperativization" was greatly accelerated, and in the fall of 1956, Chou En-lai announced with satisfaction to the Chinese Communist Party Congress: "By the end of June 1956 a total of 992,000 agricultural producers' cooperatives had been organized throughout the country. Their members make up 91.7 per cent of the country's peasant households; those joining cooperatives of the advanced type constitute 62.6 per cent of all peasant households." [60] Liao Lu-yen, Minister of Agriculture, significantly declared in the light of this development: "The small peasant economy has been changed throughout the country." [61] By the early part of 1958 the merging of smaller cooperatives reduced the national total number of cooperatives to about 750,000, each having an average of 170 households, some 300 laborers, and 2,000 mow (approximately 300 acres) of land.[62]

The attempt to collectivize a peasant economy of microscopic family farms and intensive cultivation gives rise to serious organizational problems in inculcating an impersonalized collective role conception in the peasants' minds, in developing a businesslike attitude, in creating a technically and administratively qualified leadership for the vastly expanded operational unit, in coping with interference on collective labor by such remaining private undertakings as home industries and raising vegetables on the family plot, and in satisfactorily dividing the collective income between capital accumulation, needs of the state, and remuneration for the members. Reports in Communist literature indicate that a significant number of the cooperatives failed in surmounting these difficulties, and that only some of them worked well. On the other hand, cooperatives command the general advantages of a greatly expanded pool of labor, land and resources, and a unified administrative authority. These advantages brought about the rapid extension of irrigated areas through numerous hydraulic projects, and increased adoption of improved techniques of cultivation, resulting in the Communist claim of an increase in national agricultural output since collectivization.

The experience of some successful cooperatives and certain general technical advantages of collectivism encourage the Communist leadership into believing in the universal practicability of collectivization by imposing military discipline to overcome the organizational difficulties that have plagued the poorly operated cooperatives. This is among the major considerations that have motivated the drastic merging of the country's 750,000 cooperatives into 26,500 people's communes in the last four months of 1958. As a unit of production an average commune contains some 5,000 households, 10,000 laborers and 6,000 mow (about 900 acres) of land.[63] This huge organization completely obliterates the family as a unit of production by collectivizing even the private plots previously reserved for family use under the cooperative system and by setting up communal industries to replace home industries and to diversify economic operations in rural communities.

In 1955 Mao Tse-tung declared in a speech that one of the urgent reasons behind the hastening of the collectivization program was the need to accumulate capital for industrialization.[64] The same need for industrial capital contributed to the establishment of the commune system which appears more effective than the cooperatives in extracting income from the peasantry. Aspirations for the status of an industrialized nation have been firing the imaginations of the Chinese people for a century, and Communist leadership in China, like its counterpart in the Soviet Union, dedicates itself to the realization of this popular dream. This dedication serves to mitigate some of the harsh features of the Communist power and retain the support of some of the intellectuals for it. It is obvious that industrialization on an extensive scale will have profound effects on the Chinese family system, as demonstrated by the experience of Western industrial society and the Soviet Union.

The present scale of industrial development appears small compared to that of leading Western powers, but it represents a vast acceleration when compared with progress in the pre-Communist period. The heart of the initial development is the first five-year plan (1953–1957). In the first two years of the plan, many industries failed to reach their targets owing to the initial shortage of capital, technical knowledge, organizational and administrative skill, despite limited Soviet assistance.[65] But by the third year, 1955, the program picked up momentum as increasing numbers of industries fulfilled their assigned quota.[66] The vigorous steel-making campaign by both modern and native methods in 1958 further accelerated the development of related industries and stimulated the people's awareness of the industrialization movement. The progress is shown in the following figures for four basic industries during 1952–1958.

Commodity	1952	1954	1955	1957	1958
Steel (million metric tons)	1.4	2.2	2.8	5.35	11.08
Coal (million metric tons)	63.5	80.0	93.0	130.00	270.00
Cement (million metric tons)	2.9	4.6	4.5	6.86	9.30
Electricity (billion kilowatt hours)	7.3	10.9	12.3	19.30	27.50

(Sources: State Statistical Bureau figures released by the New China News Agency, June 14, 1956, and April 14, 1959.)

At the conclusion of the first five-year plan in 1957, the country's total industrial production increased by 132.5 per cent in value over 1952.[67] The feverish leap-forward campaign in 1958 further raised the industrial output in that year by 65.0 per cent over 1957.[68]

Influence on the Family of Industrialization, Nationalization of Business, and Collectivization of Agriculture

We may summarize the significant changes in the economic position and structure of the family which are implied in the Communist nationalization of commerce and industry, acceleration of industrialization, and collectivization of agriculture.

First and foremost is the general replacement of the family as a dominant and independent unit of production in all sectors of economic production, chiefly by removing the means of production from family ownership. Second is the abolition of the head of the family as the leader and chief organizer in production activities, his traditional role being taken over by the new staff members in the state-monopolized economy.

Third, the economic status of women, and to a lesser extent that of the young, tends to be raised by the nationalized and collectivized economy since under such a system the unit for remuneration for work is not the family but the individual worker regardless of sex, age, or family position. The operation of the wage system in industry and commerce in this respect is self-evident. The remuneration system in the cooperative farm is illustrated in the following case:

> A cooperative society of agricultural production has been successfully organized in the village of Sanliushu of Kuangjao county, Shantung Province. The system of remuneration is based upon the number of labor points earned by an individual: (1) A man working a full day receives ten labor points. (2) Labor performed by women is counted in two ways: (a) Those who work in the field performing the same tasks as those performed by men get the same remuneration as men: each working day by one woman counts ten labor points. (b) Women working on special jobs such as picking cotton or preparing animal feed are remunerated according to piece rates expressed in labor points. The roasting of ten catties of animal feed is reckoned as one labor point, and the picking of fifteen catties of cotton is counted as eight labor points. (3) Remuneration for labor performed by children of both sexes is according to the same system. In the cooperative organization of auxiliary industry, such as cutting reeds from marshes, catching fish and shrimp from streams, and making sauces, individuals work and share the fruits of labor collectively according to the same system of remuneration based on labor points.[69]

Now women and children are able to see concretely how much they contribute economically to the family, as measured by wages or labor points they receive, compared to those received by the head of the family or to the total income of the family. Later, under the commune system, the children are fed and cared for by the commune, and each person receives his remuneration in kind and in wages directly from the commune administrators, no longer through the head of the family as previously done under the cooperatives. This effectively invalidates the traditional reprimands used by husbands and parents: "I feed you and you must listen to me"; "I have fed you and raised you and you must obey me." The subversive effect of this change on the structure of family status and authority based on age and sex differentiation cannot be ignored.

Here we would repeat that a deep-rooted tradition does not suddenly lose its force. One Communist report has stated:

> But, at the present, among the mutual-aid and cooperative organizations of agricultural production there is a widespread practice of giving women unequal pay for equal work with men. In a few mutual-aid organizations no labor points at all are entered into the record for women. In a large number of mutual-aid organizations the remuneration for women's labor is arbitrarily fixed as one-half that of a man's labor, regardless of the actual labor efficiency of the women. Some organizations nominally base the remuneration for women's labor upon record of work done and evaluation of labor points, but the number of labor points received by women are always somewhat below the actual labor efficiency of the women. . . .
>
> In Ch'eh Fang village of Yi county in Liaohsi Province some of the people were contemptuous of women's participation in production, regarding them as the "little worker," the "half-size worker," or remarking that "two of them cannot do the work of one [man]." As a consequence, few women participated in production. This year [1952], when the agricultural producers' cooperative was established, when women raised the question of equal pay for equal work at a meeting, many male cadres said: "Women may fool around with cooking, but they are no good for production work," or "If a man earns ten labor points in a day, a woman should earn less." At that meeting someone made the proposal that the recording of work done and the evaluation of the number of labor points should be based on actual results of labor regardless of sex, as, for example, the pulling of weeds by women and the cultivating work by men are about equal in the amount of energy exerted and in the actual result, so both cases should be rewarded with eight labor points each. Some male cadres refused to accept this argument. Failing to arrive at an agreement, both men and women went to work as an experiment. As a result, the male cadres were convinced and said, "Women's work in weeding is not any lighter than men's cultivating, and the two types of work should be rewarded with the same number of labor points." From then on, the principle of sex equality and the same pay for the same work has been implemented in that cooperative. Women in the village became enthusiastic in production, and mothers would say to the women's cadres, "Hurry up and solve the nursery problem so that I can enter into production." [70]

Similarly, there have been a large number of cases of discrimination against giving equal consideration to labor performed by children.[71] The people's commune in its present form may alter this discriminatory tradition by the egalitarian nature of its remuneration system of "free supplies" of food and other necessities of life, but this system is far from having been stabilized.

Fourth, the mobilization of women and children into collective agricultural production reduces the self-sufficiency of the family economy. This is shown concretely in the case of a mutual-aid team in the village of Wangnankou in Laiyang county of Shantung Province. This team was composed of 16 farm families which together possessed 311 mow of land (roughly 50 acres). There was a shortage of labor and 16 women were mobilized to work. "Since the women brought back material benefits in the form of labor points on an equal footing with men, the parents-in-law became pleased and began treating them with a greater measure of equality. The parents-in-law are now willing to see the home spinning and weaving stopped, and to buy cloth for the daughters-in-law the same as for other members of the family." [72]

Under guidance from the state, collectivized agriculture increasingly emphasizes the planting of high-yielding marketable crops best suited to a certain area, thus departing from the tradition of stressing home-consumption, self-sufficiency crops. For instance, a cooperative in Shansi Province reduced the varieties of crops from nineteen to eleven, devoting a large proportion of its land to corn, a high-yielding marketable item.[73] As the family no longer harvests the varieties of crops needed to sustain itself but must rely increasingly on the market, it ceases to be a self-contained unit of economic production and consumption. Family solidarity based on the economic factor is consequently reduced.

Fifth, the general character of collectivized agriculture and state-controlled enterprises is different from that of the family organization. These new organizations are not the products of biological relatedness, for membership is acquired only by the criteria of work capacity and is structured according to the need for work, not according to sex and age.[74] Hence the new pattern of economic organization not only tends to break down the traditional dominance of the family as a fundamental unit of production and its high degree of self-sufficiency, it also undermines the particularistic influence of the family.[75]

Industrialization has an additional disorganizing influence on the traditional family by providing employment and hence economic assistance for the women and the young to escape pressure from the family system of status and authority. Although in the pre-Communist period, modern factories in big cities supported young men and rebellious females deserting the old-style household, many young men and women and dissatisfied wives who left home at the beckoning of the new idealism of freedom and equality were forced to return home by the failure to find a livelihood. Industrialization developed at a slow pace, job opportunities were few, and most of the connections that might lead to jobs were in the hands of relatives who would almost invariably lead them not to a job in a factory but back home where they came from. The accelerated development of modern industries under the Communist regime makes a major difference in this respect in comparison to the pre-Communist period.

CHAPTER IX

The Shifting Center of Loyalty

The Family as the Center of Loyalty in Traditional Society

THE TRADITIONAL Chinese family organization structured on the principle of the Five Cardinal Relations, with its emphasis on the status system of age and sex differentiation, naturally lay heavy stress on loyalty between members of the family and to the family as a group. The central feature of traditional Chinese society as a whole was that the individual's loyalty toward the family transcended all his other social obligations and that the family was the determining factor in the total pattern of social organization.

The ties of affection as a basic factor of loyalty among members of the traditional family were so strongly developed that they dictated the values and outlook of social life for the individual. Thus, Liang Shu-ming wrote from the viewpoint of a traditional scholar:

> The life of a single individual is an incomplete life. A single man or a single woman can be counted only as half of a human being. There must be sexual relationship before a complete life starts. Following this come parents and children, elder brother, and younger brother. This is the so-called family. Beyond the family, social relationships bring about the tie between ruler and subjects, between friend and friend. Life exists in these relationships, and the family is the most fundamental of them by nature. The so-called Cardinal Relations center upon the relations of family which are natural relationships, for man holds closest to him what is closest by nature. Man normally rejoices over what is joyful to his loved ones, and grieves over what is grievous to them. Loved ones echo to each other physically, understand each other mentally, establish between themselves a sympathetic consonance and a mental and physical interdependence. This is affection. A beautiful and satisfying life is no other but the fulfillment of these relationships. On the contrary, the greatest misfortune of life is the lack of these relations. The widower, the widow, the orphan, the aged without children — these suffer the greatest

misfortunes of a normal life, and they are [traditionally] called the "inarticulates." They are so called because they have no loved ones to whom they can tell their stories of sickness, hardship, poverty, and misfortune. How different this is from the Western style which makes orphans out of children and makes lonely old people out of parents by having the children live apart from their parents; how different this is from the Western style which values not companionship but separation, and condones an unstable relationship of marriage.

For the Chinese, the family is the fountainhead of his life and the place which he regards as his final repose. It is extremely difficult to stabilize life except by the tie of the family. Life usually brings more grief than joy, but the family provides the sentiments of joy. To the Chinese people, the family provides consolation and encouragement, and practically performs the function of religion.[1]

Moreover, the principle of Cardinal Relations fixed the degree and depth of affection between family members according to an established scale based on the proximity of kinship. Thus the strongest affection was fostered between parents and children, and the next strongest between husband and wife; then came that between brothers, between brothers and sisters. Descending in the scale were affection between cousins, between uncles, nephews and nieces, between oneself and uncles' wives, between one's own wife and the wives of brothers, uncles, and other collaterals.

By this code, the strongest affection, that between parents and children, husband and wife, and brothers and sisters, embraced a circle that constituted the basic membership of the average family; one's affection for the more distant relatives such as grandparents, uncles, aunts, and cousins, and for the even more distantly related clansmen, was greater than one's affection for other members of society; and beyond the fringe of the kinship group lay people who were regarded with some degree of distrust and inimical interest. The family, the circle of relatives, and the clan constituted the irreplaceable warm spot of life in a harsh world. "Thinking of home" by sojourners in distant places was one of the most popular and moving themes in Chinese poetry for two thousand years. Perhaps only those who have experienced the traditional Chinese family life can fully appreciate the feeling in such well-known poetic lines as "A cup of dull liquor with home ten thousand *li* away." And perhaps only a traditional Chinese can be really overcome with joy when he meets a relative or a clansman in a distant place.

This is not to say that the traditional Chinese family made a picture of undiluted affection. We have seen that there were numerous sources of family conflict and tension. But loyalty to the family was nevertheless preserved by the dominance of the family in the individual's social and economic interest and by the classical requirement of self-sacrifice and forbearance for the interest of the group. As Liang wrote on this point:

> The principle of Cardinal Relations demands union and not separation among family members. But sometimes when it is not possible to unite, nor is it possible to separate, then each conflicting party exercises forbearance for the preservation of the group and lets the unresolved problem remain unresolved. In the actual situation, few can take the decisive step of separation [by leaving the family], and equally few can really practice the principles required for union, and eight or nine out of ten cases are those in which the family members just bear each other [in order to preserve the family as a group].[2]

The formula of compromise and self-sacrifice, not the definition or protection of the rights of the individual, traditionally preserved loyalty in the Chinese family in spite of disruptive factors. The standard line of the mediator of a family conflict was, "After all, we are all family members," and to a person threatening to take a conflict outside the family for settlement the popular exhortation was, "Family dirt should not be aired outside." The Confucian adage, "Brothers may fight within the house, but will join hands to resist insults from without," remained a valid description of the situation when the traditional family was strong.

Most important in the present context, the successful maintenance of the family as the center of the individual's loyalty requires the continued dominance of the family as an economic structure and as a unit of social interest — in other words, the continued operation of the traditional family which subordinates the role of the individual to the interest of the group; and we have seen that for the past half century the structural strength of the traditional family has been progressively weakened.

Increased Outside Contacts of the Young

In turning to loyalty as a basic element in the Chinese family we are shifting our focus essentially to a factor of family solidarity directly related to the conditioning of the young. From the preceding discussion we have seen that the converging forces of the family revolution increasingly broke down the traditional seclusion of the family members and confinement of their work and interest to family concerns, a practice which once served to exclude the development of competing centers of loyalty outside the family. It goes without saying that an inevitable result of the family revolution and its accompanying social changes was the steady increase of opportunity for youth to have contacts outside the family and therefore to be exposed to new influences which conflicted with traditional family loyalties.

In terms of factors already discussed we need only mention here the economic developments, the modernizing of education, and the increasing population mobility of the Republican period. All of these had profound effects on the attitudes of youth and acted to awaken the interest of the young in affairs and modes of thinking which diminished the traditional strength of family ties. Their effect was heightened by the dislocation of the war period, which forced millions of Chinese, the greater proportion of whom were young people, onto the roads and to distant parts of the country far from the centers of established family influence.

Another pre-Communist factor in the weakening of family loyalty was the growth of social and economic associations that absorbed an increasing proportion of the time and interest of the young. The traditional social order had few organizations for the young, especially women. Whereas the traditional fraternities and sororities were small in membership and did not steer the course of life away from the center of the family, the organizations for the young, ranging from clubs and societies to organizations of an economic and political nature, which developed in the modern period, imbued their members with an idealism inimical to the traditional order besides increasing their physical separation from family contact.

Here again, as we have seen, Communist accession to power gave added impetus to developments already under way. Large-scale Communist programs mobilizing the young for political, economic, and social activities have brought millions of young men and women, and even older children, into contact with new centers of ideology and interest that contradict the moral and organizational principles of the traditional family; and the nationalization and collectivization of economic life has progressively weakened traditional economic reliance upon the family as a factor in generating family loyalty.

More specifically, the development of modern education, which under Communism is a powerful factor undermining family loyalty, has been dramatically accelerated by the present government. The enrollment of students in higher education throughout the country under Communist rule showed a marked increase from the pre-Communist years; and under the policy of "opening school doors to workers and peasants" and the vigorous campaign to wipe out illiteracy, the enrollment of primary and middle schools, especially the former, has increased even more rapidly (see the accompanying table). Leisure-time and evening classes have appeared in growing numbers. Moreover, and of special importance, this kind of influence is now exerted on the very young as a result of women's participation in production and the accompanying development of nurseries. The weaning of the young child away from uninterrupted family care, supervision, and education at the most formative period deal a heavy blow to the traditional conception of the family as the center of one's life and one's loyalty. Under present conditions, when both parents work outside the home all day, the children are placed in nurseries and learn to become independent at the early age of five or six. For the wives there is the choice of giving up work and taking care of the children or continuing to work and letting outside contacts claim the loyalty of the children, and economic and political pressure dictate the latter.

The organization of the young for political, social, and economic activities is far more extensive under the Communist regime than ever before. Some idea of the organization of youth has been noted before. Organizational efforts are also being vigorously pushed in the age group below youth. The Young Pioneers, which organizes children 9 to 14 years of age, claimed a national membership of 5,200,000 in 1952 and 10,000,000 in 1956. Together with the 5,000,000 members in 1952 and 20,000,000 in 1956 of the New Democratic Youth League, which organizes young men and women 15 to 25, the total membership of the organized young reached 10,200,000 in 1952 and 30,000,000 in 1956. Youth of the urban business class form only a minority of the membership, as students constituted only 11 per cent of the total membership of the New Democratic Youth League in 1952.[3] Although no data on the class composition of Youth League membership is available after 1952, the continued expansion of the League among workers and peasants indicates a probable increase of their percentage in League membership since then. Every youth organization serves to dilute the traditional loyalty toward the family.

The Development of Individualism

Extensive outside contacts are, of course, not necessarily destructive to family loyalty unless accompanied by the inculcation into the individual's mind of the acceptance of a new pattern of social life that does

TABLE 1

Number of Students Enrolled in Modern Schools in Continental China, 1946–1956

Types of educational institutions	1946	1949	1950	1951	1952	1954	1956
Universities, colleges, normal colleges, other institutions of higher learning	129,366	130,058	143,267	175,284	219,750	......[a]	400,000
Middle schools and institutions of similar standing	1,878,523	1,271,342	1,576,377	2,007,781	3,078,826	3,580,000	5,000,000 (estimate)
Elementary schools and institutions of similar standing	23,683,492	24,391,033	28,923,988	43,173,540	49,034,081	51,190,000	57,000,000 (estimate)
TOTAL	25,691,351	25,792,433	30,643,632	45,356,605	52,332,657	......[a]	62,400,000

Source: *Jen-min Chiao-yü Yüeh-k'an* (People's Education Monthly), October 1952, p. 6; *Jen-min jih-pao* (People's Daily), July 23, 1955, p. 3; New China News Agency, August 31, 1956.
[a] Figures not available.

not rely upon the family as a central factor. Chinese immigrants in the United States have enjoyed extensive contacts with another culture and have lived far apart from their families for protracted periods, but the members of the first generation still preserve strong family loyalty, for they cling to the ideology of the traditional social pattern. The youth of changing modern China, by contrast, have been increasingly susceptible to a new ideology incompatible with the organizational principle and value standard of the traditional family.

An outstanding element in the new ideology is the Western concept of individualism, which runs directly counter to the spirit of the traditional Chinese family and is incompatible with the traditional loyalty devoted to it. Traditional Chinese moral standards demanded not merely self-sacrifice from the individual but also that he take responsibility for self-cultivation according to Confucian ethics and try to find the solution for all domestic disharmonies in his own efforts at self-perfection. Self-cultivation, the basic theme of Confucian ethics traditionally inculcated in the child's mind from an early age, did not seek a solution to social conflict in defining, limiting, and guaranteeing the rights and interests of the individual or in the balance of power and interests between individuals. It sought the solution from the self-sacrifice of the individual for the preservation of the group. And this responsibility of self-sacrifice fell heavily on the young and on the women. The requirements of *hsiao, ti,* and *ching-chieh* (filial submission of the children, fraternal subordination of the younger brother, and chastity of the women) formed a much greater proportion of traditional moral teachings than the obligations placed upon the head of the family, the older generation, and the men.

Western individualism as a social ideal therefore did not have much attraction for the traditional Chinese mind. Individualism as a philosophy has been a subject of protracted polemics from the days of the New Culture Movement of 1917 down to the present; and it is now the object of renewed condemnation from Communist ideology as a legacy of bourgeois culture. But there is little doubt that the greater recognition of individual rights and interests under the slogan of freedom and equality has had strong appeal for the long oppressed young men and women and has acted as a fermenting agent for China's modern revolutions, particularly the family revolution. Increased extra-familial contacts, reduced control of the family over the individual, and the development of new organizations and new centers of interest based upon the defined share of the individual's rights and privileges have all contributed to the spreading influence of the concept of individualism as a guiding principle for one's social life during the past half century.

That the majority of Chinese probably still find Western individualism a violation of their sense of moral responsibility is suggested by the number of rural Communist leaders who have resisted the idea of divorce and the claim of property rights by divorced women. But there is little doubt that the Western concept of individualism has made deep inroads on the minds of the modern intelligentsia who have been leaders in the movement towards social change. One of the many situations reflecting this has been the popular condemnation of "familism and clannism" over the past three or four decades.

Grounds for that condemnation have been many. One was that the full development of an individual's abilities and initiative was obstructed by the system of "familism and clannism." A further argument was that the individual's interests and rights must find full development in some other organizational context than the old familially oriented pattern. Spurred by the influence of nationalism and idealism for a "new society," the individual increasingly identifies his interests and rights with that of the state and the mass society, no longer solely with that of the family and clan. It is characteristic of an age of revolution that, when the established institutional framework of society fails to hold its ground against antagonistic influences, the individual is inclined to review his own position in reference groups in accordance with new ideological orientations. It was in the midst of such a revolutionary situation that individualism rapidly expanded its influence in modern China.

Control of the nation by Communist leadership has inevitably brought strong condemnation of individualism as "undisciplined liberalism" and a product of "decadent capitalism." But the present urge toward state collectivism calls upon the individual to sacrifice for a group far different from the family; and, whatever its ultimate fate under the Communist regime, individualism has already performed the function of alienating the individual from family loyalty.

The State as the New Center of Loyalty

In China's modern scene, aside from individualism based on the ideas of individual freedom and equality, there has been probably no more powerful ideological factor subversive to family loyalty than the call of nationalism. Under its pressure all modern Chinese reformers have tried to shift the center of loyalty from the family to the state.

K'ang Yu-wei in his *Ta T'ung Shu* (The Great Commonwealth) pointed out the incompatibility between family loyalty and national interest. Sun Yat-sen in his *San-min Chu-i* (Three People's Principles) exhorted his countrymen to broaden familism to nationalism by widening the center of loyalty from the family to the nation. The defeats China had suffered from foreign powers made the adoption of nationalism and patriotism a matter of urgent necessity. The Japanese invasion and the ensuing eight years of devastating war extended the influence of nationalism from the intelligentsia to other classes of the population.

The state as a morally higher center of loyalty had been an established factor in the modern trend of social, economic, and political events prior to the rise of the Communist regime, but in no previous period has the interest of the state and its machinery been more sharply defined and loyalty to it more drastically demanded than under the Communist rule. By propaganda, indoctrination, and pressure from the law the requirement of loyalty to the state and "the people" above everything else is being systematically forced into the consciousness of the population.

The effort to focus loyalty upon the state and its machinery is seen in many of the propaganda documents, giving evidence of benefits reaped by individuals who have chosen the state and its policies as the object of personal devotion. Thus, when a humble worker is elevated to a prominent position, when a brutally treated laborer sees his boss arrested, when a landless peasant gets free land, when an oppressed widow is able to remarry through enforcement of the new Marriage Law, when a slave-girl gains freedom from her purchaser, when a mistreated underdog sees the vindication of justice, the recitation inevitably ends with the uniform statement from the hero of the story: "How grateful I am to the Communist Party!" or "I have Chairman Mao to thank for this!" or " I wouldn't have this day if it were not for the Communist Party!" Whether such remarks are actually uttered by the individual or are attributed to him by the Communist script writer seems immaterial. Two things are clear. One is that the individual benefiting by the action of the regime is naturally grateful to the benefactor, and the other is that it is the intention of official propaganda to encourage the feeling of gratitude, and therefore loyalty, to the state.

Significant is the new moral value being set up by the political movement requiring individuals specifically to put the state above the family as an object of loyalty. Should any member of the family commit an offense against the state, it is one's new duty to expose that member to the government. Failing to do so is to commit the error of "sentimentalism," or "inability to break through personal feelings and face-saving," and this may bring punishment by law on the ground of knowingly harboring criminals. In the first decade of Communist administration of the country successive popular campaigns and movements have brought sharply to the people's attention this new requirement of regarding the state as the supreme object of loyalty. In the movement of punishing landlords and local bullies, in the movement of suppressing counterrevolutionaries, in the Three-Anti and the Five-Anti campaigns * against corrupt officials and "law-breaking" businessmen, high tension was created and emotional pressure exerted to compel individuals to expose any family member who had broken the Communist law and to discourage any effort to shield such a member.

To effect such a change in the object of personal loyalty and affection is of course difficult. To accomplish it, communism employs mass meetings and propaganda campaigns of great emotional tension, highlighted by the confessions of individuals. The individual and the group are thrown into tortuous emotional convulsions in the process of "thought struggle" and "thought remoulding."

During the Five-Anti movement in 1952 in Shanghai over 600 members of the New Democratic Youth League in Futan University were pressured into going home to persuade family members to confess their crimes. Many of the young men and women in the League pledged: "I am going to persuade my father to confess. Should he refuse, I will expose him to the government." As a result of their exemplary actions and campaigning, 1,146 other men and women students in that university also went home to do persuasion work.[4] The Communists alleged that the vast majority of businessmen in Shanghai and other cities had committed some degree of offense against the state — bribing officials, evasion of taxes, theft of public property, theft of state economic secrets, or cheating on government contracts. To extract confessions from such a large number of alleged lawbreakers the party enlisted young people, and while this movement was going on mobilization meetings were held in practically every school, every factory, and every organized group in the large cities throughout the country. The violence done Chinese family

* The Three-Anti campaign was against bureaucratism, receiving bribes, and wasting public funds. The Five-Anti campaign was against evasion of taxes, theft of state economic information, bribery, cheating on state contracts, and theft of state property.

traditions by communism is dramatically illustrated by reports in the official press.

One recalls that when Confucius was asked, "Should the son serve as witness against the father who has stolen a sheep?" the Master's reply was, "The son shields the father, and the father shields the son." [5] Chinese history records examples of sons pardoned for killing their parents' murderer because they were practicing filial piety, and even in the modern period the murderer of the Shantung warlord, Chang Chung-ch'ang, was pardoned by the Kuomintang government because he was avenging his father's death. It is in such a context of loyalty to parents which was held above loyalty to the law of the state that one must put the conflict inspired by Communist ideology which is typified in the case of a college student, Li Kuo-hsin, who wrote:

> My father was a bigwig in the feudalistic secret societies. Due to sup-port from the secret societies and due to his shrewdness, he was for nine years the head of Hochiang subdistrict. In March 1950 he participated in a rebellion and fled from home. At first I blamed the government for lack of understanding: my father had been forced into action by bandits, and the government was unjustly accusing him of being the leader of rebel-lious bandits. After repeated "study" (indoctrination) I finally came to see many things wrong with father. Still I did not recognize his serious crimes and the reasons for his rebellion.
>
> I joined the New Democratic Youth League. The education I received from the League helped me to take a big step forward in the improve-ment of my thought. I was deeply moved by the example of a comrade who correctly dealt with the problem of his reactionary father. With this inspiration, I began to analyze my father's rebellion. After a long search I found out the reasons for his rebellion. First, he had embezzled several thousand catties of government rice, and he was afraid of prosecution. Second, he had ignored three summonses from the local government. Thus I came to recognize that his rebellion was not the result of force by bandits but a systematic and premeditated action against the revolution and against the people.
>
> After that my attitude towards my father began to change from sym-pathy to hatred. In discussion meetings of the cell I brought up my father's counterrevolutionary activities, his embezzlement of the people's wealth, his taking of a concubine in Chengtu. I thoroughly exposed these facts, decidedly and unemotionally criticized them, thus further deepen-ing my hatred for him.
>
> I was told that the government demanded that the family look for my father. I firmly decided to take up the duty of locating him. I first con-tacted the responsible comrades in the local armed forces and planned the

work together with them. I went to my relatives for information, but to
no avail. I returned home with the armed comrades and tried to get information from mother. My mother told me that a relative had seen my
father in Siaopeichieh in Kwanghan county. I started out to find him.
When I finally arrived it was six o'clock, but because of the urgency of
the matter I did not stop to rest. Searching inside and outside the town,
I finally found him in a small teahouse.

He was sitting alone. His shrunken and pale appearance almost made
me fail to recognize him. But he recognized me. I was so happy. Was not
that my father? My heart started to beat fast, but I calmed myself. With
tears in his eyes my father told me, "Since I parted from your brothers
and sister, I have had to depend entirely on practicing medicine for a
living. Before September, business was not bad, but after that there was
hardly any business. Hunger, cold, and sickness almost took my life. For-
tunately, the owner of a medicine store next door gave me a pot of char-
coal fire and some money. The owner is willing to recomend me to the
union of Chinese doctors in Kwanghan. If I join the union, I'll have a
practicing certificate, and I can practice anywhere without restriction."

My father and I talked till late at night. We entered the city and had
dinner together. Before parting, he told me, "When you get home, be
sure to bring me some money."

When I returned to the hotel I fell into a heart-rending state. I ran a
high fever, my body trembled; I turned and tossed in bed but could not
sleep. New and old thoughts were struggling within me. I pitied my
father. All alone here, he had suddenly met his own child, and how
eagerly he was pinning his hopes on me. How could I have him taken
back to be shot? On the other hand, still without repentance, he continued
to be an enemy of the people. He was entirely selfish, only emphasizing
his own suffering, disregarding the suffering of others. . . .

Though he was hateable, he was my own father. I could not be severe
and cold, severing myself from sentiment. Wouldn't it be all right if I
went home and told people that I had gone to Kwanghan and had failed
to find my father?

That would not do. I would save my father, a local bully, a landlord,
but indirectly I would become a counterrevolutionist. I thought of getting
some poison and forcing him to take it. But this wouldn't do either. I
was sympathizing with him. I was forgetting that I was a youth of new
China, a member of the League.

After a night of conflict I finally shattered my incorrect thoughts and I
consolidated myself on the principle of "no compromise in revolution, and
no sentimentalism in struggle." I reaffirmed my stand.

I went to the police bureau and informed the responsible comrade.
Then I went to my father and demanded that he recant his past and reform. He said, "How could you do this to me?" and tried to escape by

saying that he was going to eat. By that time the armed comrades were already at the door. My father had no choice but to pretend to be willing to reform, and gave himself up.

He was taken to the county government of Kwanghan. I waited until he wrote out his repentance and confession before starting back to Chengtu. He was imprisoned in Kwanghan and later was sent back to Hwayang county by armed guards. My duty was at last done. I felt lighthearted; I was happy, for I had rid the people of a dangerous character.[6]

Cases like this one show that a new answer has been given to the old Confucian paradox. If loyalty in the parent-child relationship, so strongly guarded by filial piety and by law for centuries past, can be swept aside by the violent storm of Communist revolution, loyalty toward other family members is even more surely threatened. Although the traditional relationship between Chinese husband and wife was not so strong as that in Western culture, it was, nevertheless, a significant force in a system where women's occupations were undeveloped and where women enjoyed few property rights. In the traditional Chinese family organization the position of the husband, the only one from whom a wife could expect affection, and the strongly enforced mores of chastity conditioned her to put loyalty to her husband above everything else. There is a long tradition of Chinese wives who committed suicide when the husband died, as a demonstration of perfect loyalty and the conviction that it was better for a wife to go to heaven with her husband than go on living alone on earth. There is deep signficance, then, in this story from a Communist report:

Ou Hsiu-mei was a peasant woman in a village in Lien county in the northern part of Kwaungtung Province. She was married very young through a matchmaker to Liang Wen-chiu. Liang was a local political boss, having been the chief of a *chia* unit [a local administrative unit of one or more villages] under the Kuomintang regime, and he extorted the villagers through conscription, bribery, and other channels. Ou did not like this, but her thought was conditioned by the traditional advice to "follow a chicken when married to a chicken and follow a dog when married to a dog." After the establishment of the Communist regime, Liang went into the hills as a subleader in anti-Communist armed activities. After that, villagers ceased to communicate with her. Suffering from isolation and seeing that others whose husbands served in the Communist army had the help of neighbors in working the fields, she began to envy others and feel ashamed of herself. Meanwhile, a few party cadres, seeing that she originated from a poor family, tried to indoctrinate her.

Liang sometimes returned home from the hills secretly. Ou used the opportunity to talk to him: "What future do you have by working in the anti-Communist forces? There is still time for you to turn back, and the people's government will let you redeem your crime by making contributions to the revolution." But Liang replied, "Chiang Kai-shek will soon come back and better days will not be far off. If you tell the villagers that, it will help." She had doubts about this, but fear made her keep silent.

Women members among the village cadres and leaders of the peasants' association came to talk to her. "If millions of Chiang Kai-shek's troops have been wiped out, what chance will your husband have? One day he will be caught and shot, and then you will be a bandit's widow." Again they said to her, "You were a poor child by origin, and the victims of your husband are all poverty-stricken peasants like yourself. If you will help catch your husband, ridding the people of a dangerous character, you will win great merit, and both the people and the government will respect you and love you, and you will gain a new life. Do you want to come on the side of the people, or do you wish to follow the road to death with your husband?"

She could not sleep at night, those words turning over and over in her mind. Close to the Chinese New Year's Eve she made up her mind and went to the peasants' association to promise that she would catch her husband inside of one month.

She thought of a plot whereby she could trick her husband into being captured. When Liang came home on New Year's eve, she told him, "The present situation is tense, sentinels are posted all over the place, searching all suspected homes. Return on the second night of the New Year and hide at the foot of the hill. I will bring you some food and liquor." After he left she hastened to the peasants' association and informed them of her plan.

At the appointed time she took a basket of food and went to the foot of the hill. Liang was waiting and started to gorge himself. But he was already in the midst of soldiers who were closing in from all directions in the dark. One soldier carelessly flashed his flashlight. Liang immediately knew something was up. He threw down his chopsticks and bowl and started to run. Ou wrapped her arms around him but Liang pushed her and kicked her. The soldiers closed in with torches, lighting up the whole hillside. Liang jumped into a quagmire pond, hid himself under the surface, leaving only his nose out to breathe. After a tiresome search, one soldier pushed a stick into the mire and by chance poked him in the head. Involuntarily he screamed in pain, and was caught.

At the mass trial Ou accused Liang of his crime. She said she did not want to be the wife of a bandit any longer. She demanded that the government shoot him, and said she would eternally follow the Communist Party. Her name soon spread to the whole county. On March 30, 1951, at the county meeting of peasants' representatives, and at the meeting of the evaluation of merits in anti-bandit campaigns, she was elected anti-bandit hero, special class.[7]

When the Three-Anti and the Five-Anti movements swung into high gear in the cities throughout the country in 1952, there were widespread campaigns in urban areas to mobilize wives to persuade their hubsands to confess their crimes and to expose these crimes to the government should the husbands remain unregenerated. In the coal-mining area of Mentoukou, west of Peking, where the Committee on Wives actively led the workers' wives to participate in the Three-Anti movement, according to statistical information in February 1952, twenty-three wives had succeeded in persuading their husbands to confess their crimes, and over three hundred cases of corruption were uncovered through the grapevine of the workers' wives.[8] The psychological process in such a transference of loyalty is illustrated in the case of Chiang Shu-k'un, a woman worker in a tobacco factory, who pushed her husband into confession.

> The case took place in the interior town of Paoting of Hopei Province in North China. Chiang's husband, Ho, was an accountant in the printing plant of the provincial Bureau of Revenue of Hopei which printed tax stamps. Ho stole a large amount of newly printed tax stamps and hid them under the bed for over a year, waiting to dispose of them. The theft of the stamps aroused a sensation in the printing plant, but the thief was not discovered.
>
> Chiang discovered the stamps when the Three-Anti movement was sweeping the country in 1952. She recalled her unhappy childhood and marriage and how the State Tobacco Factory where she worked was now like a second home. Cadres and workers in the factory had helped her in learning new skills. She worked hard in literacy class. She was a model worker, a member of the New Democratic Youth League, and a member of the Communist Party.
>
> Now she knew that Ho was no longer her husband but a thief who stole state property. If she spared him, she would be ungrateful to the state and to the party. She reported him, and he was arrested on Chinese New Year's Day. This made Chiang very happy and did not spoil her New Year's holiday. The news of Chiang's exposing her husband served as encouragement to all the women workers in the factory, and at the mobilization meeting of the Three-Anti movement, a flower of honor was pinned on her.[9]

Since we have selected our illustrations on the basis of the loyalty demanded in the most important categories of traditional kinship relations, we must touch upon the loyalty between brothers and between brothers and sisters. The traditional social order placed heavy requirements of fraternal loyalty on the individual, especially on the younger brother, and the popular Chinese phrase "cooperation be-

tween hands and feet in worries and in difficulties" is a realistic reference to the traditional concept of fraternal relationship. Two cases
given emphasis in the Communist press illustrate the present mood.

Hun Yi-ch'un, head of the *Chieh-fang Jih-pao* publishing company
in Shanghai, became concerned when his elder sister was being
"struggled" against by the peasants' association in her town as a landlord and a local bully. Hun utilized his important status as the head
of an official regional newspaper to write to various official organs
concerned with the case, saying that his sister was a good person, a
widow who relied on the land for livelihood and not for exploitation,
and that the struggle against her was unjust. After investigation,
superior party organs, rejecting his protest, stated: "Hun in the land
reform failed to make a demarcation between friend and foe, lost his
proper stand, and protected the landlord." [10]

Yu Ch'uan-ming was a Communist Party member, a professor of
Western languages in Peking University, and the chief of the executive office of the Peking Municipal Committee of the All-China Union
of Educational Workers. He had an elder brother who was being
"struggled" against as a landlord, local bully, and secret agent for
the Kuomintang, allegedly having killed seventy to eighty Communist
political workers. Yu tried to protect his elder brother by advising him
to hide his property and by writing to local government organizations
for help. As a result, Yu was removed from party membership in
order to "preserve the purity of the party ranks." The party's charge
against Yu included denunciation of him as a "disloyal element to
the proletarian class who stole his way into the party." In Yu's own
open statement of self-criticism, he said, "My failure to recognize my
own error is due entirely to. . . my inability to sever thoroughly the
feudalistic fraternal sentiments and come over to the stand of the
party." [11]

One may well ask whether the drastic shift in the center of loyalty
away from the family, a shift which is being motivated by terror and
emotional tension generated in a succession of high-pressure political
movements, can possibly be permanent. As the Communist regime con-
solidates its power and begins to settle down to an established political
and social order, it may relax some of its pressures. Moreover, a
complete breakdown of family solidarity would hardly be conducive
to the social and economic order the Communists are trying to establish; and, in fact, few cases such as presented here have been reported in the Communist press since 1953. We would judge that in
the long run the degree of the transfer away from the family to the

state and to extra-familial organizations will be determined not by campaigns and exhortation but by the success or failure of communism in actual practice in assuming many of the social and economic functions of the traditional Chinese family.

CHAPTER X

Secularization of the Family Institution

Up to this point we have considered elements in Chinese family structure and relationships which in the main have their counterparts in varying degrees of strength in Western society. The unique, and possibly most basic, feature of the traditional Chinese family was its sacred character. In a variety of forms, the religious element was elaborately and inseparably woven into the fabric of the family institution; and it helps to explain why the disruptive factors, such as the excessive exercise of authority by the male and senior family members, failed in the past to shake the foundation of the family. When under strain from the authoritarian family structure and buffeted by frequent domestic conflicts, the individual tended to drift away from the family, and interdependence of utilitarian interests and the exigency of a realistic situation were not sufficient to tie him firmly to the family, the sacred concepts and symbols of the unity of the family lifted his interest and feelings above himself and focused them on the group. Thus also, especially in the traditional concept of marriage based on the perpetuation of the ancestral lineage, the ancestors religiously symbolized the collective existence of the family group, a psychological process which explains why many an unjustly treated mother in the traditional family who contemplated leaving her husband's home stopped short of action at the sight of her son playing in front of the ancestral altar.

One reason for the weakening of the traditional Chinese family has been the rise of skepticism toward that institution. Discussing and doubting the fundamental soundness of an institution as the means of meeting the problems and needs of social life is the beginning of the operation of a highly subversive influence, for in skeptical discussion there lurks an alternative that may threaten to replace the existing institution.

In the traditional Chinese social order, the sacred character of the family institution imposed a deterministic view toward it, admitted no discussion of its soundness as an institution, and tolerated no suggestion of alternatives. As in other social institutions, it enforced a dogma. A wife might blame her unhappiness on her husband's or mother-in-law's wickedness, and perhaps lament her own ill fate, but she never thought to blame the institutional arrangement of traditional family life as the cause of her sorrows. If extremely mistreated, she might commit suicide, but in so doing she would still be following the path marked out for her by the institution without questioning the theoretical soundness of traditional family relationships. Members of a community witnessing or discussing the occasional brutal treatment of a daughter-in-law tended to view the case from the standpoint of personality deviation, not from the soundness of the family institution itself.

The impact of Western science on China, which inevitably inspired skepticism, with its implication of alternatives for ancient learning and ancient institutions, has steadily increased since the 1920's. From the beginning of the modern period the young educated generation has been encouraged to penetrate through the once awesome, sacred character of the traditional family in an effort to assess its fitness and adequacy in meeting modern needs. Guiding their course of skeptical criticism has been the logic and methodology of modern science, which are hardly reconcilable with the religious factors lending a sacred character to the family institution. The modern mood has, if anything, been even more encouraged under communism.

The primary factor in lending a sacred character to the traditional family was the cult of ancestor worship, vividly demonstrated in traditional residential homes in South China. There the ancestral altar in the main hall, the general dimness of the place, and the rows of golden ancestor tablets, darkened by incense smoke and reflecting the eerie light from the flickering sacrificial lamp, created a sacred atmosphere in the family dwelling, inspiring awe in the children. The constant reminder of the relationship between the living and the dead, between the existing family and the spirits of its creators, constituted a major function of ancestor worship which imposed a sense of sacredness on the family as an institution. The principles, inspired sentiments, symbols, and rituals of ancestor worship assured a religious veneration for the departed ones.

Sharing the sacred veneration for the dead, in a sense, were the old people in the family, who resembled the ancestors in having performed the sacred function of creating and perpetuating the family lineage. Thus an elderly head of the family was sometimes addressed as *lao tsu-chung* (the old ancestor) as a form of flattery (the matriarch in "The Dream of the Red Chamber," for example, was thus addressed), and the prestige and authority of the elders possessed a sacred character. The one insult the traditional Chinese would not tolerate was any slighting reference to parents or ancestors; and the destruction of the graves of other people's ancestors was punishable by traditional Chinese law. In this connection it is significant that Communist law gives no special protection to graves. Presumably, with traditional concepts still existing in the minds of a large number of local cadres, offenders against the old law might be punished, but the formal legal ground for such punishment would be violation of private property, not sacrilege against a social institution, which is contrary to the atheistic view of Communist ideology.

For two or three decades now the strength of ancestor worship has been waning rapidly among Chinese urban intellectuals, for Western values, dominated by science and materialism, repudiate ancestor worship as a part of popular superstition. A large number of the modern educated elements no longer regularly performed the ancestor worship rituals, and those who still did regarded the ceremony as a formalistic act without the traditional attitude of sincere veneration.

In the Communist movement the note of anti-superstition is even more uncompromising than it has been in other social movements, and ancestor worship is unequivocally regarded as a superstitious act. On the traditional duty to have children as a part of ancestor worship, the opinion of a Communist court was expressed thus: "Some people just do not understand this. They regard it as an extremely grave matter to be without offspring to continue the sacrifice and the burning of incense for the ancestors. Actually, what good will it do the dead ancestors to have incense burning continued, and what does it matter to them if incense burning is discontinued? This is a kind of nonsensical, superstitious thought, and it is incorrect." [1] This is not only the attitude of the Communist court, but it also reflects the pre-Communist attitude of the agnostic younger generation of urban intelligentsia who came under the influence of modern science and materialism in modern schools. The difference is that in the pre-Communist period this attitude was not so sharply defined, not so much a conscious guide for action, and was seldom expressed in such undisguised terms by a court as a criterion for the settlement of problems of kinship relations. It would be incongruous to see a Communist stemming from the urban intelligentsia performing traditional rituals before an ancestral shrine.

The institutional framework of traditional Chinese society was characterized by the prominence of *li,* which we may translate as ritualism, denoting a *system of semi-formal norms of behavior* in all basic situations of social life. Although the family institution relied no less on *li* as an operational factor than on other institutions, *li* as a strategic component of traditional Chinese culture has remained scientifically unexplored. Here we would only point out the sacred character of ritualism so far as it concerns the family institution, and its change in the modern period.

Ritualism as the acting out according to prescribed procedures of what was considered the ideal pattern of social relations served to focus the individual's attention toward an external situation and therefore performed an important function in the integration of the family. While rituals were present in almost every aspect of the traditional family, they were particularly prominent in the critical events of birth, marriage, and death of family members. The religious element was present in the ritualistic performances for all such critical events that marked the stages in the life cycle for both the family and the individual members. The sacred character thus injected into such events inspired awe and respect for the family institution.

The sacred nature and the feeling of fatefulness in the traditional marriage ceremony has been noted previously. The religious element permeated the rituals attending the birth of a new family member, especially the first son, when rites were performed to thank the ancestral spirits and the gods for the blessed event. The exact time of the birth, the year, month, day, and hour of the arrival, was carefully noted down and interpreted in the light of the magical belief that the time of birth foretold the future luck or misfortune not merely of the child but also of those related to him. Ceremonial feasts were given and religious rites performed when the baby reached the age of one month and one year, celebrating the child's survival and thanking the gods and spirits for their auspicious influence. Thus the earthly event of birth was turned into a sacred occasion in an effort to generate a serious attitude among the family members toward adding a new member to the group by expressing hope for his future and his relation to the group and publicly demonstrating this attitude to the wider kinship circle.

Death was intimately related to the development of mysticism and religious beliefs from earliest times. More than any other ritual, mortuary rites served to impart a sacred nature to the family institution, for they were rigidly prescribed and most elaborate, lest any abbreviation or error bring anger and retaliation from the spirit of the dead. Their psychological effect can be judged from the experience of an American girl who had married a Chinese and who, when she went to her husband's interior village upon her father-in-law's death, was completely mystified and exhausted after going through rites which lasted forty-nine days — as required by tradition for a well-to-do family. A traditional Chinese going through the same experience would inevitably have been filled with awe for the supernatural significance of critical events connected with family life. Moreover, such rituals were also performed on the death anniversary of a family member as a part of the cult of ancestor worship to perpetuate that feeling and reinforce the impression of the family as an organization of the living under the blessing, guidance, and surveillance of the spirits of the dead.

For the modern educated Chinese, knowledge of and respect for the ritualistic aspect of the family has been drastically reduced for the past three decades. The New Culture Movement that started in 1917 and subsequent social movements regarded ritualism as the leading source of the harsh features, misery, and backwardness of traditional Chinese society; and the anti-superstition movement directed against ancestor worship attacked all traditional religious rituals. The modern Chinese intellectuals who still continue to perform the rituals do so to please or appease insistent parents or other members of the older generation, and not from personal acceptance of the doctrine of ritualism. It seems certain that, so far as the Chinese intellectual is concerned, there were sufficiently powerful influences some years before the advent of communism to assure that sacred rituals would disappear from family life with the dying of the older generation.

Under Communist rule the trend toward secularization is spreading slowly from the modern urban intelligentsia to other segments of the population. The Communists are making no systematic effort to suppress the performance of old rituals, but they identify traditional ritualism as a vestige of the "feudalistic culture," and the social atmosphere being created discriminates against traditional ritualism in general. The Communist anti-superstition movement adds strength to this development owing to the presence of the religious element in a large number of the old rituals.

Thus the already marked trend toward simplifying rituals concerned with critical events in family life is accelerated by the Communists; and the new marriage ceremony has dropped the religious rites, including the consultation of the oracle which gave the traditional marriage a sacred, predetermined character. Under Communist rule there is strong discouragement of elaborate funerals, discouragement which cannot remove the mysticism and religious sentiment about death but does reduce the sacred nature of death as a public event, which once had the function of confirming the unity of the family weakened by a member's death. The birth of a baby and the birthdates of old family members are likewise being increasingly treated as common secular events stripped of the ritualism and religious content which traditionally served to accentuate the significance of such events for the integration of the family group.

In view of the official Communist hostility toward private wealth and the drive against superstition it seems plain that few would now dare to continue the performance of old rituals with any degree of elaborateness on the occasions of birth, marriage, or death; and one can imagine the effect of present secularizing influences concerning the family institution on the minds of the some thirty million members of the Young Pioneers and the New Democratic Youth League who will mature into leadership in the next adult generation.

Another of the significant Chinese institutions associated with the family are the traditional festivals, which before the extensive development of urban commercialized recreation during the past half century were the major form of family recreation. Their importance lay not only in the fact that the entire family participated, thus emphasizing the family as a center of life and confirming its solidarity through periodically reconvening all the members, but also in their sacred character; for most of the traditional festivals were organized around a supernatural idea, a saint, a god, a spirit, or a supernatural legend, and they were celebrated with religious rites.

The Ch'ing Ming on the third day of the third month (for cleaning and repairing the ancestors' graves), the Dragon Boat Racing Festival on the fifth day of the fifth month, the Girls' Festival on the seventh day of the seventh month (for anticipating a happy marriage), and the Moon Festival on the fifteenth day of the eighth month (celebrating the autumn harvest) are examples of such events organized around supernatural ideas. The Chinese New Year holiday, although based on the calendar, was traditionally replete with religious rites. All such festivals were used as occasions for family reunion, and members of the family working or living away felt obligated to come home and celebrate with the family if it was humanly possible; for, whatever the nature of recreation and pleasure involved, the supernatural connotation and rituals that characterized these events inspired in the individual a sacred feeling toward the family institution.

Again, the change in this aspect of Chinese family life was started by the urban intellectuals, for whom festivals came to have less and less sacred meaning. In the modern period there has been a steady increase in the number of families who no longer celebrate many of the traditional festivals; and modern educated girls have ignored the Girls' Festival as they have come to believe in romantic love and not in predestined wedlock. But for the common people the traditional festivals have continued to be important — despite the development of commercialized recreation which offers keen competition and the development of the new system of memorial days based upon personalities and events of modern political and social significance which, claiming increasing public attention and interest, are totally devoid of any sacred significance to the family institution.

Under the Communist regime, no direct effort has been made to discourage the continued celebration of traditional festivals, except some of the highly superstitious ones like the community celebration of the birthday of a certain god. But the rapid development of new forms of group recreation, like singing, folk dancing, and community stage plays, together with mass mobilization for the celebration of a new set of memorial days of secular, social, and political character, tend to reduce the importance of traditional festivals.

It can be readily seen even from the foregoing brief discussion that the secularizing influence of the whole modern period has inevitably affected the traditionally strong Chinese allegiance to the family and the strength of the old system of family status and authority. The family as an institution for effective integration and control over individuals is being replaced by a less stable family organization, governed by the legal mechanism of the state and the secular forces of social and economic life.

However, even under Communist pressure, the trend toward secularization is developing only gradually. A part of the concept in ancestor worship is the belief that the soul of the dead must return to the home district to enjoy sacrifices offered by the offspring in order to avoid the tragedy of causing the soul to wander homelessly, a belief which led the traditional Chinese to live near home and to die at home if possible. In spite of the anti-superstition movement the Communists had difficulty in 1955 in mobilizing peasants in Shantung Province to migrate to the Amur Region partly because of the popular fear that, once migrated to that far-off territory, the soul of the dead would be prevented from returning to the old homeland by the mountain barrier of Shan Hai Kuan which divides China proper from Manchuria. It was only after vigorous persuasion that a substantial number of peasants changed their minds and migrated.[2] Religious attitudes and beliefs, unlike the economic and political structure, cannot be forcibly changed in a short time by a revolution.

CHAPTER XI

Disorganization of the Clan

THE DOMINANCE of the clan organization in Chinese village life has been noted by many observers. Composed of several hundred to upward of ten thousand members living mostly in the same community, the clan has traditionally provided the numerical base for a variety of collective social and economic functions for its members, impossible for relatively small individual families to perform. It may be said that the Chinese family derived much of its traditional social and economic importance from its membership in the numerically large clan organization.

As to the extent of the clan's influence, one needs only to note that in North China a large proportion of the villages bear clan surnames. Names like Wangchiats'un (the village of the Wang family) or Lichiats'un (the village of the Li family) represents the stereotype for the names of Chinese villages. In South China, even in villages not bearing a clan's surname, it was generally difficult for an individual or family not belonging to the local clan to live there. And it is well known that down to comparatively recent times Chinese governments relied upon the strength of the clan for the maintenance of local peace and order.

While a systematic treatment of the clan lies beyond the scope of this study, we would point out some of the main forces at work under the Communist regime concerning features of the clan organization which have been of basic importance to the family. There were no extensive changes introduced into rural clans during the Republican era; and the data in this discussion concern mainly conditions in the southern provinces where the organization of the agnate clan (or the sib) is stronger and its influence greater than in other parts of China.

It is notable that the Communist regime is the first Chinese government that has not relied upon or made use of the clan for the maintenance of local peace and order or for the consolidation of its political power. Although pre-Communist governments and political leaders expressed dissatisfaction with "familism and clannism" as a hindrance to modern developments, they made no systematic attack against the clan organization, and there is no Communist law that prohibits the clan as a legitimate form of organization; but vital forces are at work that have a disintegrating effect on it.

Change of the Age Hierarchy and Kinship Relations

The organizational framework of the clan relied heavily upon the age hierarchy and the proximity of kinship, as explained in Chapter IV,[1] since it was through these two principles, especially that of the age hierarchy, that the large membership of a clan could be structured in an orderly way and each of the individuals living in it could identify his status. Age hierarchy and proximity of kinship constituted the foundation both for the formal organization of authority in the clan and for the performance of many of its functions.

Obviously, therefore, the rise in status of the young and the women, marriage by free choice, the weakening of the family as a unit of production and as a center of loyalty — all such factors which have affected the system of status and authority of the traditional family have similarly affected the organization of the clan; for the traditional family was the basic cell of the clan organization, and whatever has weakened the family has inevitably also weakened the larger structure of the clan.

Furthermore, the fury of the class struggle in the Communist land reform had a disorganizing influence on the clan structure since the economic stratification of the clan membership became an explicit object of revolutionary destruction. Clannish authority and status based upon age hierarchy and proximity of kinship inevitably lose their effectiveness in the process of any violent class struggle; for, when a person is accused of being a local bully, a bad landlord, or a usurer, no amount of seniority of generation or age, often not even the proximity of kinship, can protect him from an outraged victim or an angry revolutionary mob. Certainly this has been dramatically demonstrated in Communist China. Reports of "accusation meetings" and public trials in the land reform show that, although kinsmen, especially the young and the women, had difficulty at first in speaking up against a relative if the latter was an older person high in status and authority based on age hierarchy and proximity of kinship, when one or two "victims" who had been carefully coached beforehand spoke up, the ice was broken, and under the pressure of emotional tension and the contagion of mass excitement others soon followed suit in pouring out anger and rage against the accused, and a long respected old aunt or uncle would be publicly beaten up, clapped into jail, or shot, depending on the seriousness of the alleged crime.

In the "struggle meeting" in Tzuchien village in Yukan county of Kiangsi Province for instance: "Liu Ch'i-sen was an old local bully and landlord. He had victimized many persons in the same clan, and some in the same fang (a sub-unit of the clan consisting of members of close relationship from common descent). During the first stage of the land reform, he had escaped punishment. But during the re-examination of the land reform, poor peasants and farm laborers of the same clan and the same fang finally arose to mete out justice to him." [2] In a village in Kwangtung Province over five hundred women formed a crowd and went to their landlord relatives to demand refunds of rent reductions and "to square off" past economic injustices. At mass meetings the same women "broke through clannish attitudes and kinship sentiments" to accuse landlord relatives in the same clan — for "what are we afraid of when we have the Communist Party as our support?" [3]

Change in the Agencies of Clan Authority

Formal control of the clan rested mainly on two agencies. One was the elders' council, vested with the formal authority of making policies and decisions. The other was a form of executive organ, a council of administrators that bore different names in different localities, for carrying out decisions made by the elders and administering the property and business of the clan. In the informal aspect of the power structure, landlords and leaders of organized armed groups and other elements whose political influence and connections usually extended beyond the village generally controlled both of these agencies either by personal participation or by putting in their own people.

That system of authority has suffered mortal blows from revolutionary activities in the land reform and subsequent reconstitution of village organization under Communist rule. There has been no formal attack by the Communists against the elders' council as an organization, but its influential members have been stripped of property and status by land reform. Members of the council of administration of clan property and business have been singled out for accusations of embezzlement of public funds by other clansmen, especially by poor peasants and farm laborers who had been consistently kept out of power in the clan organization, and being accused of such crimes brings ruinous fines, public beatings, imprisonment, and at times death. Consequently, since no one dares to serve in them now, clan agencies have either automatically disbanded or are at a standstill with many of their members classified as criminals.

Replacing the elders' council and the administrative agencies are authoritarian Communist organizations deriving their power from the peasants' associations\ controlled by the policy of "relying upon poor peasants and farm laborers, making alliances with the middle peasants, and overthrowing the landlords." The village Women's Association in some localities has come to share some of the power.[4] Youth organizations such as the New Democratic Youth League are also instrumental in the new village authority. These new agencies may still be subjected to the influence of kinship relations to some extent, but their basic principles of organization exclude kinship ties.

Finally, the traditional clan possessed its own armed forces in the form of local militia, especially in the southern provinces, forces which were wholly under the control of the landlords and other elements of power in the clan. Under communism the old militia is replaced by "people's soldiers," who are still local militia in fact but under control of the Communist government and no longer a part of the clan organization. Disarming the old militia and squeezing out hidden arms from the villages constituted a violent phase in the early period of the Communist conquest.

Change in the Economic Functions of the Clan

The clan, at least in the southern part of the country, owned common property and performed many important economic functions, and clan properties were often quite extensive.[5] Income from clan property was used to finance the village school, the maintenance of the ancestral temples, ancestral sacrifices and related functions, public works such as construction and repair of roads and bridges, military defense of the village, and at times relief for the poor. Up to the Communist accession to power in 1949 many clans in the vicinity of Canton apportioned land to poor members at nominal rent. A very important economic function of the clan was the collective undertaking of the irrigational and water control projects which formed the foundation of China's irrigational agriculture and accounted for much of the peasants' reliance upon the clan in the past. In a village in Kwangtung Province in 1936 the clan built a long dike to reclaim a large tract of tideland which added almost one-third more cultivated land to the village, and the distribution of irrigational water on this land continued to be under the clan's control until the Communists took over.

This picture has been drastically changed under Communist rule. Land reform regulations require the confiscation of clan property for redistribution to the poor and landless peasants, thus leaving the clan without funds to carry on its functions. Vital economic functions such as irrigation, water control, and local road construction and maintenance now belong to the Communist government, with assistance from new local organizations such as peasant associations. From 1955 to 1958, when agricultural producers' cooperatives became the national pattern of agricultural organization, those economic functions which the government did not take over from the clan passed on to the cooperatives, which collaborate with the government in the performance of such functions. The cooperatives have increased in size generally with one cooperative embracing an entire village, performing, aside from collective farming, a wide range of economic functions such as the reclamation of wasteland, irrigational projects, and the collective struggle against flood and drought that once were under the leadership of the clan.[6]

Changes in Social Functions of the Clan

As previously indicated, it had been a clan function to finance schools and at times to give free education to poor but worthy sons. Although the land reform regulations permit retention of part of the clan property for education, the control of this property has been transferred from the clan to the new village government and the peasant association.[7] Besides, the Communist government is directly subsidizing rural education on a large scale.

Administering ancestral sacrifices and maintaining ancestral temples was a major function of the clan, and the spring and autumn sacrifices to the ancestors once were leading events in the social life of the villages. Gathering hundreds and at times thousands of members in the ancestral temple for the solemn ceremony under the guidance of the elders, such sacrifices periodically demonstrated the tangible existence of the clan as well as the collective strength of the group, inspired strength and morale in the individual members, and stimulated loyalty to and pride in the kinship organization. Reinforcing these psychological effects were the mystical symbols of the ancestors' tablets, the incense and candles, the impressive religious rites, and the many honorific articles and inscribed exhortations left behind by worthy members of preceding generations for posterity to remember, admire, and follow. The joyous feasting which concluded this event served to heighten the spirit of solidarity and to evoke allegiance to the clan.

Now, with clan property confiscated, to find money for discharging ceremonial functions becomes a major difficulty. In many villages in Kwangtung in 1951 the clan failed to provide even for the spring and autumn sacrifices, and a few older members undertook the sacrificial ceremony from private funds, but the ceremony was far from the grand affair it used to be. Most of the ancestral temples have been taken over by peasants' associations and other new organizations as headquarters and as classrooms, and the buildings have come to serve functions unconnected with the maintenance of the sacred character of the clan and family organization. In many of the ancestral temples objects of an honorific nature, such as carved wooden plaques bearing the names and honors of worthy sons of the clans, some over a century old and given to the clan by great officials and even by the Ch'ing emperors, have been removed and burned by peasants' associations in order to eradicate the last trace of "feudalism."

Another function of the clan was to sponsor public recreation such as the celebration of traditional festivals with presentations of stage operas. This function was continued by the clan in a few places in the first two years of the Communist rule, but it is no longer common practice since the clan has no source of income to finance such undertakings. Increasingly, the peasants' associations, the village Youth Corps and the Women's Association have come to undertake the function of providing public recreation — of a very different nature and social orientation.

Organizationally and functionally crippled by land reform and agricultural collectivization, the clan no longer retains its traditional dominance as the core of rural community life. Finally the people's commune provides a systematic replacement for the clan's structural-functional position in the rural community, for the commune system combines local political, military, economic, educational, recreational, and welfare service functions into a unified organization.

In urban communities the clan has long been weakened by population mobility and by the non-kinship nature of the economy. In the pre-Communist period it still retained a partial existence in the form of surname associations which owned income-yielding properties or collected dues from members, held annual membership meetings, and performed the function of consolidating kinship ties as a basis for mutual assistance, and such associations are still active in non-Communist Hong Kong.[8] In Communist China even this diluted form of the clan, the surname association, has passed out of existence under the vigorous attack on "familism and clannism."

CHAPTER XII

Ideology and Propaganda in the Change of the Family

CONSTRUCTIVE REVOLUTIONARY change in the institutional framework of a society proceeds both from disruptive influences which cripple the structure and functions of established institutions and from the creative influences of a new ideology which offers an ideal picture of a different set of institutions to be constructed on the foundations of the old.

That disruptive forces alone, without an accompanying creative concept, will not lead to the rapid development of new institutions is demonstrated by the limitation of the function of modern industrial development as an influence on the traditional Chinese family institution. Modern industrial employment in China provided an avenue of escape from traditional family control and thus disrupted the traditional pattern of family life, but it did not produce any immediate change in the traditional family or set in motion any conscious movement toward the development of a new family institution. It was a notable characteristic of the Chinese who emigrated to Southeast Asia to work in modern mines and factories that, although they remained away from home for protracted periods of time, they adhered ideologically to the traditional family and remained faithful to it. It was the second generation Chinese, educated in modern schools where the ideal of the Western family pattern was impressed upon them, who first made the shift away from the traditional mode of family life.

An interesting case history is provided by the silk workers in Kwangtung Province in South China, where in the early 1900's modern silk factories were established in and around Shunteh district which almost exclusively employed female workers on the mechanized jobs, in raising silkworms and preparing the worms' food from the leaves of mulberry trees — in short, where women were the main workers and gained economic independence in an industry outside of the home. Since the factories were in a rural area quite isolated from contacts with modern ideas, these women became deviant types of individuals, particularly the unmarried girls who developed a cult of collective spinsterhood, leading a pseudo-family life in highly organized sororities. Some of them who had been forced into marriage either by their parents' authority or by the superstition that a woman must be married in order to obtain a home for one's spirit after death used their wages to reimburse the husband's family for the marriage expense, told the husband to take another wife or a concubine, and left the husband's family to continue with their independent livelihood. Some of them turned to homosexuality. As a group they developed an attitude of disdain and contempt toward women who married, lived with the husband's family, and accepted the low status traditionally assigned to a wife and a daughter-in-law. Similar conditions also prevailed among professional female servants in southern cities.

Thus, without the influences from any new ideology, the economic independence of these women workers resulted in mock marriage, in their refusal to live with their husbands, in actual spinsterhood, in pseudo-family life through sorority organization, in homosexuality — all destructive to the traditional family; but their rebellious and independent spirit created no new family institution to replace the old one, and their deviating behavior could hardly be said to constitute a part of the constructive influence in the modern family revolution.

The true significance of modern economic development lies not in its providing economic independence to oppressed members of the family but in the convergence of such new economic independence with the intellectual and emotional drive of a new social idealism that promises a better social order, including a new form of family. Only in the building of a different family institution in accordance with the new ideological pattern does the new economic independence become a positive influence. Hence the importance of the ideological aspect of the Chinese family revolution and of the mass communication of a new ideology.

In the pre-Communist period new idealism in a loosely organized form was derived from the feminist movement and the family pattern in modern Europe and the United States. By 1930 it was partly formulated into a legal statute, the law of marriage and kinship, under the Nationalist government; but throughout the pre-Communist period the primary means of popularizing the ideas of the family revolution and in familiarizing the people with the new legal standards was not political action but the written language — hence the confinement of the family revolution largely to the urban intelligentsia who could read. Personal discussions, motion pictures of modern love and marriage, and living examples of modern marriages and incidents of rebellion against the family all served as lesser means of communication in carrying certain aspects of the new idealism to the illiterate segment of the population who remained impervious to the huge volume of modern literature on the family revolution. But their influence was limited and did not travel far beyond the metropolitan areas. The family revolution was thus confined to the urban centers, leaving the vast countryside in the tight grip of the traditional family institution.

Under the Communist regime, the new Marriage Law emerges as a more systematic embodiment of the new idealism concerning marriage and the family. With the Marriage Law as the ideological base, the storm of the family revolution has spread from the urban intelligentsia to members of the working class, from the urban areas to the broad countryside, as shown by the foregoing facts of increasing family instability, mounting figures of divorce, and the growing number of new marriages in the larger section of the population beyond the restricted circle of the former urban upper and middle classes. The significant feature of this development has been neither the requirement of the registration of all new marriages nor the many legal decisions settling family conflicts according to new legal stipulations which are in harmony with the revolutionary idealism but the extensive use of mass propaganda by the Communist regime.

Literature, the chief means of spreading the family revolution in the pre-Communist period, remains a major instrument under communism. Articles in newspapers and magazines, pamphlets, and books continue to incite rebellion against the old family and to invite acceptance of the new ideal, but much of the substance of such literature, particularly works of fiction, has changed. Marriage and the family life of the worker, peasant, and the lower-middle class have become substitutes for those of the upper and upper-middle class as leading subjects for discussion and fictionalization. If the illiterate masses still cannot read these reflections of themselves, at least the attention of those who can read is being turned to the family problems among the broader segment of the population. So far as the literate segment of the population still constitutes the main carrier of the new influence and the basic group from which the elite are recruited for the enforcement of Communist policies, this change of content in the literature is instrumental in spreading the family revolution from the urban intelligentsia to the other classes.

A major difference from pre-Communist literature on the family problem has been the far greater use made by the Communists of folk literature and printed materials simple enough for the common people to understand. Folk stories based on themes of the new marriage and the new family are turned out in large quantity by organizations such as the Democratic Women's League, not only for reading by people with a low level of literacy, but also for storytellers in the market places to recite to illiterates. Folk ballads on the family problem have also been a new form of literature aimed not at the intelligentsia but at the "broad masses." "Newspaper-reading groups," where a literate leader reads to an illiterate group, have been another means by which the message of the family revolution is travelling in wider circles.

Distinctly new and effective on the Chinese scene as an instrument of propaganda for the common people are the serial pictorial pamphlets in the style of American comic books. Serial drawings depicting traditional stories had come into wide circulation among the common people in the last two pre-Communist decades, but they are now being utilized for changing the family institution and are published in daily newspapers such as the *Chieh-fang Jih-pao* in Shanghai and the *Su-nan Jih-pao* circulating in the southern part of Kiangsu Province. A large number of propaganda leaflets and handbooks on the subject of the problems of marriage and the family are written in the simple, daily language of the common people.[1] "The family revolution expressed in literature has definitely shed its bourgeois frivolousness and has gone to the people." [2]

The wide use of "blackboard newspapers" and "wall newspapers," which are bulletins written on blackboards and on papers posted on walls, is another cheap and effective means of utilizing the medium of the written language in propaganda for the Marriage Law. As both these forms are hand-written, they need not rely on the printing press, which remains scarce in rural areas, and are easily adaptable to rural settings.

In the pre-Communist period motion pictures on the family problem seen by the common people, literate or illiterate, were confined to the urban areas, and stage plays were mostly for the intelligentsia, the modern stage play emphasizing dialogue and unaccompanied by music being a new form introduced from the West. Communist scripts for stage plays are written against the background of the common people and deal with specific points of the new Marriage Law. Such typical pieces as "The Thousand-Year-Old Glacier Begins to Thaw," "The Little Son-in-Law," "The Marriage of Little Dark No. 2," "New Ways for a New Event," and "New Conditions" present concrete problems and solutions along lines laid down by the Marriage Law. Moreover, theater audiences are no longer limited to the modern urban intelligentsia; nor are the performances limited to those given by theatrical groups of students from modern schools. Commercial theatrical companies and large numbers of skilled theatrical groups of the government's Recreation and Culture Corps, are now producing such plays in rural towns for the first time.[3] The modern stage play has thus been popularized by the Communists and utilized as a form of propaganda which reaches all classes of people.

The Communists' skillful use of the theater arts for propaganda purposes is clearly revealed in the rise of theatrical groups in all parts of the country, particularly in rural communities, almost from the beginning of the Communist regime. In 1951 it was officially reported that there were 1,500 amateur theatrical groups in Laiotung Province alone. In Lushan county of Honan Province, there were 240 amateur theatrical groups in 1952. During the years 1951 and 1952, "25 per cent of all the plays put on by the 240 theatrical groups dealt with the theme of the Marriage Law."[4]

Besides creating their own version of modern stage drama, the Communists are attempting to reduce the influence of the traditional operas which have so long been a popular means of enforcing the traditional values of the family institution. "The government is planning to outlaw the continued performance of traditional operas that emphasize the virtue of chastity, praise polygamy, and teach sex inequality."[5] Municipal governments in Hankow, Nanking, and other cities have suppressed many "feudalistic" operas. Where specific legal action has not been taken in this respect, indoctrination of the actors and actresses in all parts of the country and the censorship of the theater is bringing about similar effects. In addition, a large number of playwrights are assigned the task of revising the old operas in order to eliminate the "feudalistic values" and to fit the stories into the revolutionary setting, and by 1956 the vast majority of the popular old operas had been thus revised.

An outstanding accomplishment of the Communist regime in propagandizing the Communist concept of the new family is the ultilization of the extensive organizational system of the young and the women, the two groups most dissatisfied with their treatment under the traditional system of family status and authority. The Communist organizations of the young, which comprised a national membership of some 30,000,000 in 1956, reach into every class and every part of the country. Organization of the women appears to be even more extensive, for as early as the fall of 1950 it was reported that 30,000,000 women had become affiliated directly or indirectly with the All-China Democratic Women's League in 31 provinces, 83 cities, and 1,287 counties,[6] and membership is certain to have increased since then. Members of such extensive organizations are among the first to "learn" the new Marriage Law and to be baptized by its idealism.[7]

Ideas of the new Marriage Law travel not only through the youth and women's organizations but also through the channels of other organizations with staggering figures of membership, such as the Communist Party, the labor union system, and the armed forces, members of all such organizations being required to participate in organized sessions to "study" the Marriage Law.[8]

Then there is what is called the "propaganda network," organized by volunteers (generally members of the Communist Party or the New Democratic Youth League) to publicize all official policies and ideas, including the new Marriage Law, to co-workers in offices, shops, factories, urban neighborhoods, and villages. It was officially claimed that there were in excess of five million of these volunteers in 1952. That they are instrumental in spreading the new ideas of marriage and the family among the common people, particularly in the hitherto isolated villages, is illustrated in the case of Lushan county of Honan Province in Central China, where in 1952 there were over three thousand members in the county's propaganda network who tried to acquaint the masses in every village with the Marriage Law through "broadcasting platforms, labor recruiting units, newspaper-reading units, blackboard newspapers, and in market places and teahouses." [9]

Members of the various organizations such as the Youth Corps, the Democratic Women's League, and the Communist Party act not only as propaganda agents in many ways, but are also active in counseling on marriage and family problems in factories, shops, and in villages.[10] Sessions are organized to acquaint the public with the Marriage Law. In the East China region fifteen million peasants heard lectures on the Marriage Law when it was made the central subject of study by government order for the winter literacy classes for peasants in that region.[11]

Whatever the reaction from a traditional people to lectures and other forms of propaganda, the striking fact is that a vast number of them have now heard about an arrangement of family life at sharp odds with all they were taught and accustomed to in the past. Even if a part of the peasant public do not accept such strange ideas, they have come to feel that a major change of family life is impending. The present vast organized effort to acquaint the public with the new ideas on the family institution is a situation never before encountered in China.

A totally new propaganda device is the "exhibition of marriage problems," a Communist invention. Such exhibitions, first organized in large numbers from 1951 to 1953, display pictures and drawings to dramatize the "unreasonableness" and tragedies of the old institution of family and marriage and to show the happiness brought to couples married in accordance with the Marriage Law. Speakers talk to the crowd as they file past the exhibits, and they give counsel to individuals in a separate room.

In an exhibition in Shaohsing, a rural town in Chekiang Province, a converted traditional woman was used as a living sample; she poured out her tale of misfortune to the visitors. She was a woman who with her little daughter had been chased out of the family by the mother-in-law. She took her daughter and went into a Buddhist convent for eight years. After the Communist government promulgated the Marriage Law, she heard about it and appealed her case in court. The court punished the mother-in-law and gave the complainant a job in a tea factory. According to the official report, "She is now a happy woman, full of gratitude to the Communist government and deep conviction for the principles of the Marriage Law as well as the wickedness of the traditional family institution. Whenever a crowd of visitors gathers in front of her, she gives her talk and wipes away her tears as she tells her heart-rending story of mistreatment by the mother-in-law and husband, and her listeners are deeply moved." [12] Undoubtedly, such living examples of suffering from the traditional family are effective in arousing resentment against the age-old institution and in gaining converts to the new ideas as displayed in the highly dramatized pictures and drawings. This exhibition drew over 10,000 visitors in five days. An exhibition of the same kind in Shanghai, sponsored by the local Democratic Women's League, lasted for ten days in October of 1951 and drew 160,000 visitors.

In the rural communities of Shantung Province a more modest version of the city exhibitions, the "exhibition sheds for the propaganda of the Marriage Law," has been used with visible effect. In such sheds there are the same types of pictures and drawings and the same setup of speakers and counselors. It is estimated that the majority of the visitors to the sheds are young people of both sexes, but there are also middle-aged and old people. In Laiwu county of that province it was officially reported that about half of all the adult population of the county had visited the exhibition shed. Several young women demanded divorces after visiting the shed, and some parents after being exposed to the new ideas also permitted their children to obtain divorces.[13] In Wenteng county of the same province, when an agricultural fair was held in May 1951, an exhibition shed for the marriage problem attracted fifteen thousand visitors in six days. An old man went into the shed to look at the pictures and drawings depicting incidents of the "wickedness of the feudalistic marriage and family" and the "happy new marriages." He returned with his family to look at the pictures again. After that, he brought a group of neighbors to view the same thing. After looking at the drawings and listening to the lectures, many young men and women sought counsel from the counselors and asked about the new procedures of marriage or divorce, "fully ready to carry their new-gained ideas into action."[14]

Lastly, the Communists have shown effective skill in "setting the masses in motion," in focusing public attention on an objective, and in employing group pressure to induce individuals to march toward that objective. While this is a process deserving fuller analysis, the only intention here is to point out that the mass meeting is the beginning of a collective process of implanting in the public mind a new motivation for group behavior and that it constitutes a cornerstone of the Communist mass propaganda technique.

A mass meeting may serve any ulterior purpose, such as popularizing the idea in the Marriage Law by utilizing the striking effect of an "unusual" issue or incident, for instance, the tragic death of a person on account of family conflict; for any unusual issue switches the attention of the audience from their routinized daily behavior and thought and focuses it on the issue which is magnified and dramatized for emotional effect. In the mass meeting the emotions of an unruly crowd are unleashed to throw the routinized thought and behavior further out of balance, to release institutionally inhibited feelings, to heighten the sense of popular justice by circular reaction induced by slogan-shouting, yelling, and repetitive speeches and stories, and finally to pass an unconventional resolution to settle an "unusual" issue. Immediately after passing the resolution as a "popular demand" comes the moralization of the lesson, which is the real aim of the whole show. Still reeling from the high emotional tension generated, the audience is induced to accept not only the solution to the issue but also the moral lesson as interpreted by the masters of the show, the chairman, and the directors of the mass meeting. Thus a new rule is set up to govern an aspect of social life that used to be governed by a very different rule, and the formerly inviolate traditional pattern is broken.

This generalized process of mass meetings, which has served to destroy age-old patterns of behavior, is being applied explicitly to change the institution of the family and marriage. The following is the summary of a concrete case:

In Ts'angshan county of Shantung Province a young peasant woman, P'an Shi, was tortured to death by her mother-in-law, Ch'i Sung Shi, and the latter's common-law husband, Kuo Yu-shan. The torturing was extremely cruel, but no one dared to protest publicly, for Kuo was the village head and a Communist Party cadre. After all, torturing a daughter-in-law to death had happened before.

The case was discovered by superior government authorities of the T'eng county Special District. In view of the cruelty of the case and in view of the current policy of enforcing the Marriage Law, the higher authorities decided to make an issue out of the case as an example to the local population and unregenerated cadres.

The two murderers were arrested and were made to confess the full details of their crime. The second step was to call a meeting of "representatives" of the local population in the several surrounding counties. Among the several hundred gathered representatives were village and subdistrict cadres, such as village heads and other local officials, local progressive elements, and some die-hard, ancient-minded mothers-in-law and older people. At the meeting the carefully prepared case was reported with full dramatic details to the audience. The story acquired real life and emotional character by bringing in the prisoners to rehearse the confession. The audience was horrified and moved by the story. What should be done in this case to vindicate justice? It was "decided by the meeting" to take the next step: calling a "public trial" mass meeting to be attended by local people. Meanwhile, the full moral of the story, the wickedness of the ancient institution of family and marriage and the necessity for introducing a new pattern as delineated by the Marriage Law and motivated by the spirit of personal freedom on the basis of sex equality, was fully elucidated. After the meeting of representatives Wang Hung-yi, a party cadre representing the second subdistrict of Ts'angshan county, related the effect of the meeting on his own thinking:

"In the past, I felt that the freedom of divorce stipulated in the Marriage Law was looking for unnecessary trouble, shattering people's predestined matrimonial ties. I did not recognize that the Marriage Law aims at the harmony of family life and the development of production. Now, after listening to the explanations on the Marriage Law, I am beginning to recognize the error of my past thought.

"I am a newly liberated peasant. I have a daughter. When she was very young, I found a husband for her. The husband's family was a feudalistic one and would not give her enough to eat and to wear, but constantly scolded and beat her. My daughter could not stand it and in 1949 tried to obtain a divorce from the subdistrict government. The subdistrict government refused her request. At that time I said to my wife, 'She is married into the family, how could she think of a divorce?' In this situation, not only was the divorce attempt a failure, but the husband's family also increased the cruelty of treatment toward her and said that 'it would matter very little even if she were beaten to death.' Finally, through struggle, my daughter obtained a divorce, found someone to love, remarried, and now she is quite happy. Right along, I felt that this was a disreputable event. Now I know that, as a subdistrict cadre, if I do not first dig out my own feudalistic thoughts, I cannot thoroughly enforce the Marriage Law for the government."

Besides Wang Hung-yi, other representatives also spoke up along the same vein. Altogether, the representatives uncovered in the meeting 119 cases of mistreated child brides and 91 cases of mistreated wives. "Thus, all the participating representatives and cadres gained a good education."

Then at a great mass meeting came the "public trial" of the murderers. As "planned," upward of ten thousand people came. After inflaming speeches and personal confessions by the murderers, the chairman asked for opinions regarding the sentence from the audience. "Mass emotions swelled to a high tide, there was a deafening roar in unison for 'Drastic punishment for the brutal murderers!' The people's court accepted the demand of the masses and announced the death penalty for the brutal murderers, Kuo Yu-shan and Ch'i Sung Shi." . . .

When the mass trial and the shooting were over, both the representatives and the participants of the mass meeting returned to their respective villages to set off the secondary effect of the exciting event. For three or four days individual village mass meetings were held to hear the reports of the event from those who had participated and to discuss the problems of the Marriage Law in the light of the event. "There was a general recognition of the injustice of the institution that the people were accustomed to." The happy ending to cases of freedom of divorce and freedom of marriage served as models of the new way in the discussions. As a consequence of the village mass meetings and discussions, "many brutal characters who were used to mistreating women lost their courage and became humbled, and many oppressed women were emboldened, starting legal procedure to get a divorce." [15]

This is but one of a large number of similarly significant cases illustrating the part played by mass meetings as a means towards changing the popular attitude toward the traditional family institution. There was a similar case in Pishan county in the neighborhood of the scene of the foregoing case. After the mass meeting and the shooting of the murderer, a leader said, "In my village there are many brutal mothers-in-law. Previously, the oppressed women just took the mistreatment and did not dare to protest. After having the experience of this mass meeting, I now know how to tell them to rebel." [16] In Kwangtung Province there have been many such cases. Particularly significant is a case in which the technique of the mass meeting was used to overcome the public anger of a whole village in Fukien Province against the enforcement of the Marriage Law on a divorce case, driving a wedge into the solid opposition of the village leaders and the village population and gaining popular acceptance for the principles of the new law.[17]

In analyzing such cases of public exhibitions and mass meetings, the change of attitudes among some of the older people and local leaders seems significant, but perhaps even more important is the beckoning of a new idealism and new means to realize it as dramatized to the young. For it is the young men and women who, once converted, are the members of a new family institution which is acquiring real life in the developing Chinese social order, as the institutional authority once vested in the older group is now being replaced by the formal political authority of a regime that no longer operates on the principles of the institutional framework of traditional society. The conservatism of the older people can slow down but cannot prevent the development of a new family institution once the new concept has claimed the young minds.

The propaganda activities we have cited took place between 1950 and 1953, since which time there has been a cooling off of agitation to introduce drastic and speedy change in the family system. Certain propaganda work, such as the elimination of "feudalistic" family values from traditional operas, is still carried on. But other types of propaganda such as public exhibitions, mass meetings, and even general publicity work for the family revolution have noticeably slowed down and in some places stopped altogether since 1953. Since that year, the "high tide" of the family revolution has been retreating — but only, as will be discussed later, because the urgency of the problem of economic development has relegated family reform to a secondary place.

CHAPTER XIII

Recession of the "High Tide" and Long Term Trends

AN EFFORT has been made in the previous chapters to an-
alyse the major aspects of the traditional Chinese family system which
have undergone change in the past half century, especially under Communist leadership. We have noted that during the years from 1950 to
1953, the early years of Communist rule, the tempo of the family revolution was especially rapid, affecting a larger section of the population
than in any previous period. In its broad sweep of recasting the institutional framework of Chinese society, the fury of a newly successful
revolution bore down hard on the family as on other aspects of traditional social life. We have noted also that since 1953 the organized
mass campaign to change the family system has noticeably slowed
down in its pace, and Communist leadership has directed its full
strength to other issues deemed more immediately urgent for the
construction of the socialist state, namely, the first five-year plan of
economic development, the collectivization of agriculture, and the
nationalization of industry and commerce. Although the family revolution is being presently eclipsed, we should not assume that the traditional family system is to be spared from further change. In conclusion,
therefore, it seems relevant first to review the current situation and
then to make a summary with implications for the future.

Modern changes in the Chinese family system have been the result
of both ideological motivation and environmental pressure from new
socio-economic developments. As an ideological movement, the family
revolution has developed in the form of a pulsative process, waxing
and waning with the greater movement of the socio-political revolution of which it is a part. Each pulsation in the process has consisted
of an initial upsurge, a steady rise of the movement to a "high tide,"
in the Communist terminology, and a recession in which some mem-

bers of the movement fell back in disillusionment but others re-formed their ranks in preparation for another assault, with a repetition of the cycle until a new institutional order succeeded in replacing the old one. During each high tide the social atmosphere was charged with tense emotions and revolutionary acts carried to a level which could not be sustained over a long period because of the lack of coordinated support from revolutionary developments in other related aspects of social life.

The general operation of this process has been suggested in the body of this study. The first wave of the family revolution began with the initial upsurge in the last decade of the nineteenth century, rose to a high tide in the Republican revolution of 1911, but retreated soon afterwards into a period of placid advocation and moderate reforms. A resurgence of the movement came with the New Culture Movement of 1917 and the May 4th Movement of 1919, reaching its crescendo in the Second Revolution during the mid-1920's. A recession of the movement followed the Kuomintang-Communist split, and the restorationist counter-current temporarily drowned out the battle cry of the family revolution. The confusion and disappointment of the revolutionists were vividly portrayed in the works of modern fiction of the late 1920's and early 1930's. A good example of such fiction is Mao T'un's *Disillusionment*, which depicts the demoralization and decadence of the frustrated revolutionary youth. The resuscitation of the Communist movement during the great national crisis of the Japanese invasion in 1937 brought renewed strength to the smoldering family revolution as an organized radical drive for the remaking of the family institution. The movement advanced and spread as a part of the Communist revolution, and its development from 1950 to 1953 undoubtedly represents another of its high tides, especially the large-scale campaign for enforcement of the new Marriage Law in 1953. After that year the movement once more entered into a recession which has continued to 1958 when the communes were set up.

The Communist period clearly demonstrates that a major reason for recession is the lack of coordinated support from other related aspects of the social revolution. Preoccupied with the building of the socialist economic order, Communist leadership has been unable to give sustained attention to the family revolution on a mass-organized scale. The lack of coordinated support is seen in the shortage of nurseries to facilitate employment and economic independence for women both in the cities and in the countryside, in the loud condemnations by feminist leaders of discrimination against employing female workers in Com-

munist state enterprises due to the added expense in providing assistance for childbirth and child care, and in the Communists' inability
to provide enough jobs for the women newly emancipated from the confines of the "feudalistic family."

Whereas women were told before 1953 that their only road to liberation was to "participate in productive labor," in 1955 they were advised to wait for the call by the state to take part in production, and
that meanwhile they should recognize the social value of being a
"family woman." As unemployment spread in the urban areas in the
spring of 1957, there was even the proposal of sending some of the
employed women back to the family in order that unemployed men
could have jobs; and the new propaganda line in urban areas was:
"If women who stay at home can encourage their husbands and children to take part in socialist reconstruction, and educate their children
to become members for the next shift in the work of socialist reconstruction, then their domestic service already contains revolutionary
and social value, and the salaries and income of their husbands and
other family members already contain their own labor." [1] In the countryside, emancipation of women from "feudalistic family oppression"
has lost its priority to the dominant national drive toward complete
collectivization of agriculture, and the most important advice for
women is to participate in the collectivization movement.[2] The Democratic Women's League in a rural coastal town reported in 1955 that
it had great difficulty in trying to distribute to the public four hundred
copies of the *Hun-yin Fa T'u-chieh* (Popular Pictorial Edition of the
Marriage Law) for not even the popular organizations were willing
to accept them.[3] This is certainly in sharp contrast to the widespread
enthusiasm with which documents relating to the Marriage Law were
handled before 1953.

Since 1953, the Communist press has published little factual information about the problems of marriage and the family, and it has not
been clear how the new trend is expressed in the actual marriage and
family situation in the country as a whole, but a report on the interior
province of Shensi in 1956 exemplifies the recession of the last high
tide.[4] According to this report, which came out of a field survey, the
wide publicity of the Marriage Law in 1953 produced many new marriages based on free choice, but since then there has been a general
revival of the arranged marriage in the province, especially in the
rural communities where it is practiced on a cash-and-carry basis as
in the old rural tradition, in two rural counties more than 90 per cent
of the marriages being consummated in this traditional manner. The

report quotes many cases, the character of which appears humorous to modern eyes but serious to the traditional-minded peasants. Here are a few of them, all from localities in Shensi Province:

> Cases wherein marriageable girls are handled like a commodity by their parents and sold to the highest bidder have been known. . . . In one village in Chi-shan county . . . the village chief bought his son a wife with money he got by selling a cow and two huts. . . . In another village [in the same county] a girl was offered for sale twice. The last price was 240 yuan [about a hundred dollars]. When the buyer came up with something like 100 yuan, he was shouted out of the house. . . . In a village of Shang county a boy and a girl were much in love. The girl's parents demanded a wedding gift of 150 yuan. All the boy could produce was 100 yuan. This amount was rejected, and the girl was forcibly sold to an older man who was better off. An old villager in Fu-p'ing county sold his divorced daughter for 1,200 yuan plus a good coffin. The deal, however, was called off when the coffin ordered was found to be of inferior quality. In another village in Yen-yang county a man had already sold two of his three daughters. The third, who happened to be an activist, objected to the cash deal and wanted love her own way. She was locked up in the house by her father.

Since such cash deals, long an institutionalized practice in poor rural areas, are ruled out by the Communist Marriage Law, they "have gone underground under various disguised names and procedures," according to the Shensi report; and the people charge that, since the Marriage Law has come into operation, they have had to pay more than previous prices in undercover deals. The report further states that since 1953 the Women's Association, the Youth League, the courts, and the Communist Party branches and People's Councils have not bothered much about the Marriage Law unless homicide cases are involved in family conflicts, and that those who resist the cash-down, arranged marriage eventually lose courage for lack of public support. People have referred to the vigorous publicity of the Marriage Law in 1953 as "a light breeze that leaves no traces at all."

There is some degree of authenticity in this report, for it was made by a correspondent for an official Communist newspaper which would be eager to publicize the success of the Marriage Law if there had been such success. The unresolved question it raises is how far does the condition in Shensi Province represent the situation in other parts of the country? Since cash-down, arranged marriage has been most common in poverty-stricken rural areas, and Shensi is one of the poorest provinces in China proper, the high percentage of return to traditional marriage in Shensi may be exceptional. We would judge that what is happening in Shensi is in harmony with the general national picture, in which the noticeable slow down in organized mass campaigns to change the system of marriage and the family permits reassertion of the traditional pattern; and that, therefore, the Shensi report hints at what may be happening in other parts of the country although the degree of revival of the traditional system of marriage may differ from place to place.

This is not to say that the revival of traditional marriage indicates a tendency toward reconsolidation of the old family system so that it will constitute a component of the socialist society that the Communists are trying to build. Although there may not be another series of mass campaigns to disorganize the traditional family and to bring about a new one, ideological and environmental factors in operation converge toward continued and steady weakening of the traditional system and the development of a new institution of marriage and family organization.

As our study has shown, the process of family change in China, including the new family idealism encouraged by structural alteration of the political, economic, and social factors, has gathered too much momentum to be halted. We have seen that this spreading process began in the closing years of the last century with the lone voices of a few non-conforming young men and women and grew in the subsequent four decades to engulf the whole modern educated segment of the urban population, the segment which held a dominant position in modern China, and that Communism has augmented its strength by extending support for it to the urban working class and to the peasants. There is still in motion, then, a long term process which will survive temporary setbacks and which works inevitably toward three principal ends: the breakdown of the traditional family system, the development of a new family institution, and the decline of the family as the core of Chinese social organization. It is in such a context of continuing change that we would summarize our study.

In the past half century there has been a growing loss of stability and organizational integrity of the traditional Chinese family system caused by such converging factors as the extending influence of romantic love, the changing procedure of marriage, the freedom of divorce, the rebellion of the women and the young against the traditional stratification of family status and authority, the shrinking family function in economic production, the rising competition of extra-familial centers of loyalty, the secularizing influences that quietly strip the family of its sacred character and remove its belief in group perpetuation, and the contagious spirit of a new family idealism being disseminated by modern education and propaganda in the midst of a violent social revolution.

The sphere of these influences is steadily widening. Even in the period of recession marked by the report we have cited on Shensi Province in 1956 the Communist courts in that province handled 8,163 cases involving marital discord during the period from January to June, and 4,980 of these cases, or 61 per cent, ended in divorce.[5] Such a recession as the temporary continuation of a past in which the parents obtain compensation for the economic investment in raising a daughter who is to be married out of the family is sure to be reversed if the Communists can achieve economic betterment of the peasantry, including nation-wide development of an old-age pension system; and it is already countered by the spreading influence of romantic love, the continued protest and rebellion of the young, and the declining authority of the parents over the children's marriages due to interference from the Marriage Law and to the general weakening of the authority of the elders.

With a firm Communist policy of the collectivization of agriculture and nationalization of commerce and industry, the individual's economic dependence upon the family, so dominant a factor in the structure and solidarity of the traditional family, is being increasingly replaced by the economic organization of the state. Save for those too young yet to earn an independent livelihood, the individual's economic security no longer weighs as heavily as before in compelling the preservation of family unity in the face of domestic conflict or in upholding the family as the supreme center of loyalty in one's social existence; and it is difficult to see how the traditional family economic system can retain its functional and structural integrity. The older generation may retain the traditional concept of the family, together with its system of authority and status as shaped by the past economic order, but the young generation is growing up in a collectivized and nationalized economy.

As the inevitable disorganization of the traditional family system continues, there is still uncertainty as to the new form of family institution which would be developed to replace the old one, especially in agrarian communities. The new family idealism distinctly calls for two renovations, namely, alteration of the traditional system of family authority and status, and the establishment of a monogamous marriage based on free choice of partners. But marriage is only a part of the family institution, and what form the alteration of the authority and status structure will take has not been clearly indicated. Neither the Communist law nor the vaguely presented new family ideology gives any clear definition as to the function and structure of the new family to be set up.

Whereas the traditional family had a clearly defined functional orientation, that is, to perpetuate the ancestral lineage, to raise the young, and to support the old, and its pattern of authority and status was carefully geared to that orientation, no such clarity of function-structure definition is found in the new ideology of the family system. Since 1952 the Communist slogan has called for the building of a "democratic, harmonious, and united new family for production," but it is obvious that the family is no longer an organizational unit of production under the collectivized and nationalized economy, and that the role structure among the members cannot be geared to the needs of a function that the family no longer performs as an organized unit. There is also the difficult problem of developing practicable means to achieve the "democratic, harmonious, and united" features for the new family under a socio-economic milieu that favors the detachment of the individual from family ties.

The lack of a specifically defined idealistic form of family as conscious guidance leaves the development of a new family institution to the shaping influence of a spontaneous process resulting from the interplay between ideological values and the new socio-economic structure. In the urban environment which is conducive to the development of an universalistic economy, this process has already resulted in a large number of two-generation conjugal families in which the married son and his family set up an independent household away from his parents where the parents may come to visit but not as permanent members exercising authority and control in the new family. In the countryside it has been common in the past to find an arrangement similar to the French *famille souche*, "in which one of the sons marries and continues to live with the parents while the other sons and daughters marry and go out of the family unit," [6] and which worked successfully chiefly because of the institutionalized authority and status of the parents over the married son and his family. The present Communist policy tends to try to preserve this type of family while at the same time seeking to promote "democratic harmony" by curbing the parents' authority on the one hand and urging the young couple to respect the parents on the other, the object being to avoid disruption of economic production resulting from mass development of family conflicts. The Communist press has publicized many cases in which the son and his wife live "democratically and harmoniously" with the parents on the basis of "mutual affection and mutual respect." [7]

It seems doubtful that the *famille souche* on a "democratic and harmonious" basis can become generally successful at the same time that the "feudalistic" system of family authority and status is brought under vigorous attack, and the individuals, particularly the daughters-in-law, are finding economic independence outside of the family. An economically independent daughter-in-law would be unwilling to use her own earnings to help support the traditionally despotic parents-in-law, especially the mother-in-law. A common result is the breakup of the three-generation family, as shown in the following which occurred in 1953.[8]

In Toukan village in Shaho county of Hopei Province K'ang Ch'ing-ho was a peasant with a petty business on the side. He took a wife, and they got along well at first. Then the mother-in-law started to abuse the wife and told the son to beat her; later the mother-in-law joined in the beating. Finally, the daughter-in-law took her child and ran away. K'ang was unhappy both over his personal loss and the difficulty of finding money to get another wife. Then came the Communist regime, and K'ang became progressive and joined the Communist Party. Later, he fell in love with a female party member and married her. The same conflict arose between the new daughter-in-law and the mother-in-law. This time, the Communist wife, who was a full-fledged agricultural worker, asked for a divorce in the subdistrict government after being beaten up by the husband. The officials in the subdistrict government tried to reconcile the couple by lecturing both parties. K'ang remembered the misfortune of his first marriage and was willing to compromise, but the wife was insistent upon separation from the mother-in-law. The mother-in-law was furious, reminding her son of the traditional filial obligations. However, separation was effected, with the mother-in-law given her own portion of the family land and a separate house around the same courtyard. The son still helped her do the heavy farm work necessary for her support. Later, the daughter-in-law and the mother-in-law became fairly amicable to each other.

There is ample evidence from urban experience that separation from the parents-in-law and the setting up of an independent household, which reduces the traditional extended family to a conjugal form, is encouraged by the social atmosphere developed under Communist rule. There are families in which the parents-in-law live successfully with the married son and his wife, but the controlling position in the family has passed from the parents to the young couple, with the parents as adjuncts and not masters. Such families may retain the three-generation membership, but its internal structure departs radically from the traditional pattern. There now seems to be a trend toward the conjugal family and a weakened form of the three-generation family even in the rural areas if the above story is at all representative.

With the traditional family institution being progressively weakened, and with the present trend, so far as it can be discerned, toward the two-generation family or a weakened form of the three-generation family, there is a plainly visible decline in the vital position of the kinship system which, as we have pointed out, is a central factor in the traditional Chinese social order. We have seen that just as Western society is characterized by an industrial pattern, traditional Chinese society is marked by a familial pattern of social relations. The "blood and flesh" bond took precedence over all other social ties, and the identity of surname between individuals generated a spontaneous feeling of kinship and imposed a compelling sense of mutual obligation. In this sense, then, the changes in the family and the clan not only affect the structure of the kinship system itself but also cripple its functional position in Chinese society, and the present process of change alters the basic pattern of Chinese society.

Our analysis has shown that the kinship system owed its former importance in the web of social relations to many of its functions which are being reduced or removed by Communist socio-economic developments. We have seen that the larger kinship system was an extensive group for mutual aid. An especially important economic aspect of the traditional family was the fitting of its structural features to the function of giving material care and security to the individual throughout his entire life cycle — raising him from infancy, providing him with the means or channels of livelihood in his adult years, and supporting him in old age — functions which made the family the very root of his social life and which have been progressively reduced by the rise of modern urban economy in the pre-Communist period, the steady subversion of the whole system of family authority and status over the past half century, and now by the collectivization of farms and nationalization of businesses by the Communists.

It has also become clear that the former family and extended kinship system as an informal but basic political unit in the sense that it was indispensable for the maintenance of peace and order has little or no meaning in the Communist political system, which extends its direct control down to the level of the individual, and under which, in fact, the systematic destruction of the political function of the kinship system has been a major measure taken to clear the way for the development of a new social order.

Lastly, we have seen that the accelerated development of modern schools, first under the Republic and now in the Communist state, has increasingly replaced the family as the basic educational center for learning occupational skills and for moral and citizenship training at the same time that the trend towards secularization is making deep inroads into ancestor worship, the family religion and the most universal cult in China, which contributed not merely stability to the family institution but also an attitude of piety in the religious life of the Chinese people.

In considering implications for the future we would note that the reduction of functions results not only in the decrease of dominance of the family and the clan in the organizational scheme of Chinese society as a whole but also in the diminishing size, solidarity, and stability of the family itself.

Although the membership of the two-generation or the weakened three-generation family does not appear to be much smaller than that in the former common people's average household, each of such individual families now must stand on its own limited numerical strength, as the rapidly disintegrating extended kinship system is unable to give it the former strong collective support. And a new factor having possible effect on the size of the family is the increasingly vigorous birth control movement since 1956. In March of 1957 editorials and articles in the Communist press, including the leading official organ, *Jen-min Jih-pao* (People's Daily) in Peking, openly put aside the anti-Malthusian tradition of Marxism and expressed alarm at the prospect of further increase at the annual rate of 2 to 3 per cent of the already excessive population of six hundred million. While the idea of birth control had already been accepted by the urban intelligentsia for several decades, Communist leadership now finds it urgent to develop a birth control movement among the workers and peasants who have not heard of it before. Should the propaganda drive and available medical facilities eventually succeed in making birth control effective among the common people, there would be possible reduction in the size of the family. As reduction in membership would decrease the collective strength of the family in the performance of many of its social and economic functions, the birth control movement portends a further weakening of the functional position of the family system.

That the reduction of family functions weakens the interdependence among family members, with the consequent decrease in solidarity in the family group, is clearly indicated in the high divorce rate among the new marriages under Communist rule. When romantic interest shifts from the spouse to a third party, there is now no strong socio-economic bond to hold the couple together, as emphasized by accounts in the Communist press.[9]

Most important in the long run, in addition to the functional and structural features of the Chinese family institution emerging under communism, is the incompatibility between the social dominance of the kinship system and the basic features of a modern industrial society under authoritarian socialism. The contrast between the particularistic and the universalistic pattern of social organization has been pointed out by Talcott Parsons. When kinship relations as a particularistic factor play a dominant role in social life, they result in a national society which is subdivided into numerous small, semi-autonomous, and mutually exclusive kinship cells. This localized, un-coordinated subdivision of the social structure is contradictory to the nature of a sensitively integrated mass society with a highly centralized control which intimately coordinates all the component parts down to the level of the single individual. The dynamic nature, the functional diversity, and the high degree of integration of such a mass society impose on the individual the requirement of specialization and universalism, the development of which would be hampered should the particularistic kinship relations retain the dominant position in the web of social relations. Thus, when Communist authorities assign specialized jobs to each college graduate throughout China as they have done every year since 1951, the individual's kinship ties play no part in the decision of job assignments. In some cases, husband and wife are assigned jobs in different localities in knowing disregard of the family relationship in order to meet the requirement of the state. Sharp indeed is the contrast between this system and the traditional situation in which nepotism based on kinship ties was condoned and even socially obligatory.

Modern Chinese intellectuals and the Communists are aware of the fact that a society subdivided into numerous self-containing kinship groups is neither conducive to centralized control nor favorable to the development of an industrial social order. The attack for half a century against familism and clannism, the numerous cases of political accusations against one's own kin with Communist encouragement, and the cultivation of a large number of extra-familial socio-economic ties are aspects of a conscious or unconscious social effort at detaching individuals from the firmest of traditional Chinese social ties, the kinship tie, in order to refit them into the mesh of new social relations based on the requirements of an industrial economy and a centralized political state.

When we examine this fundamental change, with its obviously profound meaning for the future, we see that it is taking place at various tempos in different types of communities and among different groups of the population. It is being materialized rapidly in the urban environment, the cities having been the staging center of the family revolution for half a century. In the country, in spite of Communist ideological encouragement and pressure from agricultural collectivization, change of the kinship system among the peasants faces the counterforces of the immobility of the agrarian population and the lack of diversity of the agricultural economy; as family members stay together and the bulk of the peasantry remain earthbound to the same village as kinship groups, the old kinship relations have many occasions to reassert themselves whenever the untested socio-economic pattern fails to meet the infinitely varied needs of the individual. Even in an agricultural producers' cooperative, with its obliteration of private ownership of land and heavy farm equipment, there are still many aspects of social and economic life in which the individual must turn to other fellowmen for assistance not provided for by the cooperative organization or other non-kinship bodies; and traditional experience will influence a person to turn to close kin in such circumstances. Under pressure from Communist ideology and adverse socio-economic factors, the rural kinship system will weaken, but it may not disintegrate to the same degree as in the urban community with its mobile population and its diversified economy, which continuously detaches individuals from their kinship groups and reshuffles them into widely separate compartments in the social and economic structure.

Counteracting these conservative features of agrarian life are the new influences from the people's commune system which completely separates the means of production from family ownership, enforces compulsory collective labor outside the family, furnishes direct economic support to all commune members including children and the aged, transfers cooking, child care, and other domestic chores to collective organizations, and reduces contact and interaction between family members as parents work at separate sites and children go to nurseries or schools during the day. This structural pattern of communal living compels far-reaching alterations in the organization of family life, despite the slackening of ideological motivation in family reform. Since the adoption of the commune system, there has been widespread voicing of fear for the "impending disappearance of the family," a fear which the Communists try hard to allay.

The acceptance of fundamental social change is faster among the younger than the older generation. Those who were under the age of twenty when the Communists took over the country in 1949 accept the new family pattern and become adjusted to non-kinship organizations more readily than those over this age. In terms of educational levels, those with higher education yield to the influence of modern trends more rapidly than the uneducated or the poorly educated because of the difference in opportunity in absorbing the new family idealism. In terms of economic gradations, change develops more readily among higher than among lower income groups, as the spreading of the family revolution from upper and middle classes to the workers and peasants has shown. The higher economic groups not only enjoy more contacts with new ideas through education, but they can also better afford the risk of experimenting with a new arrangement of life as there is a greater margin of economic security to cushion the shock from possible failure. A wealthy family can better afford than a poor one to let a son or a daughter enter marriage without insisting upon obtaining a return for the economic investment in raising her.

Taken as a whole, the general materialization of the long-term trends depends on the eventual success of the new socio-economic order in adequately assuming many of the vital functions which formerly were performed by the traditional family and its extended kinship system. Before the new social system has thoroughly proved its worth and dependability, the people, especially the older people, will not lightly risk giving up their time-tested system of social relations, which not merely has demonstrated its material benefits to them but is also deeply woven into their emotional disposition. The system of arranged marriage being driven underground by the enforcement of the Communist Marriage Law is a case in point. As the gigantic experiment of the Communist revolution gropes along its uncharted path, the course of development of these trends will be marked with cycles of advance, halt, and reversal, as it has in the past turbulent half century. Should these trends eventually come to take root among the larger proportion of the Chinese population, Chinese society will by then have permanently shifted from the age-old organizational pattern centered upon the kinship system as the core, the pattern which so long characterized Chinese civilization.

The Marriage Law of the People's Republic of China

Promulgated by the Central People's Government on May 1, 1950

Chapter One: General Principles

Article 1.

The arbitrary and compulsory feudal marriage system, which is based on the superiority of man over woman and which ignores the children's interests, is abolished.

The New Democratic marriage system, which is based on free choice of partners, on monogamy, on equal rights for both sexes, and on protection of the lawful interests of women and children, shall be put into effect.

Article 2.

Polygamy, concubinage, child betrothal, interference with the remarriage of widows and the exaction of money or gifts in connection with marriage shall be prohibited.

Chapter Two: Contracting of Marriage

Article 3.

Marriage shall be based upon the complete willingness of the two parties. Neither party shall use compulsion and no third party shall be allowed to interfere.

Article 4.

A marriage can be contracted only after the man has reached twenty years of age and the woman has reached eighteen years of age.

Article 5.

No man or woman in any of the following instances shall be allowed to marry:

(a) Where the man and woman are lineal relatives by blood or where the man and woman are brother and sister born of the same parents or where the man and woman are half-brother and half-sister. The question of prohibiting marriage between collateral relatives by blood within the fifth degree of relationship is to be determined by custom.

(b) When one party, because of certain physical defects, is sexually impotent.

(c) Where one party is suffering from venereal disease, mental disorder, leprosy, or any other disease which is regarded by medical science as rendering the person unfit for marriage.

Article 6.

In order to contract a marriage, both the man and the woman shall register in person with the people's government of the subdistrict or village in which they reside. If the marriage is found to be in conformity with the provisions of this law, the local people's government shall, without delay, issue a marriage certificate.

If the marriage is found to be incompatible with the provisions of this law, no registration shall be granted.

Chapter Three: Rights and Duties of Husband and Wife

Article 7.

Husband and wife are companions living together and shall enjoy equal status in the home.

Article 8.

Husband and wife are in duty bound to love, respect, assist, and look after each other, to live in harmony, to engage in production, to care for the children, and to strive jointly for the welfare of the family and for the building up of a new society.

Article 9.

Both husband and wife shall have the right to free choice of occupations and free participation in work or in social activities.

Article 10.

Both husband and wife shall have equal rights in the possession and management of family property.

Article 11.

Both husband and wife shall have the right to use his or her own family name.

Article 12.

Both husband and wife shall have the right to inherit each other's property.

Chapter Four: Relations between Parents and Children

Article 13.

Parents have the duty to rear and to educate their children; the children have the duty to look after and to assist their parents. Neither the parents nor the children shall maltreat or desert one another.

The foregoing provision also applies to stepparents and stepchildren. Infanticide by drowning and similar criminal acts are strictly prohibited.

Article 14.

Parents and children shall have the right to inherit one another's property.

Article 15.

Children born out of wedlock shall enjoy the same rights as children born in lawful wedlock. No person shall be allowed to harm or to discriminate against children born out of wedlock.

Where the paternity of a child born out of wedlock is legally established by the mother of the child, by other witnesses, or by other material evidence, the identified father must bear the whole or part of the cost of maintenance and education of the child until it has attained the age of eighteen.

With the consent of the natural mother, the natural father may have custody of the child.

With regard to the maintenance of a child whose natural mother marries, the provisions of Article 22 shall apply.

Article 16.

A husband or wife shall not maltreat or discriminate against a child born of a previous marriage.

Chapter Five: Divorce

Article 17.

Divorce shall be granted when husband and wife both desire it. In the event of either the husband or the wife insisting upon divorce, it may be granted only when mediation by the subdistrict people's government and the subdistrict judicial organ has failed to bring about a reconciliation.

In the case where divorce is desired by both the husband and wife, both parties shall register with the subdistrict people's government in order to obtain a certificate of divorce. The subdistrict government, after establishing that divorce is desired by both parties and that appropriate measures have been taken for the care of children and property, shall issue the certificate of divorce without delay.

When only one party insists on divorce, the subdistrict people's government may try to effect a reconciliation. If such mediation fails, it should, without delay, refer the case to the district or city people's court for decision. The subdistrict people's government shall not attempt to prevent or to obstruct either party from appealing to the district or city people's court.

In dealing with a divorce case, the district or city people's court must, in the first instance, try to bring about a reconciliation between the parties. In case such mediation fails, the court shall render a verdict without delay.

In the case where, after divorce, both husband and wife desire the resumption of matrimonial relations, they should apply to the subdistrict people's government for a registration of remarriage. The subdistrict people's government should accept such a registration and issue a certificate of remarriage.

Article 18.

The husband shall not apply for a divorce when his wife is with child. He may apply for divorce only one year after the birth of the child. In the case of a woman applying for divorce, this restriction does not apply.

Article 19.

The spouse of a member of the revolutionary army on active service who maintains correspondence with his (or her) family must first obtain his (or her) consent before he (or she) can ask for a divorce.

As from the date of the promulgation of this law, divorce may be granted to the spouse of a member of the revolutionary army who does not correspond with his (or her) family for a subsequent period of two years. Divorce may also be granted to the spouse of a member of the revolutionary army who has not maintained correspondence with his (or her) family for over two years prior to the promulgation of this law and who fails to correspond with his (or her) family for a further period of one year subsequent to the promulgation of the present law.

Chapter Six: Support and Education of Children after Divorce

Article 20.

The blood ties between parents and children do not end with the divorce of the parents. No matter whether the father or the mother acts as guardian of the child or children, they still remain the children of both parties.

After divorce, both parents still have the duty to support and educate their children.

After divorce, the guiding principle is to allow the mother to have custody of a baby still being breast-fed. After the weaning of the child, if a dispute arises between the two parties over the guardianship and an agreement cannot be reached, the people's court shall render a decision in accordance with the best interests of the child.

Article 21.

After divorce, if the mother is given custody of a child, the father shall be responsible for the whole or part of the necessary cost of the maintenance and education of the child. Both parties shall reach an agreement regarding the amount of the cost and the duration of such maintenance and education. In the case where the two parties fail to reach an agreement, the people's court shall render a decision.

Payment must be made in cash, in kind, or by tilling the land allocated to the child.

Such an agreement reached between the parents or decision rendered by the people's court in connection with the maintenance and educational expenses for a child shall not prevent the child from requesting either parent to increase the amount above that fixed by agreement or by judicial decision.

Article 22.

In the case where a divorced woman remarries and her husband is willing to pay the whole or part of the cost of maintenance and education for the child or children by her former husband, the father of the child or children is entitled to have such cost of maintenance and education reduced or is entitled to be exempt from bearing such cost in accordance with the circumstances.

Chapter Seven: Property and Maintenance after Divorce

Article 23.

In case of divorce, the wife shall retain such property as belonged to her prior to her marriage. The disposal of other household properties shall be subject to agreement between the two parties. In the case where an agreement cannot be reached, the people's court shall render a decision after taking into consideration the actual state of the family property, the interests of the wife and the child or children, and the principle of benefiting the development of production.

In the case where the property allocated to the wife and her child or children is sufficient for the maintenance and education of the child or children, the husband may be exempt from bearing further maintenance and education costs.

Article 24.

After divorce, debts incurred during the period of marriage shall be paid out of the property acquired by husband and wife during this period. In the case where no such property has been acquired or in the case where such property is insufficient to pay off such debts, the husband shall be held responsible for paying these debts. Debts incurred separately by the husband or wife shall be paid off by the party responsible.

Article 25.

After divorce, if one party has not remarried and has difficulties in maintenance, the other party should render assistance. Both parties shall work out an agreement with regard to the method and duration of such assistance; in case an agreement cannot be reached, the people's court shall render a decision.

Chapter Eight: Bylaws

Article 26.

Persons violating this law shall be punished in accordance with law. In the case where interference with the freedom of marriage has caused death or injury, the person guilty of such interference shall bear criminal responsibility before the law.

Article 27.

This law shall come into force from the date of its promulgation. In regions inhabited by national minorities, the Military and Political Council of the Administrative Area of the provincial people's government may enact certain modifications of supplementary articles in conformity with the actual conditions prevailing among national minorities in regard to marriage. But such measures must be submitted to the Government Administration Council for ratification before enforcement.

Reference Notes

Chapter I. The Communist Revolution and the Change of Chinese Social Institutions

1. *Hun-yin fa chih ch'i yu-kuan wen-chien* (The Marriage Law and Related Documents), Peking, 1950, pp. 1–21.
2. *The Works of Mencius* (tr. James Legge), Shanghai, 1949, Book III, Part I, ch. 4.
3. *Chung-hua min-kuo t'ung-chih t'i-yao* (Statistical Abstract of the Republic of China), Nanking; 1947 ed., p. 4, 1935 ed., p. 219.
4. *Chia tzu hsin-shu* (New Book on Chia Tzu), quoted in *Tz'u yuan* (Source of Phrases), Shanghai, 1949, p. 173.
5. See Talcott Parsons, *The Social System*, Glencoe, Illinois, 1951, pp. 85–87.
6. K'ang Yu-wei, *Ta t'ung shu* (The Great Commonwealth), Shanghai, 1923, Part I.
7. *The Civil Code of the Republic of China* (tr. Hsia Tsin-lin), Shanghai, 1931, pp. 249–291.
8. See, for example, "Absolute Proof of the Communists' Practice in Communal Wives," in *Kuang-ming chih-lu* (The Road of Light), Nanking, vol. I, no. 7–8, June 1931, pp. 1–7.

Chapter II. Freedom of Marriage

1. *Works of Mencius* (tr. Legge), Book III, Part II, ch. 4, p. 268.
2. *Ibid.*, Book V, Part I, ch. 1, p. 345.
3. *Hun-yin fa hsuan-ch'uan shou-ts'e* (Propaganda Handbook of the Marriage Law), Peking, 1951, pp. 9–11.
4. *Jen-min jih-pao* (People's Daily), Peking, March 9, 1950, p. 3.
5. *Hun-yin fa chih ch'i yu-kuan wen-chien* (The Marriage Law and Related Documents), Peking, 1950, p. 89.
6. Ta Chen, *Population in Modern China*, Chicago, 1946, p. 114.
7. Hsü Chen, *Chung-kuo fu-nü yün-tung shih* (The History of the Chinese Women's Movement), Shanghai, 1930, pp. 34–60.
8. See, for example, the "Hsiu-cheng shen-kan-ning pien-ch'ü chan-hsing t'iao-li" (Revised Temporary Marriage Regulations in the Border Region of Shensi, Kansu, and Ninghsia Provinces), *Shen-kan-ning pien-ch'ü cheng-ts'eh*

t'iao li lei-chih (Collection of Policies and Regulations of the Border Region of Shensi, Kansu, and Ninghsia Provinces), 1944.

9. Marriage Law, Article 1 (see Appendix).

10. *Ibid.*, Article 3.

11. *Ibid.*, Article 2.

12. *Ibid.*, Article 6.

13. *Ibid.*, Article 3.

14. *Ibid.*, Article 3.

15. *Ibid.*, Article 2.

16. *Ibid.*, Article 4.

17. *Ibid.*, Article 5.

18. *Shing-tao jih-pao*, Hong Kong, December 11, 1951, p. 4.

19. *Jen-min jih-pao*, Peking, June 3, 1955, p. 2.

20. *Ibid.*, March 29, 1951, p. 2.

21. *Ibid.*, August 9, 1951, p. 2.

22. *Ibid.*, March 29, 1951, p. 2.

23. *Ibid.*, September 29, 1951, p. 3.

24. Liu Mien-chih, "The Policy of Simultaneous Mobilization of Men and Women Peasants and of Effective Protection for Women's Legitimate Rights Must be Thoroughly Enforced in the Land Reform," *Hsin Chung-kuo fu-nü* (New Chinese Women), no. 25–26, December 1951, p. 16.

25. *Jen-min jih-pao*, September 29, 1951, p. 3.

26. *Chieh-fang jih-pao*, February 11, 1952, p. 5.

27. *Hun-yin fa hsin-hua* (New Talks on the Marriage Law), Shanghai, 1950, pp. 9–10.

28. *Hun-yin wen-t'i shou-ts'e* (Handbook on the Marriage Problem), Peking, 1951, p. 24.

29. *Hsin Chung-kuo yueh-k'an* (New China Monthly), no. 24, October 1951, pp. 1245–1246.

30. *Hun-yin fa hsin-hua*, p. 19.

31. *Hsin Chung-kuo yueh-k'an*, vol. 4, no. 5, October 1951, p. 1249.

32. Propaganda Handbook of the Marriage Law, 1951, pp. 13–16.

33. *Ch'ang-chiang jih-pao*, Hankow, January 8, 1952, p. 2.

34. *Jen-min jih-pao*, October 9, 1951, p. 3.

35. *Ch'ang-chiang jih-pao*, January 8, 1952, p. 2.

36. Yen Yung-chieh, "A Good Way of Making Propaganda on the Marriage Law," *Hsin Chung-kuo fu-nü* no. 25–26, December 1951, p. 44.

37. "Studying the Marriage Law and Enforcing It," *Hsin Chung-kuo fu-nü*, no. 12, July 1950, p. 4.

38. *Jen-min jih-pao*, May 13, 1953, p. 3.

39. Marriage Law, Articles 6 and 7.

40. Some local courts in the rural areas still rule in favor of returning the price of the bride in case the divorce is initiated by the wife, but such courts are manned by "unregenerated" cadres who are the object of criticism by the Ministry of Justice of the Central Government of the Communist regime. See "Judicial Workers Ignoring Women's Interests and Being Irresponsible toward Matrimonial Cases," *Jen-min jih-pao*, November 10, 1951, p. 3.

41. *Wah-kiu yat-po*, Hong Kong, May 9, 1951, p. 4.

42. Marriage Law, Article 2.

43. See statement by Shih Liang, Minister of Justice, in *Hun-yin fa chih ch'i yu-kuan wen-chien*, p. 16.

Chapter III. Associated Problems of Marriage

1. Ta Chen, *Population in Modern China*, Chicago, 1946, pp. 112–113; *Chung-hua min-kuo t'ung-chih t'i-yao* (Statistical Abstract of the Republic of China), Nanking, 1947, p. 244.

2. *Chung-hua min-kuo t'ung-chih t'i-yao*, p. 9.

3. Ratios computed from Table 43, Ta Chen, p. 112.

4. Fifteenth census, vol. IV, Part I, p. 11. In this comparison, there is also the age factor at the time when the women became widowed. In the United States, the median age at which women become widowed is 51 (Statistical Bulletin, vol. 33, no. 8, August 1952, published by the Metropolitan Life Insurance Company). This means that widowhood in the United States is largely dictated by late age and not imposed by institutional restriction. Unfortunately no comparable data is available on the age of Chinese widows.

5. P. K. Wattol, *Population Problem in India*, p. 36, quoted in Ta Chen, p. 112.

6. "Report on Widow Ch'en's Case by the Huai-yang County Court," *Hun-yin fa chih ch'i yu-kuan wen-chien* (The Marriage Law and Related Documents), Peking, 1950, p. 52.

7. *Ibid.*; also, "A Directive from the Central-South Regional Military and Political Committee," *Shing-tao jih-pao*, Hong Kong, September 4, 1951, p. 2.

8. *Ch'ang-chiang jih-pao*, Hankow, January 12, 1952, p. 2.

9. *Chieh-fang jih-pao* (Liberation Daily), Shanghai, January 9, 1952, p. 3.

10. *Hun-yin fa chih ch'i yu-kuan wen-chien*, pp. 29 ff.

11. "Marriage Law Being thoroughly Enforced in Various Parts of North China," *Jen-min jih-pao*, March 9, 1951, p. 2.

12. *Jen-min jih-pao*, September 29, 1951, p. 3.

13. Marriage Law, articles 13, 15, 16, 22; also, *Hun-yin fa hsin-hua* (New Talks on the Marriage Law), Shanghai, 1950, p. 51.

14. *Hun-yin fa hsuan-ch'uan shou-ts'e* (Propaganda Handbook of the Marriage Law), Peking, 1951, pp. 7–8.

15. *Ibid.*, pp. 6–7.

16. "Change of the Marriage Institution in Rural Communities in Shansi and Suiyuan Provinces through Land Reform," *Hun-yin wen-t'i tso-t'an* (Symposium on the Marriage Problem), Canton, 1951, pp. 49–51.

17. *Hun-yin fa hsin-hua*, Shanghai, 1950, p. 5.

18. Florence Ayscough, *Chinese Women Yesterday and Today*, Boston, 1937, pp. 57–61.

19. *Hun-yin fa hsuan-ch'uan shou-ts'e*, pp. 24–26.

20. *Hun-yin wen-t'i shou-ts'e* (Handbook on the Marriage Problem), Peking, 1951, pp. 41–42.

21. *Jen-min jih-pao*, October 15, 1951, p. 3.

22. See major Chinese newspapers such as the *Jen-min jih-pao* of Peking, *Ch'ang-chiang jih-pao* of Hankow, and *Chieh-fang jih-pao* of Shanghai, issues from January to June, 1952.

Chapter IV. Freedom of Divorce

1. *Hun-yin fa hsuan-ch'uan shou-ts'e* (Propaganda Handbook of the Marriage Law), Peking, 1951, pp. 60–62.

2. "Questions and Answers on the Enforcement of the Marriage Law," by the Committee on Laws and Institutions, in the *Hun-yin fa chih ch'i yu-kuan wen-chien* (The Marriage Law and Related Documents), Peking, 1950, p. 27.

3. Ch'en Shao-yü, "Report on the Process and Reasons in the Drafting of the Marriage Law of the People's Republic of China," *Hun-yin fa chih ch'i yu-kuan wen-chien*, pp. 69–70.

4. *Hun-yin fa hsin-hua* (New Talks on the Marriage Law), Shanghai, 1950, pp. 3–4.

5. *Hun-yin chuang-k'uang mu-ch'ien fa-chan li-an* (Sample Cases on the Present Development of Marital Conditions), by the People's Court of Shansi Province, January, 1950.

6. Computed from Ta Chen, *Population in Modern China*, Chicago, 1946, Table 43, p. 112.

7. Computed from Table 3, census of nine counties in Szechwan Province, *Chung-hua min-kuo t'ung-chi t'i-yao* (Statistical Abstract of the Republic of China), Nanking, 1947, p. 9.

8. Shih Liang, "Seriously and Thoroughly Enforce the Marriage Law," *Jen-min jih-pao* (People's Daily), Peking, October 13, 1951, p. 3.

9. *Wah-kiu yat-po*, Hong Kong, April 17, 1953, p. 4.

10. Ch'en Shao-yü, cited note 3.

11. *Jen-min jih-pao*, September 29, 1951, p. 3.

12. *Wah-kiu yat-po*, Hong Kong, September 8, 1952, p. 4.

13. *Hun-yin fa chih ch'i yu-kuan wen-chien*, pp. 70–71.

14. *Wah-kiu yat-po*, April 20, 1953, p. 4.

15. *Hun-yin fa chih ch'i yu-kuan wen-chien*, p. 72.

16. *Jen-min jih-pao*, September 29, 1951, p. 3.

17. *Ibid.*

18. *Hun-yin fa chih ch'i yu-kuan wen-chien*, p. 74.

19. Teng Yung-ch'ao, "A Report on the Marriage Law of the People's Republic of China," *Hun-yin wen-t'i shou-ts'e* (Handbook on the Marriage Problem), Peking, 1951, pp. 7–8.

20. See note 13.

21. Report by Kuo Hsin-lan, woman judge in the People's Court of Canton, March 8, 1951, *Shing-tao jih-pao*, Hong Kong, March 10, 1951.

22. *Hun-yin wen-t'i shou-ts'e*, p. 34; *Hun-yin fa hsin-hua*, pp. 43–45.

23. *Hun-yin wen-t'i shou-ts'e*, pp. 37–39.

24. *Hun-yin fa hsin-hua*, p. 56.

25. Ch'en Yu-t'ung, "Liquidation of the Old Legal View as a Condition for Thorough Implementation of the Marriage Law," *Hsin Chung-kuo fu-nü* (New Chinese Women), no. 9, September, 1952, pp. 7–8.

26. *Hun-yin wen-t'i shou-ts'e*, pp. 38–39.

27. *Ibid.*, p. 40.

28. Shih Liang, cited note 8.

29. Li Cheng, "Strengthen the Learning of the Marriage Law Among Village and Subdistrict Cadres," *Jen-min jih-pao*, October 9, 1951, p. 3.

30. Hsü Teh-hsing, "Let Us Correctly Enforce the Marriage Law to Abolish the Feudalistic Marriage Institution," *Hsin Chung-kuo yueh-k'an* (New China Monthly), no. 19, May 1951, p. 34.

31. *Hun-yin fa hsuan-ch'uan shou-ts'e*, p. 60.

32. "Examples of Court Decisions on Matrimonial Cases," *Hun-yin wen-t'i shou-ts'e*, pp. 34–35.

33. *Ibid.*, p. 36; also, *Hun-yin fa hsin-hua*, pp. 46–48, and the Marriage Law, Article 19.

34. *Jen-min jih-pao*, October 13, 1951, p. 3.

35. *Chieh-fang jih-pao*, Shanghai, January 14, 1952, p. 3.

36. *Jen-min jih-pao*, October 9, 1951, p. 3.

37. Hsü Teh-hsing, cited note 30.

38. *Jen-min jih-pao*, September 30, 1951, p. 3.

39. "Statement by the Preparatory Committee of the Democratic Women's League," *Hsin Chung-kuo yueh-k'an*, October 1951, p. 1248.

40. Ch'en Yu-t'ung, cited note 25.

41. Tso Chung-fen, "Representatives' Conference of Model Laborers Implementing the Marriage Law in Lushan County," *Hsin Chung-kuo fu-nü*, no. 12, December 1952, pp. 10–12.

Chapter V. Crumbling of the Age Hierarchy

1. Meng Tzu, Book II, Part II, ch. 2. The quotation represents a slight alteration by the author from James Legge's translation, *The Works of Mencius*, pp. 213–214.

2. Han-yi Feng, "The Chinese Kinship System," *Harvard Journal of Asiatic Studies*, vol. 2, no. 2, July 1937, p. 160, reprinted separately in 1948. An explanation of the terms in the chart follows:

Lineal relatives:
Fu — Father
Mu — Mother
Tsu fu — grandfather
Tsu mu — grandmother
Tseng tsu fu — great grandfather
Tseng tsu mu — great grandmother
Kao tsu fu — great great grandfather
Kao tsu mu — great great grandmother
Tsu — son
Nü — daughter
Sun — grandson
Sun nü — granddaughter
Tseng sun — son of grandson
Tseng sun nü — daughter of grandson
Hsuan sun — son of "son of grandson"
Hsuan sun nü — daughter of "son of grandson"

First collaterals descended from males through males:
Hsiung — elder brother

Sao — wife of elder brother
Ti — younger brother
Ti fu — wife of younger brother
Po fu — elder brother of father
Po mu — wife of elder brother of father
Shu fu — younger brother of father
Shu mu — wife of younger brother of father
Po tsu fu — elder brother of grandfather
Po tsu mu — wife of elder brother of grandfather
Shu tsu fu — younger brother of grandfather
Shu tsu mu — wife of younger brother of grandfather
Tseng po tsu fu — elder brother of great grandfather
Tseng po tsu mu — wife of elder brother of great grandfather
Tseng shu tsu fu — younger brother of great grandfather
Tseng shu tsu mu — wife of younger brother of great grandfather
Chi — son of brother
Chi nü — daughter of brother
Chi sun — grandson of brother
Chi sun nü — granddaughter of brother
Tseng chi sun — great grandson of brother
Tseng chi sun nü — great granddaughter of brother

Second collaterals descended from males through males:
T'ang hsiung — son of father's brother, older than ego (wife — sao)
T'ang ti — son of father's brother, younger than ego (wife — t'ang ti fu)
T'ang tzu — daughter of father's brother, older than ego
T'ang mei — daughter of father's brother, younger than ego
T'ang po fu — son of grandfather's brother, older than father
T'ang shu fu — son of grandfather's brother, younger than father
T'ang ku mu — wife of son of grandfather's brother
T'ang po tsu fu — son of great grandfather's brother, older than grandfather
T'ang shu tsu fu — son of great grandfather's brother, younger than grandfather
T'ang ku tsu mu — wife of son of great grandfather's brother
T'ang chi — son of "son of father's brother"
T'ang chi nü — daughter of "son of father's brother"
T'ang chi sun — grandson of "son of father's brother"
T'ang chi sun nü — granddaughter of "son of father's brother"

Third collaterals descended from males through males:
Tsai ts'ung hsiung — grandson of grandfather's brother, older than ego
Tsai ts'ung ti — grandson of grandfather's brother, younger than ego
Tsai ts'ung tzu — granddaughter of grandfather's brother, older than ego
Tsai ts'ung mei — granddaughter of grandfather's brother, younger than ego
Tsai ts'ung po fu — grandson of great grandfather's brother, older than father
Tsai ts'ung shu fu — grandson of great grandfather's brother, younger than father
Tsai ts'ung ku mu — wife of grandson of great grandfather's brother
Tsai ts'ung chi — great grandson of grandfather's brother
Tsai ts'ung chi nü — great granddaughter of grandfather's brother

Fourth collaterals descended from males through males:
Tsu hsiung — great grandson of grandfather's brother, older than ego
Tsu ti — great grandson of grandfather's brother, younger than ego
Tsu tzu — great granddaughter of grandfather's brother, older than ego
Tsu mei — great granddaughter of grandfather's brother, younger than ego
    (The above four terms also apply to relatives of ego's generational level beyond
    the fourth collateral on the male side.)

First collaterals descended from females through males:
Tzu — elder sister
Tzu fu — husband of elder sister
Mei — younger sister
Mei fu — husband of younger sister
Ku mu — father's sister
Ku fu — husband of father's sister
Ku tsu mu — grandfather's sister
Ku tsu fu — husband of grandfather's sister
Tseng tsu ku mu — great grandfather's sister
Tseng tsu ku fu — husband of great grandfather's sister
Wai sheng — son of sister
Wai sheng nü — daughter of sister
Wai sheng sun — sister's grandson
Wai sheng tseng sun — sister's great grandson

Second collaterals descended from females through males:
Piao hsiung — son of father's sister, older than ego
Piao ti — son of father's sister, younger than ego
Piao tzu — daughter of father's sister, older than ego
Piao mei — daughter of father's sister, younger than ego
Piao ku mu — daughter of grandfather's sister
Piao po fu — husband of daughter of grandfather's sister, older than father
Piao shu fu — husband of daughter of grandfather's sister, younger than father
Piao tsu mu — daughter of great grandfather's sister
Piao tsu fu — husband of daughter of great grandfather's sister
Piao chih — son of father's sister's son
Piao chih nü — daughter of father's sister's son
Piao chih sun — grandson of father's sister's son

Third collaterals descended from females through males:
T'ang piao hsiung — son of daughter of grandfather's sister, older than ego
T'ang piao ti — son of daughter of grandfather's sister, younger than ego
T'ang piao tzu — daughter of daughter of grandfather's sister, older than ego
T'ang piao mei — daughter of daughter of grandfather's sister, younger than ego
T'ang paio ku mu — daughter of "daughter of great grandfather's sister"
T'ang piao po fu — husband of daughter of "daughter of great grandfather's sister," older than father
T'ang piao shu fu — husband of daughter of "daughter of great grandfather's sister," younger than father
T'ang piao chih — son of "son of daughter of grandfather's sister"
T'ang piao chih nü — daughter of "son of daughter of daughter of grandfather's sister"

Fourth collaterals descended from females through males:
Tsai ts'ung piao hsiung — son of "daughter of daughter of great grandfather's sister," older than ego
Tsai ts'ung piao ti — son of "daughter of daughter of great grandfather's sister," younger than ego
Tsai ts'ung piao tzu — daughter of "daughter of daughter of great grandfather's sister," older than ego
Tsai ts'ung piao mei — daughter of "daughter of daughter of great grandfather's sister," younger than ego

3. Feng's study gave 41 groups of relatives each with a distinct category of kinship terminology. *Ch'ing Wei Lu* (A Collection of Nomenclature) in volumes 1 to 8, gave 160 different kinship terms, with each term capable of further subdivision by the ranking of physical age. As Feng did not use the *Ch'ing Wei Lu* in his research, there may be some disagreement between his results and the listing in the *Ch'ing Wei Lu*. Nevertheless, both works show vast numbers of people that could be included in the traditional hierarchy of status and authority based primarily on the factors of generation, age, and proximity of kinship.

4. See Ch'ü T'ung-tsu, *Chung-kuo fa-lu yü Chung-kuo sheh-hui* (Law and Chinese Society), Kunming, 1944.

5. See the presentation of this point in Marion J. Levy, Jr.'s *The Family Revolution in Modern China*, Cambridge, 1949, pp. 127–133.

6. Fan Tz'u asked Confucius how to farm, and the reply was, "I do not know as much as an old farmer." See Confucius, *Analects*, Book XIII, ch. 4.

7. See *Ch'ing-ch'ao Hsü Wen-hsien T'ung-k'ao* (Compendium of Documents of the Ch'ing Dynasty), Shanghai, 1934, ch. 242, pp. 9861.

8. Edgar Snow, *Red Star Over China*, New York, 1944, p. 292.

9. Feng Wen-pin, "Present Conditions and Work of the Youth League," *Ch'ang-chiang Daily*, January 8, 1952, p. 4; New China News Agency, Peking, May 12, 1957.

10. Feng Min-pin, "The Chinese New Democratic Youth League as the Standard Bearer of the Tradition of Revolutionary Struggle of the Chinese Youth," *Hsin Chung-kuo yueh-k'an* (New China Monthly), no. 19, May 1951, p. 52.

11. *Hsin Chung-kuo jen-wu chih* (Who's Who in New China), 1950, Hong Kong, pp. 2–3.

12. *Nan-fang jih-pao*, Canton, April 19, 1950, p. 3.

13. Feng Wen-pin, in *Chang-chiang jih-pao*, January 8, 1952, p. 4.

14. *Hsin chung-kuo yueh-k'an*, no. 19, May 1951, p. 52.

15. Marriage Law, Article 13.

16. *Ibid.*, Articles 13, 14, 15, 16, 20, 21, 22.

17. *Ibid.*, Article 13.

18. Of the 73 cases in which young family members brought public accusation against relatives from March 1 to September 25, 1951, in the province of Kwangtung, 26 were against parents. See *Wah-kiu yat-po*, Hong Kong, September 25, 1951, p. 4.

19. *Jen-min jih-pao*, May 5, 1951, p. 6.

20. *Hun-yin fa hsin-hua* (New Talks on the Marriage Law), pp. 29–30.

Chapter VI. The Ascendancy of the Status of Women in the Family

1. K'ang Yu-wei, *Ta T'ung Shu* (The Great Commonwealth), Shanghai, 1923, Part I.

2. Marion Levy, *The Family Revolution in Modern China*, Cambridge, 1949, pp. 106–118.

3. *Chung-hua Min-kuo t'ung-chi t'i-yao* (Statistical Abstract of the Republic of China), Nanking, 1935, pp. 360–361.

4. Directive by the Council of Administration on the Conditions of Enforcement of the Marriage Law, *Hsin Chung-kuo yueh-k'an* (New China Monthly), no. 23, September 1951, p. 1244.

5. "A Preliminary Survey of the Enforcement of the Marriage Law in the Past Year and Opinion on its Further Thorough Enforcement," by the Preparatory Committee of the Democratic Women's League of the Central-South Region, *Hsin Chung-kuo yueh-k'an*, no. 24, October 1951, p. 1247.

6. *Jen-min jih-pao* (People's Daily), Peking, September 29, 1951, p. 3.

7. *Ibid.*, December 6, 1951, p. 6.

8. Li Ai-min, "Use Typical Cases to Educate the Cadres and the People," *Hsin Chung-kuo fu-nü* (New Chinese Women), no. 25–26, December 1951, p. 45.

9. *Jen-min jih-pao*, December 6, 1951, p. 3.

10. Ch'en Yu-t'ung, "Liquidation of the Old Legal View as a Condition for Thorough Implementation of the Marriage Law," *Hsin Chung-kuo fu-nü*, no. 9, September 1952, pp. 7–8.

11. *Jen-min jih-pao*, September 29, 1951, p. 3.

12. *Ibid.*, May 7, 1951, p. 2.

13. *Chieh-fang jih-pao*, Shanghai, January 9, 1952, p. 3.

14. *Ibid.*, September 1, 1951, p. 3.

15. *Hsien-tai fu-nü* (Modern Women), no. 9, August 1950, pp. 13–14.

16. Wu Ch'uen-heng, "Beating, Scolding and Mistreatment of Women Should Not be Allowed to Continue," *Hsin Chung-kuo fu-nü*, no. 25–26, December 1951, pp. 20–21.

17. *Chung-hua Min-kuo t'ung-chih t'i-yao* (Statistical Abstract of the Republic of China), Nanking, 1947, pp. 10–11.

18. "Samples of Court Decisions on Matrimonial Cases by the People's Court of Tientsin," *Hun-yin wen-t'i shou-ts'e* (Handbook on the Marriage Problem), Peking, 1951, pp. 31–32.

19. Hsü Teh-hsing, "Let Us Correctly Enforce the Marriage Law to Abolish the Feudalistic Marriage Institution," *Hsin Chung-kuo yueh-k'an*, no. 19, May 1951, p. 34.

20. Li Ai-min, cited note 8.

21. Marriage Law, Article 2.

22. Yang Chih-hua, "Work on Women Labor in the Past Year," *Hsin Chung-kuo fu-nü*, no. 15, October 1950, p. 22.

23. "New China's Lucky Women Workers," *Jen-min jih-pao*, March 6, 1951, p. 2.

24. "Women's Enthusiastic Participation in Literacy Short Courses in Tientsin," by the Tientsin Branch of Democratic Women's League, *Hsin Chung-kuo fu-nü*, no. 14, September 1950, p. 20.

25. Sun Chu-feng, "Experiences in Mobilizing Educated Family Women to Teach Literacy Short Courses," *Hsin Chung-kuo fu-nü*, no. 9, September 1952, p. 8.

26. *Wah-kiu yat-po*, Hong Kong, March 13, 1951, p. 4.

27. *Hsien-tai fu-nü*, no. 9, August 1950, p. 2.

28. *Ta Kung Pao*, Hong Kong, March 19, 1956, p. 1.

29. *Jen-min jih-pao*, March 31, 1956, p. 1.

Chapter VII. The Ascendancy of Women's Status
Through the Women's Movement

1. "How Should Family Women Better Serve Socialist Reconstruction," *Hsin Chung-kuo fu-nü* (New Chinese Women), no. 10, October 1955, pp. 18–19.
2. *Shing-tao jih-pao*, Hong Kong, March 8, 1951, p. 2.
3. *Ta Kung Pao*, Hong Kong, March 8, 1951, p. 3.
4. *Ibid.*, August 20, 1951, p. 3.
5. *Ibid.*, March 8, 1951, p. 3.
6. *Nan-fang jih-pao*, Canton, April 14, 1950, p. 2.
7. *Shing-tao jih-pao*, March 8, 1951, p. 2.
8. *Hsin Chung-kuo fu-nü*, no. 10, October 1955, p. 28.
9. *Shing-tao jih-pao*, March 15, 1951, p. 2.
10. *Fu-nü tai-piao ta-hui tsu-chi kang-ning* (Principles of Organization of Conference of Women Representatives), Peking, 1950, ch. 1, article 2.
11. *Ibid.*, ch. 2, article 3, sections a, b, c and d.
12. *Ibid.*, ch. 2, article 8, sections a and b.
13. *Shing-tao jih-pao*, March 7, 1951, p. 2.
14. Liu Mien-chi, "The Necessity of Simultaneous Mobilization of Peasant Men and Women in Land Reform and of Effective Protection of Women's Legal Rights," *Hsin Chung-kuo fu-nü*, no. 25–26, 1951, p. 16.
15. Chang Yün, "Women's Movement in Shanghai in the Past Year and its Mission from Now On," *Hsien-tai fu-nü* (Modern Women), no. 10, September 1950, p. 6.
16. "A Letter from the Preparatory Committee for the Democratic Women's League of Hunan," *Hsin Chung-kuo fu-nü*, no. 11, November 1952, p. 36.
17. *Ta Kung Pao*, Hong Kong, March 13, 1951.
18. *Wah-kiu yat-po*, Hong Kong, March 7, 1951, p. 2.
19. Lo Ch'iung, "The Principles of Development of the Chinese Women's Movement," *Hsin Chung-kuo fu-nü*, no. 1, January 1953, p. 31.
20. Teng Yung-ch'ao, "New China's Women Advance Again and Again," *Jen-min jih-pao* (People's Daily), September 24, 1952, p. 2.
21. *Nan-fang jih-pao*, May 2, 1951, p. 2.
22. *Shing-tao jih-pao*, April 18, 1951, p. 2.
23. *Ibid.*, August 20, 1951, p. 2.
24. *Ibid.*, June 17, 1951, p. 6.
25. "How Should Family Women Better Serve Socialist Reconstruction," *Hsin Chung-kuo fu-nü*, no. 10, October 1955, pp. 18–23.
26. *Jen-min jih-pao*, editorial, April 8, 1956, p. 1.

Chapter VIII. Changing Family Economic Structure

1. John L. Buck, *Land Utilization in China, Statistics*, Chicago, 1937, pp. 301–303.
2. *Ibid.*, p. 303.
3. *Ibid.*
4. *The Civil Code of the Republic of China* (tr. Hsia Tsin-lin), Shanghai, 1931, Article 1138.

5. *Chih-hsing hun-yin fa wen ta* (Questions and Answers on the Enforcement of the Marriage Law), Central People's Committee on Laws and Institutions, Peking, 1950, pp. 41–66.

6. *Hun-yin fa hsuan-ch'uan shou-ts'e* (Propaganda Handbook of the Marriage Law), 1951, pp. 31–32; *T'u-ti Kai-ke Chung-yao Wen-hsien Lei-chih* (Collection of Important Documents on Land Reform), Peking, 1951, p. 69.

7. *Hsin Chung-kuo fu-nü* (New Chinese Women), no. 25–26, December 1951, p. 28.

8. *Hun-yin fa hsuan-ch'uan shou-ts'e* see note 6, p. 39.

9. *Shing-tao jih-pao*, Hong Kong, March 18, 1951, p. 2.

10. *Jen-min jih-pao* (People's Daily), Peking, March 7, 1951, p. 2.

11. "How Should Family Women Better Serve Socialist Reconstruction" (A Conclusion from Discussions), *Hsin Chung-kuo fu-nü*, no. 10, October 1955, pp. 18–19.

12. *Hsin Chung-kuo fu-nü*, editorial, no. 3, March 1956, p. 4.

13. New China News Agency (hereafter referred to as NCNA), September 24, 1956.

14. Ts'ai Ch'iang, "Take a Further Step to Organize the Masses of Women under the Flag of Patriotism," *Hsin Chung-kuo yueh-k'an* (New China Monthly), no. 19, March 1951, pp. 1020–1021.

15. NCNA, September 13, 1956.

16. Fan Fu, "Peasant Women's Contribution to Land Reform," *Hsin Chung-kuo fu-nü*, no. 15, September 1950, pp. 12–13.

17. *Jen-min jih-pao*, March 5, 1951, p. 1.

18. *Ibid.*, March 7, 1951, p. 2.

19. *Shing-tao jih-pao*, Hong Kong, March 8, 1951, p. 2.

20. Fan Fu, cited note 16; also *Wah-kiu yat-po*, Hong Kong, March 13, 1951.

21. *Jen-min jih-pao*, March 5, 1951, p. 1.

22. *Ta Kung Pao*, Hong Kong, March 4, 1953, p. 2.

23. See note 11.

24. *Jen-min jih-pao*, May 16, 1956.

25. "Let Us Concentrate on the Home-Chore Problem of the Women Textile Workers," the Department of Woman Labor, All-China Labor Federation, *Hsin Chung-kuo fu-nü*, no. 25–26, December 1951, pp. 8–9.

26. "Various Means of Child Care for Working Mothers," Democratic Women's League of Tientsin, *Hsin Chung-kuo fu-nü*, no. 8, August 1952, p. 10.

27. *Jen-min jih-pao*, December 14, 1951, p. 4.

28. "For a General Development of Child Welfare Enterprises," Child Welfare Department, All-China Democratic Women's League, *Hsin Chung-kuo fu-nü*, no. 25–26, December 1951, pp. 12–13.

29. *Ta Kung Pao*, Hong Kong, April 29, 1953, p. 3.

30. Hsü Chuan, *Jen-min jih-pao*, letter from a reader, March 8, 1952, p. 2.

31. *Jen-min jih-pao*, August 5, 1955, p. 2.

32. NCNA, September 26, 1956.

33. *Kung-shang jih-pao*, June 25, 1956, p. 3.

34. NCNA, September 24, 1956.

35. *Ibid.*, September 26, 1956.

36. Huang Lien-hai, "A Survey of Early Marriages among Young Factory Workers," *Chung-kuo ch'ing-nien pao* (Chinese Youth), Peking, September 6, 1956.

37. NCNA, March 7, 1959.

38. *Ibid.*, March 5, 1959.

39. *Ibid.*, March 6, 1959.

40. *Ibid.*, March 7, 1959.

41. See note 28.

42. *Chieh-fang jih-pao*, Shanghai, March 14, 1951, p. 2.

43. "Popularize the Experience of the 30,000-odd Mutual-aid Child Care Units," the Democratic Women's League of Northern Anhwei, *Hsin Chung-kuo fu-nü*, no. 8, August 1952, pp. 12–13.

44. *Jen-min jih-pao*, May 29, 1955, p. 6.

45. *Jen-min jih-pao*, editorial, May 16, 1956, p. 1.

46. *Ibid.*

47. Yen Ling, "Cooperativization Is the Road to Thorough Emancipation for Rural Women," *Hsin Chung-kuo fu-nü*, no. 12, September 1955, pp. 3–4.

48. Lo Chin-fan, "Whither Private Enterprise?" *Nan-fang jih-pao*, Canton, August 6, 1950, p. 1.

49. "Graphic Presentation of the First Five-year Plan," *Jen-min jih-pao*, July 8, 1955, p. 2.

50. Li Fu-ch'un, "Report on the First Five-year Plan," *Jen-min jih-pao*, July 8, 1955, p. 2.

51. *Jen-min jih-pao*, January 22, 1956, p. 2.

52. Chou En-lai, "Report on the Second Five-year Plan," NCNA, September 20, 1956.

53. NCNA, September 10, 1956.

54. *Ta Kung Pao*, Hong Kong, April 28, 1956, p. 1.

55. Chou En-lai, see note 52; also, Chinese Communist Party Congress, "Proposals on the Second Five-year Plan for the Development of the National Economy," NCNA, September 28, 1956.

56. Chou En-lai, cited note 52; also, comments and reports on the second five-year plan, *Wah-kiu yat-po*, Hong Kong, October 13 and 15, 1955, p. 4.

57. Liao Lu-yen, "The Great Victory for Three Years of Land Reform Movement," *Hua-ch'iao jih-pao*, New York, October 22–24, 1952.

58. "Is There Any Difference between a Higher Agricultural Producers' Cooperative and a Collective Farm?" *Cheng-chih hsueh-hsi* (Political Study), no. 6, June 1956.

59. Wang Keng-chin, "The Great Accomplishments of New China's Agriculture in the Past Three Years," *Hsin Chung-kuo fu-nü*, no. 10, 1952, pp. 28–29; Mao Tse-tung, "On the Problem of Cooperativization of Agriculture," *ibid.*, no. 10, October 1955, pp. 2–8.

60. Chou En-lai, cited note 52.

61. Liao Lu-yen, "Explanations on the Model Regulations for the Advanced Type of Agricultural Producers' Cooperatives," *Jen-min jih-pao*, June 17, 1956, p. 2.

62. Liao Lu-yen, "The Task for 1959 on the Agricultural Front," *Hung Ch'i* (Red Flag), no. 1, January 1959.

63. *Ibid.*

64. Mao Tse-tung, "On the Problem of Cooperativization of Agriculture," cited note 59.

65. Ronald Hsia, *Economic Planning in Communist China,* Institute of Pacific Relations, New York, 1955, especially ch. 5.

66. NCNA, September 11, 13, October 3, 1956; also, Chou En-lai, cited note 52.

67. State Statistical Bureau figures released by NCNA, December 31, 1957.

68. *Ibid.,* April 17, 1959.

69. *Chieh-fang jih-pao,* Shanghai, March 25, 1952, p. 2.

70. "Agricultural Cooperatives and Mutual-aid Organizations Should Practice the Principle of Same Pay for Same Work," *Hsin Chung-kuo fu-nü,* no. 9, September 1952, p. 6.

71. *Nung-yeh sheng-ts'an Hu-tso-tsu Ts'an-k'ao Tzu-liao* (Source Book on Mutual-aid Teams of Agricultural Production), vol. 1, Ministry of Agriculture, Peking, 1952, p. 9.

72. *Chieh-fang jih-pao,* Shanghai, March 22, 1952, p. 2.

73. *Jen-min jih-pao,* May 15, 1955; also, May 20, 1956, p. 2.

74. "The Growth of Hanyin Mutual-aid Team," *Hsin kuan-ch'a* (New Observer), Peking, February 16, 1952, pp. 18–19.

75. Marion Levy, *Family Revolution in Modern China,* Cambridge, 1949, ch. 8.

Chapter IX. The Shifting Center of Loyalty

1. Liang Shu-ming, *Chung-kuo min-tsu tzu-chiu yün-tung chui-hou chi chüeh-wu (*The Final Awakening of the Chinese National Self-salvation Movement), Peking, 1932, pp. 67–68.

2. *Ibid.,* p. 70.

3. Li Wen, "The New Mission of Youth Organizations," *Nan-fang chou-k'an* (Nan-fang Weekly), Canton, no. 37, October 1, 1952, p. 6.

4. *Chieh-fang jih-pao* (Liberation Daily), Shanghai, April 28, 1952, p. 3.

5. *Lun Yü,* Book VIII, ch. 18.

6. Li Kuo-hsin, "How I Weathered my Family Crisis," *Ta Kung Pao,* Hong Kong, April 18, 1951, p. 2.

7. *Shing-tao jih-pao,* Hong Kong, April 15, 1951, p. 2.

8. Ch'en Yi-ching, "Some Experiences in Mobilizing Wives of Workers and Staff Members to Participate in the Struggle against Corruption," *Hsin Chung-kuo fu-nü* (New Chinese Women), no. 25–26, December 1951, p. 8.

9. Wen Ying, "He Is Not my Husband, but a Thief Stealing State Property," *ibid.,* p. 10.

10. *Chieh-fang jih-pao,* March 10, 1952, p. 1.

11. *Jen-min jih-pao* (People's Daily), Peking, December 1, 1951, p. 3.

Chapter X. Secularization of the Family Institution

1. *Hun-yin fa hsuan-ch'uan shou-ts'e* (Propaganda Handbook of the Marriage Law), Peking, 1951, p. 25.

2. *Jen-min jih-pao* (People's Daily), Peking, July 3, 1955, p. 2.

Chapter XI. Disorganization of the Clan

1. Hu Hsien-chin, *Common Descent Group in China and Its Functions,* New York, 1948, chs. 1 to 2.
2. "Ancestral Clannish Attitude and Feudalistic Influence Collapsed under the Reexamination of Land Reform in Tzu-chien Village of Yukan County, Kiangsi Province," *Ch'ang-chiang jih-pao,* Hankow, January 10, 1952, p. 2.
3. *Nan-fang chou-k'an* (Nan-fang Weekly), Canton, no. 9, March 3, pp. 14–15.
4. See ch. 4 for figures and cases of women rising to political power.
5. Hu Hsien-chin, cited note 1.
6. *Ta Kung Pao,* Hong Kong, April 23, 1956, p. 1.
7. *Ch'ang-chiang jih-pao,* January 12, 1952, p. 2.
8. *Wah-kiu yat-po,* Hong Kong, April 18, 1955, p. 4.

Chapter XII. Ideology and Propaganda in the Change of the Family

1. *Jen-min jih-pao* (People's Daily), Peking, October 28, 1951, p. 3.
2. T'ao Chih, *Hun-yin hsin kuan-tien* (New View of Marriage), Peking, 1951, p. 58.
3. *Ch'ang-chiang jih-pao,* Hankow, February 9, 1952, p. 4; "Commentaries on Cultural Life," *Jen-min jih-pao,* December 4, 1951, p. 3; "A Report on Hui-an County of Fukien Province," *Hsin Chung-kuo yueh-k'an* (New China Monthly), no. 24, October 1951, p. 1050.
4. Tso Chung-fen, "Representatives' Conference of Model Laborers Implementing the Marriage Law in Lushan County," *Hsin Chung-kuo fu-nü* (New Chinese Women), no. 12, December 1952, pp. 10–12.
5. *Jen-min jih-pao,* December 4, 1951, p. 3; New China News Agency, July 25, 1956.
6. Ts'ai Ch'iang, "The Work of the All-China Democratic Women's League during the Past Year and Its Main Missions for This Winter and the Coming Spring," *Hsin Chung-kuo fu-nü,* no. 15, October 1950, pp. 19–21.
7. See the directives issued to local branches and membership by the Youth Federation and the Democratic Women's League, *Hun-yin fa chih ch'i yu-kuan wen-chien* (The Marriage Law and Related Documents), Peking, 1950, pp. 14–18.
8. *Ibid.,* pp. 11–13, 19.
9. Tso Chung-fen (cited note 4), pp. 9–10.
10. There was the case of a female party member claiming to have changed the traditional attitude of a whole village towards the problem of family and marriage, reported in the *Chieh-fang jih-pao,* Shanghai, January 14, 1952, p. 2.
11. *Jen-min jih-pao,* October 28, 1951, p. 3.
12. *Ibid.*
13. *Chieh-fang jih-pao,* February 9, 1952, p. 3.
14. "The Propaganda Shed for the Marriage Law in Wenteng County of Shantung Province," *Hsin Chung-kuo fu-nü,* no. 24, October 1951, p. 1248.
15. *Jen-min jih-pao,* October 22, 1951, p. 3.
16. *Ibid.*
17. *Chieh-fang jih-pao,* August 9, 1951, p. 3.

Chapter XIII. Recession of the "High Tide" and Long Term Trends

1. "How Should Family Women Better Serve Socialist Reconstruction," *Hsin Chung-kuo fu-nü* (New Chinese Women), no. 10, October 1955, pp. 18–19.

2. Yen Ling, " 'Cooperativization' Is the Road to Thorough Emancipation for Rural Women," *Hsin Chung-kuo fu-nü*, no. 12, 1955, pp. 3–4.

3. Hsia Kuang, "The Vicissitudes of the *Popular Pictorial Edition of the Marriage Law,*" *Hsin Chung-kuo fu-nü*, no. 10, October 1955, p. 22.

4. *Chung-kuo ch'ing-nien pao* (Chinese Youth), Peking, August 30, 1956.

5. *Ibid.*

6. F. Le Play, *Les Ouvriers Européens*, Tours, 1879, I, 457, quoted in Marion Levy, *Family Revolution in Modern China*, Cambridge, 1949, pp. 55–56.

7. Lin Chen, "Husband-wife Harmony and Harmony in the Whole Family," *Ch'ang-chiang jih-pao*, Hankow, February 4, 1952, p. 2; *Hun-yin fa hsuan-ch'uan shou-ts'e* (Propaganda Handbook of the Marriage Law), Peking, 1951, p. 62; Hsieh Chuio-tsai, "Let Us All Take Part in the Campaign to Implement the Marriage Law," *Hsin Chung-kuo fu-nü*, no. 10, October 1955, p. 19.

8. *Jen-min jih-pao* (People's Daily), Peking, June 13, 1953, p. 2.

9. Liu Lo-ch'ün, "Why Did Our Husband-wife Relationship Break Up?" *Hsin Chung-kuo fu-nü*, no. 11, November 1955, pp. 6–7.

Index